Cotton Mather.

THE WONDERS OF THE INVISIBLE WORLD.

BEING AN ACCOUNT OF THE TRYALS OF SEVERAL WITCHES LATELY EXECUTED IN NEW-ENGLAND.

BY COTTON MATHER, D.D.

TO WHICH IS ADDED

A FARTHER ACCOUNT OF THE TRYALS OF THE NEW-ENGLAND WITCHES.

BY INCREASE MATHER, D.D.
PRESIDENT OF HARVARD COLLEGE.

LONDON:
JOHN RUSSELL SMITH,
SOHO SQUARE.
1862.

INTRODUCTION.

The two very rare works reprinted in the present volume, written by two of the most celebrated of the early American divines, relate to one of the most extraordinary cases of popular delusion that modern times have witnessed. It was a delusion, moreover, to which men of learning and piety lent themselves, and thus became the means of increasing it. The scene of this affair was the puritanical colony of New England, since better known as Massachusetts, the colonists of which appear to have carried with them, in an exaggerated form, the superstitious feelings with regard to witchcraft which then prevailed in the mother country. In the spring of 1692 an alarm of witchcraft was raised in the family of the minister of Salem, and some black servants were charged with the supposed crime. Once started, the alarm spread rapidly, and in a very short time a great number of people fell under suspicion, and many were thrown into prison on very frivolous grounds, supported, as such charges usually were, by very unworthy witnesses. The new governor of the colony, Sir William Phipps, arrived from England in the middle of May, and he seems to have been carried away by the excitement, and authorized judicial prosecutions. The trials began at the commencement of June; and the first victim, a woman named Bridget Bishop, was hanged. Governor Phipps, embarrassed by this extraordinary state of things, called in the assistance of the clergy of Boston.

There was at this time in Boston a distinguished family of puritanical ministers of the name of Mather. Richard Mather, an English non-conformist divine, had emigrated to America in 1636, and settled at Dorchester, where, in 1639, he had a son born, who was named, in accordance with the peculiar nomenclature of the puritans, Increase Mather. This son distinguished himself much by his acquirements as a scholar and a theologian, became established as a minister in Boston, and in 1685 was elected president of Harvard College. His son, born at Boston in 1663, and called from the name of his mother's family, Cotton Mather, became more remarkable than his father for his scholarship, gained also a distinguished position in Harvard College, and was also, at the time of which we are speaking, a minister of the gospel in Boston. Cotton Mather had adopted all the most extreme notions of the puritanical party with regard to witchcraft, and he had recently had an opportunity of displaying them. In the summer of the year 1688, the children of a mason of Boston named John Goodwin were suddenly seized with fits and strange afflictions, which were at once ascribed to witchcraft, and an Irish washerwoman named Glover, employed by the family, was suspected of being the witch. Cotton Mather was called in to witness the sufferings of Goodwin's children; and he took home with him one of them, a little girl, who had first displayed these symptoms, in order to examine her with more care. The result was, that the Irish woman was brought to a trial, found guilty, and hanged; and Cotton Mather published next year an account of the case, under the title of "Late Memorable Providences, relating to Witchcraft and Possession," which displays a very extraordinary amount of credulity, and an equally great want of anything like sound judgment. This work, no doubt, spread the alarm of witchcraft through the whole colony, and had some influence on the events which followed. It may be supposed that the panic which had now arisen in Salem was not likely to be appeased by the interference of Cotton Mather and his father.

The execution of the washerwoman, Bridget Bishop, had greatly increased the excitement; and people in a more respectable position began to be accused. On the 19th of July five more persons were executed, and five more experienced the same fate on the 19th of August. Among the latter was Mr. George Borroughs, a minister of the gospel, whose principal crime appears to have been a disbelief in witchcraft itself. His fate excited considerable sympathy, which, however, was checked by Cotton Mather, who was present at the place of execution on horseback, and addressed the crowd, assuring them that Borroughs was an impostor. Many people, however, had now become alarmed at the proceedings of the prosecutors, and among those executed with Borroughs was a man named John Willard, who had been employed to arrest the persons charged by the accusers, and who had been accused himself, because, from conscientious motives, he refused to arrest any more. He attempted to save himself by flight; but he was pursued and overtaken. Eight more of the unfortunate victims of this delusion were hanged on the 22nd of September, making in all nineteen who had thus suffered, besides one who, in accordance with the old criminal law practice, had been pressed to death for refusing to plead. The excitement had indeed risen to such a pitch that two dogs accused of witchcraft were put to death.

A certain degree of reaction, however, appeared to be taking place, and the magistrates who had conducted the proceedings began to be alarmed, and to have some doubts of the wisdom of their proceedings. Cotton Mather was called upon by the governor to employ his pen in justifying what had been done; and the result was, the book which stands first in the present volume, "The

Wonders of the Invisible World;" in which the author gives an account of seven of the trials at Salem, compares the doings of the witches in New England with those in other parts of the world, and adds an elaborate dissertation on witchcraft in general. This book was published at Boston, Massachusetts, in the month of October, 1692. Other circumstances, however, contributed to throw discredit on the proceedings of the court, though the witch mania was at the same time spreading throughout the whole colony. In this same month of October, the wife of Mr. Hale, minister of Beverley, was accused, although no person of sense and respectability had the slightest doubt of her innocence; and her husband had been a zealous promoter of the prosecutions. This accusation brought a new light on the mind of Mr. Hale, who became convinced of the injustice in which he had been made an accomplice; but the other ministers who took the lead in the proceedings were less willing to believe in their own error; and equally convinced of the innocence of Mrs. Hale, they raised a question of conscience, whether the devil could not assume the shape of an innocent and pious person, as well as of a wicked person, for the purpose of afflicting his victims. The assistance of Increase Mather, the president or principal of Harvard College, was now called in, and he published the book which is also reprinted in the present volume: "A Further Account of the Tryals of the New England Witches.... To which is added Cases of Conscience concerning Witchcrafts and Evil Spirits personating Men." It will be seen that the greater part of the "Cases of Conscience" is given to the discussion of the question just alluded to, which Increase Mather unhesitatingly decides in the affirmative. The scene of agitation was now removed from Salem to Andover, where a great number of persons were accused of witchcraft and thrown into prison, until a justice of the peace named Bradstreet, to whom the accusers applied for warrants, refused to grant any more. Hereupon they cried out upon Bradstreet, and declared that he had killed nine persons by means of witchcraft; and he was so much alarmed that he fled from the place. The accusers aimed at people in higher positions in society, until at last they had the audacity to cry out upon the lady of governor Phipps himself, and thus lost whatever countenance he had given to their proceedings out of respect to the two Mathers. Other people of character, when they were attacked by the accusers, took energetic measures in self-defence. A gentleman of Boston, when "cried out upon," obtained a writ of arrest against his accusers on a charge of defamation, and laid the damages at a thousand pounds. The accusers themselves now took fright, and many who had made confessions retracted them, while the accusations themselves fell into discredit. When governor Phipps was recalled in April, 1693, and left for England, the witchcraft agitation had nearly subsided, and people in general had become convinced of their error and lamented it.

But Cotton Mather and his father persisted obstinately in the opinions they had published, and looked upon the reactionary feeling as a triumph of Satan and his kingdom. In the course of the year they had an opportunity of reasserting their belief in the doings of the witches of Salem. A girl of Boston, named Margaret Rule, was seized with convulsions, in the course of which she pretended to see the "shapes" or spectres of people exactly as they were alleged to have been seen by the witch-accusers at Salem and Andover. This occurred on the 10th of September, 1693; and she was immediately visited by Cotton Mather, who examined her, and declared his conviction of the truth of her statements. Had it depended only upon him, a new and no doubt equally bitter persecution of witches would have been raised in Boston; but an influential merchant of that town, named Robert Calef, took the matter up in a different spirit, and also examined Margaret Rule, and satisfied himself that the whole was a delusion or imposture. Calef wrote a rational account of the events of these two years, 1692 and 1693, exposing the delusion, and controverting the opinions of the two Mathers on the subject of witchcraft, which was published under the title of "More Wonders of the Invisible World; or the Wonders of the Invisible world displayed in five parts. An Account of the Sufferings of Margaret Rule collected by Robert Calef, merchant of Boston in New England." The partisans of the Mathers displayed their hostility to this book by publicly burning it; and the Mathers themselves kept up the feeling so strongly that years afterwards, when Samuel Mather, the son of Cotton, wrote his father's life, he says sneeringly of Calef: "There was a certain disbeliever in Witchcraft who wrote against this book" (his father's 'Wonders of the Invisible World'), "but as the man is dead, his book died long before him." Calef died in 1720.

The witchcraft delusion had, however, been sufficiently dispelled to prevent the recurrence of any other such persecutions; and those who still insisted on their truth were restrained to the comparatively harmless publication and defence of their opinions. The people of Salem were humbled and repentant. They deserted their minister, Mr. Paris, with whom the persecution had begun, and were not satisfied until they had driven him away from the place. Their remorse continued through several years, and most of the people concerned in the judicial proceedings proclaimed their regret. The jurors signed a paper expressing their repentance, and pleading that they had laboured under a delusion. What ought to have been considered still more conclusive, many of those who had confessed themselves witches, and had been instrumental in accusing others, retracted all they had said, and confessed that they had acted under the influence of terror. Yet the vanity of superior intelligence and knowledge was so great in the two Mathers that they resisted all conviction. In his *Magnalia*, an ecclesiastical history of New England, published in 1700, Cotton Mather repeats his original view of the doings of Satan in Salem, showing no regret for the part he had taken in this affair, and making no retraction of any of his opinions. Still later, in 1723, he repeats them again in the same strain in the chapter of the "Remarkables" of his father entitled "Troubles from the Invisible World." His father, Increase Mather, had died in that same year at an advanced age, being in his eighty-fifth year. Cotton Mather died on the 13th of February, 1728.

Whatever we may think of the credulity of these two ecclesiastics, there can be no ground for charging them with acting otherwise than conscientiously, and they had claims on the gratitude of their countrymen sufficient to overbalance their error of judgment on this occasion. Their books relating to the terrible witchcraft delusion at Salem have now become very rare in the original editions, and their interest, as remarkable monuments of the history of superstition, make them well worthy of a reprint.

The Wonders of the Invisible World:
Being an Account of the
TRYALS
OF
Several Witches,
Lately Excuted in
NEW-ENGLAND:
And of several remarkable Curiosities therein Occurring.

Together with,

I. Observations upon the Nature, the Number, and the Operations of the Devils.

II. A short Narrative of a late outrage committed by a knot of Witches in *Swede-Land*, very much resembling, and so far explaining, that under which *New-England* has laboured.

III. Some Councels directing a due Improvement of the Terrible things lately done by the unusual and amazing Range of *Evil-Spirits* in *New-England*.

IV. A brief Discourse upon those *Temptations* which are the more ordinary Devices of Satan.

By *COTTON MATHER.*

Published by the Special Command of his EXCELLENCY the Govenour of the Province of the *Massachusetts-Bay* in *New-England*.

Printed first, at *Bostun* in *New-England*; and Reprinted at *London*, for *John Dunton*, at the *Raven* in the *Poultry*. 1693.

THE AUTHOR'S DEFENCE.

Tis, as I remember, the Learned *Scribonius*, who reports, That one of his Acquaintance, devoutly making his Prayers on the behalf of a Person molested by *Evil Spirits*, received from those *Evil Spirits* an horrible Blow over the Face: And I may my self expect not few or small Buffetings from Evil Spirits, for the Endeavours wherewith I am now going to encounter them. I am far from insensible, that at this extraordinary Time of the *Devils coming down in great Wrath upon us*, there are too many Tongues and Hearts thereby *set on fire of Hell*; that the various Opinions about the Witchcrafts which of later time have troubled us, are maintained by some with so much cloudy Fury, as if they could never be sufficiently stated, unless written in the Liquor wherewith Witches use to write their Covenants; and that he who becomes an Author at such a time, had need be *fenced with Iron, and the Staff of a Spear*. The unaccountable Frowardness, Asperity, Untreatableness, and Inconsistency of many Persons, every Day gives a visible Exposition of that passage, *An evil spirit from the Lord came upon Saul*; and Illustration of that Story, *There met him two possessed with Devils, exceeding fierce, so that no man might pass by that way*. To send abroad a Book, among such Readers, were a very unadvised thing, if a Man had not such Reasons to give, as I can bring, for such an Undertaking. Briefly, I hope it cannot be said, *They are all so:* No, I hope the Body of this People, are yet in such a Temper, as to be capable of applying their Thoughts, to make a *Right Use* of the stupendous and prodigious Things that are happening among us: And because I was concern'd, when I saw that no abler Hand emitted any Essays to engage the Minds of this People, in such holy, pious, fruitful Improvements, as God would have to be made of his amazing Dispensations now upon us. Therefore it is, that One of the Least among the Children of *New-England*, has here done, what is done. None, but *the Father, who sees in secret*, knows the Heart-breaking Exercises, wherewith I have composed what is now going to be exposed, lest I should in any one thing miss of doing my designed Service for his Glory, and for his People; but I am now somewhat comfortably assured of his favourable acceptance; and, *I will not fear, what can a Satan do unto me!*

Having performed something of what God required, in labouring to suit his Words unto his Works, at this Day among us, and therewithal handled a Theme that has been sometimes counted not unworthy the Pen, even of a King, it will easily be perceived, that some subordinate Ends have been considered in these Endeavours.

I have indeed set myself to countermine the whole PLOT of the Devil, against *New-England*, in every Branch of it, as far as one of my *darkness*, can comprehend such a *Work of Darkness*. I may add, that I have herein also aimed at the Information and Satisfaction of Good Men in another Country, a thousand Leagues off, where I have, it may be, more, or however, more considerable Friends, than in my own: And I do what I can to have that Country, now, as well as always, in the best Terms with my own. But while I am doing these things, I have been driven a little to do something likewise for myself; I mean, by taking off the false Reports, and hard Censures about my Opinion in these Matters, the *Parter's Portions* which my *pursuit of*

Peace has procured me among the *Keen*. My hitherto *unvaried Thoughts* are here published; and I believe, they will be owned by most of the Ministers of God in these Colonies; nor can amends be well made me, for the wrong done me, by other sorts of *Representations*.

In fine: For the Dogmatical part of my Discourse, I want no Defence; for the Historical part of it, I have a Very Great One; the Lieutenant-Governour of *New-England* having perused it, has done me the Honour of giving me a Shield, under the Umbrage whereof I now dare to walk abroad.

Reverend and Dear Sir,

You very much gratify'd me, as well as put a kind Respect upon me, when you put into my hands, your elaborate and most seasonable Discourse, entituled, *The Wonders of the Invisible World*. And having now perused so fruitful and happy a Composure, upon such a Subject, at this Juncture of Time; and considering the place that I hold in the Court of *Oyer* and *Terminer*, still labouring and proceeding in the Trial of the Persons accused and convicted for Witchcraft, I find that I am more nearly and highly concerned than as a meer ordinary Reader, to express my Obligation and Thankfulness to you for so great Pains; and cannot but hold myself many ways bound, even to the utmost of what is proper for me, in my present publick Capacity, to declare my *singular Approbation* thereof. Such is your Design, most plainly expressed throughout the whole; such your Zeal for God, your Enmity to Satan and his Kingdom, your Faithfulness and Compassion to this poor People; such the Vigour, but yet great Temper of your Spirit; such your Instruction and Counsel, your *Care of Truth*, your Wisdom and Dexterity in allaying and moderating that among us, which needs it; such your clear discerning of Divine Providences and Periods, now running on apace towards their Glorious Issues in the World; and finally, such your good News of *The Shortness of the Devil's Time*, that all Good Men must needs desire, the making of this your Discourse publick to the World; and will greatly rejoyce, that the *Spirit of the Lord* has thus enabled you to *lift up a Standard* against the Infernal Enemy, that hath been *coming in like a Flood upon us*. I do therefore make it my particular and earnest Request unto you, that as soon as may be, you will commit the same unto the *Press* accordingly. I am,

Your assured Friend,

William Stoughton.

I live by *Neighbours* that force me to produce these undeserved Lines. But now, as when Mr. *Wilson* beholding a great Muster of Souldiers, had it by a Gentleman then present, said unto him, *Sir, I'll tell you a great Thing: Here is a mighty Body of People; and there is not* Seven *of them all, but what loves Mr.* Wilson. That gracious Man presently and pleasantly reply'd: *Sir, I'll tell you as good a thing as that; here is a mighty Body of People, and there is not so much as* One *among them all, but Mr.* Wilson *loves him.* Somewhat so: 'Tis possible, that among this Body of People, there may be few that love the Writer of this Book; but give me leave to boast so far, there is not one among all this Body of People, whom this *Mather* would not study to serve, as well as to love. With such a *Spirit of Love*, is the Book now before us written: I appeal to all *this World*; and if *this* World will deny me the Right of acknowledging so much, I appeal to the *other*, that it is *not written with an Evil Spirit*: for which cause I shall not wonder, if *Evil Spirits* be exasperated by what is written, as the *Sadduces* doubtless were with what was discoursed in the Days of our Saviour. I only demand the *Justice*, that others *read* it, with the same Spirit wherewith I *writ* it.

ENCHANTMENTS ENCOUNTERED.

Section I.

It was as long ago as the Year 1637, that a Faithful Minister of the Church of *England*, whose Name was Mr. *Edward Symons*, did in a Sermon afterwards Printed, thus express himself; 'At *New-England* now the Sun of Comfort begins to appear, and the glorious Day-Star to show it self;—*Sed Venient Annis Sæculæ Seris*, there will come Times in after Ages, when the *Clouds will overshadow and darken the Sky there*. Many now promise to themselves nothing but successive Happiness there, which for a time through God's Mercy they may enjoy; and I pray God, they may a long time; but in this World there is no Happiness perpetual.' An *Observation*, or I had almost said, an *Inspiration*, very dismally now verify'd upon us! It has been affirm'd by some who best knew *New-England*, That the World will do *New-England* a great piece of Injustice, if it acknowledge not a measure of Religion, Loyalty, Honesty, and Industry, in the People there, beyond what is to be found with any other People for the Number of them. When I did a few years ago, publish a Book, which mentioned a few memorable Witchcrafts, committed in this country; the excellent *Baxter*, graced the Second Edition of that Book, with a kind Preface, wherein he sees cause to say, *If any are Scandalized, that* New-England, *a place of as serious Piety, as any I can hear of, under Heaven, should be troubled so much with Witches; I think, 'tis no wonder: Where will the Devil show most Malice, but where he is hated, and hateth most:* And I hope, the Country will still deserve and answer the Charity so expressed by that Reverend Man of God. Whosoever travels over this Wilderness, will see it richly bespangled with Evangelical Churches, whose Pastors are holy, able, and painful Overseers of their Flocks, lively Preachers, and vertuous Livers; and such as in their several Neighbourly Associations, have had their Meetings whereat Ecclesiastical Matters of common Concernment are considered: *Churches,* whose Communicants have been seriously examined about their Experiences of Regeneration, as well as about their Knowledge, and Belief, and blameless Conversation, before their admission to the Sacred Communion; although others of less but hopeful Attainments in Christianity are not ordinarily deny'd Baptism for themselves and theirs; Churches, which are shye of using any thing in the Worship of God, for which they cannot see a Warrant of God; but with whom yet the Names of *Congregational, Presbyterian, Episcopalian,* or *Antipædobaptist,* are swallowed up in that of *Christian;* Persons of all those Perswasions being taken into our Fellowship, when visible Goodliness has recommended them: Churches, which usually do within themselves manage their own Discipline, under the Conduct of their Elders; but yet call in the help of *Synods* upon Emergencies, or Aggrievances: *Churches,* Lastly, wherein Multitudes are growing ripe for Heaven every day; and as fast as these are taken off, others are daily rising up. And by the Presence and Power of the Divine Institutions thus maintained in the Country, We are still so happy, that I suppose there is no Land in the Universe more free from the debauching, and the debasing Vices of Ungodliness. The Body of the People are hitherto so disposed, that

Swearing, Sabbath-breaking, Whoring, Drunkenness, and the like, do not make a Gentleman, but a Monster, or a Goblin, in the vulgar Estimation. All this notwithstanding, we must humbly confess to our God, that we are miserably degenerated from the first Love of our Predecessors; however we boast our selves a little, when Men would go to trample upon us, and we venture to say, *Wherein soever any is bold (we speak foolishly) we are bold also.* The first Planters of these Colonies were a chosen Generation of Men, who were first so pure, as to disrelish many things which they thought wanted Reformation elsewhere; and yet withal so peaceable, that they embraced a voluntary Exile in a squalid, horrid, *American* Desart, rather than to live in Contentions with their Brethren. Those good Men imagined that they should leave their Posterity in a place, where they should never see the Inroads of Profanity, or Superstition: And a famous Person returning hence, could in a Sermon before the Parliament, profess, *I have now been seven Years in a Country, where I never Saw one Man drunk, or heard one Oath sworn, or beheld one Beggar in the Streets all the while.* Such great Persons as *Budæus*, and others, who mistook Sir *Thomas Moor's* Utopia, for a Country really existent, and stirr'd up some Divines charitably to undertake a Voyage thither, might now have certainly found a Truth in their Mistake; *New-England* was a true *Utopia*. But, alas, the Children and Servants of those old Planters must needs afford many, degenerate Plants, and there is now risen up a Number of People, otherwise inclined than our *Joshua's*, and the Elders that out-liv'd them. Those two things our holy Progenitors, and our happy Advantages make Omissions of Duty, and such Spiritual Disorders as the whole World abroad is overwhelmed with, to be as provoking in us, as the most flagitious Wickednesses committed in other places; and the Ministers of God are accordingly severe in their Testimonies: But in short, those Interests of the Gospel, which were the Errand of our Fathers into these Ends of the Earth, have been too much neglected and postponed, and the Attainments of an handsome Education, have been too much undervalued, by Multitudes that have not fallen into Exorbitances of Wickedness; and some, especially of our young Ones, when they have got abroad from under the Restraints here laid upon them, have become extravagantly and abominably Vicious. Hence 'tis, that the Happiness of *New-England* has been but for a time, as it was foretold, and not for a long time, as has been desir'd for us. A Variety of Calamity has long follow'd this Plantation; and we have all the Reason imaginable to ascribe it unto the Rebuke of Heaven upon us for our manifold *Apostasies*; we make no right use of our Disasters: If we do not, *Remember whence we are fallen, and repent, and do the first Works*. But yet our Afflictions may come under a further Consideration with us: There is a further Cause of our Afflictions, whose due must be given him.

§ II.

The *New-Englanders* are a People of God settled in those, which were once the *Devil's* Territories; and it may easily be supposed that the *Devil* was exceedingly disturbed, when he perceived such a People here accomplishing the Promise of old made unto our Blessed Jesus, *That He should have the Utmost parts of the Earth for his Possession.* There was not a greater Uproar among the *Ephesians*, when the Gospel was first brought among them, than there was among, *The Powers of the Air* (after whom those *Ephesians* walked) when first the *Silver Trumpets* of the Gospel here made the *Joyful Sound.* The Devil thus Irritated, immediately try'd all sorts of Methods to overturn this poor Plantation: and so much of the Church, as was *Fled into this Wilderness,* immediately found, *The Serpent cast out of his Mouth a Flood for the carrying of it away*. I believe, that never were more *Satanical Devices* used for the Unsetling of any People under the Sun, than what have been Employ'd for the Extirpation of the *Vine* which God has here *Planted, Casting out the Heathen, and preparing a Room before it, and causing it to take deep Root, and fill the Land, so that it sent its Boughs unto the* Atlantic *Sea* Eastward, *and its Branches unto the* Connecticut *River* Westward, *and the Hills were covered with the shadow thereof.* But, All those Attempts of Hell, have hitherto been Abortive, many an *Ebenezer* has been Erected unto the Praise of God, by his Poor People here; and, *Having obtained Help from God, we continue to this Day.* Wherefore the Devil is now making one Attempt more upon us; an Attempt more Difficult, more Surprizing, more snarl'd with unintelligible Circumstances than any that we have hitherto Encountred; an Attempt so *Critical,* that if we get well through, we shall soon Enjoy *Halcyon* Days with all the *Vultures* of Hell *Trodden under our Feet.* He has wanted his *Incarnate Legions* to Persecute us, as the People of God have in the other Hemisphere been Persecuted: he has therefore drawn forth his more *Spiritual* ones to make an Attacque upon us. We have been advised by some Credible Christians yet alive, that a Malefactor, accused of *Witchcraft* as well as *Murder,* and Executed in this place more than Forty Years ago, did then give Notice of, *An Horrible* PLOT *against the Country by* WITCHCRAFT, *and a Foundation of* WITCHCRAFT *then laid, which if it were not seasonally discovered, would probably Blow up, and pull down all the Churches in the Country.* And we have now with Horror seen the *Discovery* of such a *Witchcraft!* An Army of *Devils* is horribly broke in upon the place which is the *Center,* and after a sort, the *First-born* of our *English* Settlements: and the Houses of the Good People there are fill'd with the doleful Shrieks of their Children and Servants, Tormented by Invisible Hands, with Tortures altogether preternatural. After the Mischiefs there Endeavoured, and since in part Conquered, the terrible Plague, of *Evil Angels,* hath made its Progress into some other places, where other Persons have been in like manner Diabolically handled. These our poor Afflicted Neighbours, quickly after they become *Infected* and *Infested* with these *Dæmons*, arrive to a Capacity of Discerning those which they conceive the *Shapes* of their Troublers; and notwithstanding the Great and Just Suspicion, that the *Dæmons* might Impose the *Shapes* of Innocent Persons in their *Spectral Exhibitions* upon the Sufferers, (which may perhaps prove no small part of the *Witch-Plot* in the issue) yet many of the Persons thus Represented, being Examined, several of them have been Convicted of a very Damnable *Witchcraft*: yea, more than One *Twenty* have *Confessed*, that they have Signed unto a *Book*, which the Devil show'd them, and Engaged in his Hellish Design of *Bewitching*, and *Ruining* our Land. *We* know not, at least *I* know not, how far the *Delusions* of Satan may be Interwoven into some Circumstances of the *Confessions*; but one would think, all the Rules of Understanding Humane Affairs are at an end, if after so many most Voluntary Harmonious *Confessions*, made by Intelligent Persons of all Ages, in sundry Towns, at several Times, we must not Believe the *main strokes* wherein those *Confessions* all agree: especially when we have a thousand preternatural Things every day before our eyes, wherein the *Confessors* do acknowledge their Concernment, and give Demonstration of their being so Concerned. If the Devils now can strike the minds of men with any *Poisons* of so fine a Composition and Operation, that Scores of Innocent People shall Unite, in *Confessions* of a Crime, which we see actually committed, it is a thing prodigious, beyond the Wonders of the former Ages, and it threatens no less than a sort of a Dissolution upon the World. Now, by these *Confessions* 'tis Agreed, *That* the Devil has made a dreadful Knot of *Witches* in the Country, and by the help of *Witches* has dreadfully increased that Knot: *That* these *Witches* have driven a Trade of Commissioning their *Confederate Spirits*, to do all sorts of Mischiefs to the

Neighbours, whereupon there have ensued such Mischievous consequences upon the Bodies and Estates of the Neighbourhood, as could not otherwise be accounted for: yea, *That* at prodigious *Witch-Meetings*, the Wretches have proceeded so far, as to Concert and Consult the Methods of Rooting out the Christian Religion from this Country, and setting up instead of it, perhaps a more gross *Diabolesm*, than ever the World saw before. And yet it will be a thing little short of *Miracle*, if in so *spread* a Business as this, the Devil should not get in some of his Juggles, to confound the Discovery of all the rest.

§ III.

Doubtless, the Thoughts of many will receive a great Scandal against *New-England*, from the Number of Persons that have been Accused, or Suspected, for *Witchcraft*, in this Country: But it were easie to offer many things, that may Answer and Abate the Scandal. If the Holy God should any where permit the Devils to hook two or three wicked *Scholars* into *Witchcraft*, and then by their Assistance to Range with their *Poisonous Insinuations* among Ignorant, Envious, Discontented People, till they have cunningly decoy'd them into some sudden *Act*, whereby the Toyls of Hell shall be perhaps inextricably cast over them: what Country in the World would not afford *Witches*, numerous to a Prodigy? Accordingly, The Kingdoms of *Sweden*, *Denmark*, *Scotland*, yea and *England* it self, as well as the Province of *New-England*, have had their Storms of *Witchcrafts* breaking upon them, which have made most Lamentable Devastations: which also I wish, may be *The Last*. And it is not uneasie to be imagined, That God has not brought out all the *Witchcrafts* in many other Lands with such a speedy, dreadful, destroying *Jealousie*, as burns forth upon such *High Treasons*, committed here in *A Land of Uprightness*: Transgressors may more quickly here than elsewhere become a Prey to the Vengeance of Him, *Who has Eyes like a Flame of Fire*, and, *who walks in the midst of the Golden Candlesticks.* Moreover, There are many parts of the World, who if they do upon this Occasion insult over this People of God, need only to be told the Story of what happen'd at *Loim*, in the Dutchy of *Gulic*, where a Popish Curate having ineffectually try'd many Charms to Eject the Devil out of a Damsel there possessed, he passionately bid the Devil come out of her into himself; but the Devil answered him, *Quid mihi Opus, est eum tentare, quem Novissimo die, Jure Optimo, sum possessurus?* That is, *What need I meddle with one whom I am sure to have, and hold at the Last-day as my own for ever!*

But besides all this, give me leave to add, it is to be hoped, That among the Persons represented by the *Spectres* which now afflict our Neighbours, there will be found *some* that never explicitly contracted with any of the *Evil Angels*. The Witches have not only intimated, but some of them acknowledged, That they have plotted the Representations of *Innocent Persons*, to cover and shelter themselves in their Witchcrafts; now, altho' our good God has hitherto generally preserved us from the Abuse therein design'd by the Devils for us, yet who of us can exactly state, *How far our God may for our Chastisement permit the Devil to proceed in such an Abuse?* It was the Result of a Discourse, lately held at a Meeting of some very Pious and Learned Ministers among us, *That the Devils may sometimes have a permission to Represent an Innocent Person, as Tormenting such as are under Diabolical Molestations: But that such things are Rare and Extraordinary; especially when such matters come before Civil Judicature.* The Opinion expressed with so much Caution and Judgment, seems to be the prevailing Sense of many others, who are men Eminently Cautious and Judicious; and have both *Argument* and *History* to Countenance them in it. It is *Rare and Extraordinary*, for an Honest *Naboth* to have his Life it self Sworn away by two

Children of Belial, and yet no Infringement hereby made on the Rectoral Righteousness of our Eternal Soveraign, whose *Judgments are a Great Deep*, and who *gives none Account of His matters*. Thus, although the Appearance of Innocent Persons in *Spectral Exhibitions* afflicting the Neighbour-hood, be a thing *Rare and Extraordinary*; yet who can be sure, that the great *Belial* of Hell must needs be always *Yoked* up from this piece of Mischief? The best man that ever lived has been called a *Witch*: and why may not this too usual and unhappy Symptom of A *Witch*, even a Spectral Representation, befall a person that shall be none of the worst? Is it not possible? The *Laplanders* will tell us 'tis possible: for Persons to be unwittingly attended with officious *Dæmons*, bequeathed unto them, and impos'd upon them, by Relations that have been *Witches. Quæry*, also, Whether at a Time, when the Devil with his Witches are engag'd in a War upon a people, some certain steps of ours, in such a War, may not be follow'd with our appearing so and so for a while among them in the Visions of our afflicted *Forlorns*! And, Who can certainly say, what other Degrees or Methods of sinning, besides that of a *Diabolical Compact*, may give the Devils advantage to act in the Shape of them that have miscarried? Besides what may happen for a while, to try the *Patience* of the Vertuous. May not some that have been ready upon feeble grounds uncharitably to Censure and Reproach other people, be punished for it by *Spectres* for a while exposing them to Censure and Reproach? And furthermore, I pray, that it may be considered, Whether a World of Magical Tricks often used in the World, may not insensibly oblige *Devils* to wait upon the Superstitious Users of them. A Witty Writer against *Sadducism* has this Observation, That persons who never made any express Contract with *Apostate Spirits*, yet may Act strange Things by *Diabolick Aids*, which they procure by the use of those wicked *Forms* and *Arts*, that the Devil first imparted unto his Confederates. And he adds, *We know not but the Laws of the*

Dark Kingdom may Enjoyn a particular Attendance upon all those that practice their Mysteries, whether they know them to be theirs or no. Some of them that have been cry'd out upon as imploying *Evil Spirits* to hurt our Land, have been known to be most bloody *Fortune-Tellers*; and some of them have confessed, That when they told *Fortunes*, they would pretend the Rules of *Chiromancy* and the like Ignorant Sciences, but indeed they had no Rule (they said) but this, *The things were then Darted into their minds. Darted!* Ye Wretches; By whom, I pray? Surely by none but the *Devils*; who, tho' perhaps they did not exactly *Foreknow* all the thus Predicted Contingencies; yet having once *Foretold* them, they stood bound in Honour now to use their Interest, which alas, in *This World*, is very great, for the Accomplishment of their own Predictions. There are others, that have used most wicked *Sorceries* to gratifie their unlawful Curiosities, or to prevent Inconveniencies in Man and Beast; *Sorceries*, which I will not *Name*, lest I should by Naming, *Teach* them. Now, some *Devil* is evermore Invited into the Service of the Person that shall Practise these *Witchcrafts*; and if they have gone on Impenitently in these Communions with any *Devil*, the *Devil* may perhaps become at last a *Familiar* to them, and so assume their *Livery*, that they cannot shake him off in any way, but that One, which I would most heartily prescribe unto them, Namely, That of a deep and long *Repentance*. Should these *Impieties* have been committed in such a place as *New-England*, for my part I should not wonder, if when *Devils* are Exposing the *Grosser* Witches among us, God permit them to bring in these *Lesser* ones with the rest for their perpetual Humiliation. In the Issue therefore, may it not be found, that *New-England* is not so stock'd with *Rattle Snakes*, as was imagined.

§ IV.

But I do not believe, that the progress of *Witchcraft* among us, is all the Plot which the Devil is managing in the *Witchcraft* now upon us. It is judged, That the Devil rais'd the Storm, whereof we read in the Eighth Chapter of *Matthew*, on purpose to over-set the little Vessel wherein the Disciples of Our Lord were Embarqued with Him. And it may be fear'd, that in the *Horrible Tempest* which is now upon ourselves, the design of the Devil is to sink that Happy Settlement of Government, wherewith Almighty God has graciously enclined Their Majesties to favour us. We are blessed with a Governour, than whom no man can be more willing to serve Their Majesties, or this their Province: He is continually venturing his *All* to do it: and were not the Interests of his Prince dearer to him than his own, he could not but soon be weary of the *Helm*, whereat he sits. We are under the Influence of a Lieutenant Governour, who not only by being admirably accomplished both with Natural and Acquired Endowments, is fitted for the Service of Their Majesties, but also with an unspotted Fidelity applies himself to that Service. Our Councellours are some of our most Eminent Persons, and as Loyal Subjects to the Crown, as hearty lovers of their Country. Our Constitution also is attended with singular Priviledges; All which Things are by the Devil exceedingly *Envy'd* unto us; And the Devil will doubtless take this occasion for the raising of such complaints and clamours, as may be of pernicious consequence unto some part of our present Settlement, if he can so far *Impose*. But that which most of all Threatens us, in our present Circumstances, is the *Misunderstanding*, and so the *Animosity*, whereinto the *Witchcraft* now Raging, has Enchanted us. The Embroiling, first, of our *Spirits*, and then of our *Affairs*, is evidently as considerable a Branch of the Hellish Intrigue which now vexes us as any one Thing whatsoever. The Devil has made us like a *Troubled Sea*, and the *Mire* and *Mud* begins now also to heave up apace. Even Good and Wise Men suffer themselves to fall into their *Paroxysms*; and the Shake which the Devil is now giving us, fetches up the *Dirt* which before lay still at the bottom of our sinful Hearts. If we allow the Mad Dogs of Hell to poyson us by biting us, we shall imagine that we see nothing but such things about us, and like such things fly upon all that we see. Were it not for what is IN US, for my part, I should not fear a thousand Legions of Devils: 'tis by our Quarrels that we spoil our Prayers; and if our humble, zealous, and united Prayers are once hindred: Alas, the *Philistines* of Hell have cut our Locks for us; they will then blind us, mock us, ruine us: In truth, I cannot altogether blame it, if People are a little transported, when they conceive all the secular Interests of themselves and their Families at the Stake; and yet at the sight of these Heartburnings, I cannot forbear the Exclamation of the Sweet-spirited *Austin*, in his Pacificatory Epistle to *Jerom*, on the Contest with *Ruffin*, *O misera &miseranda Conditio!* O Condition, truly miserable! But what shall be done to cure these Distractions? It is wonderfully necessary, that some healing Attempts be made at this time: And I must needs confess (if I may speak so much) like a *Nazianzen*, I am so desirous of a share in them, that if, being thrown overboard, were needful to allay the *Storm*, I should think Dying, a Trifle to be undergone, for so great a Blessedness.

§ V.

I would most importunately in the first place, entreat every Man to maintain an holy Jealousie over his Soul at this time, and think; May not the Devil make me, though ignorantly and unwillingly, to be an Instrument of doing something that he would have to be done? For my part, I freely own my Suspicion, lest something of Enchantment, have reach'd more Persons and Spirits among us, than we are well aware of. But then, let us more generally agree to maintain a kind Opinion one of another. That Charity without which, even our giving our Bodies to be burned would profit nothing, uses to proceed by this Rule; It is kind, it is not easily provok'd, it thinks no Evil, it believes all things, hopes all things. But if we disregard this Rule of Charity, we shall indeed give our Body Politick to be burned. I have heard it affirmed, That in the late great Flood upon *Connecticut*, those Creatures which could not but have quarrelled at another time, yet now being driven together very agreeably stood by one another. I am sure we shall be worse than *Brutes* if we fly upon one another at a time when the Floods of Belial make us afraid. On the one side; There are very worthy Men, who having been call'd by God, when and where this Witchcraft first appeared upon the Stage to encounter it, are earnestly desirous to have it sifted unto the bottom of it. And I pray, which of us all that should live under the continual Impressions of the Tortures, Outcries, and Havocks which Devils confessedly Commissioned by Witches make among their distressed Neighbours, would not have a Biass that way beyond other Men? Persons this way disposed have been Men eminent for Wisdom and Vertue, and Men acted by a noble Principle of Conscience: Had not Conscience (of Duty to God) prevailed above other Considerations with them, they would not for all they are worth in the World have medled in this Thorny business. Have there been any disputed Methods used in discovering the Works of Darkness? It may be none but what have had great Presedents in other parts of the World; which may, though not altogether justifie, yet much alleviate a Mistake in us if there should happen to be found any such mistake in so dark a Matter. They have done what they have done, with multiplied Addresses to God for his Guidance, and have not been insensible how much they have exposed themselves in what they have done. Yea, they would gladly contrive and receive an expedient, how the shedding of Blood, might be spared, by the Recovery of Witches, not gone beyond the Reach of Pardon. And after all, they invite all good Men, in Terms to this purpose, 'Being amazed at the Number and Quality of those accused of late, we do not know but Satan by his Wiles may have enwrapped some innocent Persons; and therefore should earnestly and humbly desire the most Critical Enquiry upon the place, to find out the Falacy; that there may be none of the Servants of the Lord, with the Worshippers of *Baal*.' I may also add, That whereas, if once a Witch do ingeniously confess among us, no more *Spectres* do in their Shapes after this, trouble the Vicinage; if any guilty Creatures will accordingly to so good purpose confess their Crime to any Minister of God, and get out of the Snare of the Devil, as no Minister will discover such a Conscientious Confession, so I believe none in the Authority will press him to discover it; but rejoyc'd in a Soul sav'd from Death. On the other side there are very worthy Men, who are not a little dissatisfied at the Proceedings in the Prosecution of this Witchcraft. And why? Not because they would have any such abominable thing, defended from the Strokes of Impartial Justice. No, those Reverend Persons who gave in this Advice unto the Honourable Council; 'That Presumptions, whereupon Persons may be Committed, and much more Convictions, whereupon Persons may be Condemned, as guilty of Witchcrafts, ought certainly to be more considerable, than barely the Accused Persons being represented by a *Spectre* unto the Afflicted; Nor are Alterations made in the Sufferers, by a Look or Touch of the Accused, to be esteemed an infallible Evidence of Guilt; but frequently liable to be abused by the Devils Legerdemains': I say, those very Men of God most conscientiously Subjoined this Article to that Advice,—'Nevertheless we cannot but humbly recommend unto the Government, the speedy and vigorous Prosecution of such as have rendred themselves Obnoxious; according to the best Directions given in the

Laws of God, and the wholsome Statutes of the *English* Nation for the Detection of Witchcraft.' Only 'tis a most commendable Cautiousness, in those gracious Men, to be very shye lest the Devil get so far into our Faith, as that for the sake of many Truths which we find he tells us, we come at length to believe any Lyes, wherewith he may abuse us: whereupon, what a Desolation of Names would soon ensue, besides a thousand other pernicious Consequences? and lest there should be any such Principles taken up, as when put into Practice must unavoidably cause the *Righteous to perish with the Wicked*; or procure the Bloodshed of any Persons, like the *Gibeonites*, whom some learned Men suppose to be under a false Notion of Witches, by *Saul* exterminated.

They would have all due steps taken for the Extinction of Witches; but they would fain have them to be sure ones; nor is it from any thing, but the real and hearty goodness of such Men, that they are loth to surmise ill of other Men, till there be the fullest Evidence for the surmises. As for the Honourable Judges that have been hitherto in the Commission, they are above my Consideration: wherefore I will only say thus much of them, That such of them as I have the Honour of a Personal Acquaintance with, are Men of an excellent Spirit; and as at first they went about the work for which they were Commission'd, with a very great aversion, so they have still been under Heart-breaking Sollicitudes, how they might therein best serve both God and Man? In fine, Have there been faults on any side fallen into? Surely, they have at worst been but the faults of a well-meaning Ignorance. On every side then, why should not we endeavour with amicable Correspondencies, to help one another out of the Snares wherein the Devil would involve us? To wrangle the Devil out of the Country, will be truly a New Experiment: Alas! we are not aware of the Devil, if we do not think, that he aims at inflaming us one against another; and shall we suffer our selves to be Devil-ridden? or by any unadvisableness contribute unto the Widening of our Breaches?

To say no more, there is a published and credible Relation; which affirms, That very lately in a part of *England*, where some of the Neighbourhood were quarrelling, a *Raven* from the Top of a Tree very articulately and unaccountably cry'd out, *Read the Third of Colossians and the Fifteenth!* Were I my self to chuse what sort of Bird I would be transformed into, I would say, *O that I had wings like a Dove!* Nevertheless, I will for once do the Office, which as it seems, Heaven sent that Raven upon; even to beg, *That the Peace of God may Rule in our Hearts.*

§ VI.

'Tis necessary that we unite in every thing: but there are especially two Things wherein our Union must carry us along together. We are to unite in our Endeavours to deliver our distressed Neighbours, from the horrible Annoyances and Molestations with which a dreadful Witchcraft is now persecuting of them. To have an hand in any thing, that may stifle or obstruct a Regular Detection of that Witchcraft, is what we may well with an holy fear avoid. Their Majesties good Subjects must not every day be torn to pieces by horrid Witches, and those bloody Felons, be left wholly unprosecuted. The Witchcraft is a business that will not be sham'd, without plunging us into sore Plagues, and of long continuance. But then we are to unite in such Methods for this deliverance, as may be unquestionably safe, lest *the latter end be worse than the beginning.* And here, what shall I say? I will venture to say thus much, That we are safe, when we make just as much use of all Advice from the invisible World, as God sends it for. It is a safe Principle, That when God Almighty permits any Spirits from the unseen Regions, to visit us with surprizing Informations, there is then something to be enquired after; we are then to enquire of one another, What Cause there is for such things? The peculiar Government of God, over the unbodied Intelligences, is a sufficient Foundation for this Principle. When there has been a Murder committed, an Apparition of the slain Party accusing of any Man, altho' such Apparitions have oftner spoke true than false, is not enough to Convict the Man as guilty of that Murder; but yet it is a sufficient occasion for Magistrates to make a particular Enquiry, whether such a Man have afforded any ground for such an Accusation. Even so a Spectre exactly resembling such or such a Person, when the Neighbourhood are tormented by such Spectres, may reasonably make Magistrates inquisitive whether the Person so represented have done or said any thing that may argue their confederacy with Evil Spirits, altho' it may be defective enough in point of Conviction; especially at a time, when 'tis possible, some over-powerful Conjurer may have got the skill of thus exhibiting the Shapes of all sorts of Persons, on purpose to stop the Prosecution of the Wretches, whom due Enquiries thus provoked, might have made obnoxious unto Justice.

Quære, Whether if God would have us to proceed any further than bare *Enquiry*, upon what Reports there may come against any Man, from the World of *Spirits*, he will not by his Providence at the same time have brought into our hands, these more evident and sensible things, whereupon a man is to be esteemed a Criminal. But I will venture to say this further, that it will be safe to account the Names as well as the Lives of our Neighbors; two considerable things to be brought under a Judicial Process, until it be found by Humane Observations that the Peace of Mankind is thereby disturbed. We are Humane Creatures, and we are safe while we say, they must be

Humane Witnesses, who also have in the particular Act of Seeing, or Hearing, which enables them to be Witnesses, had no more than Humane Assistances, that are to turn the Scale when Laws are to be executed. And upon this Head I will further add: A wise and a just Magistrate, may so far give way to a common Stream of Dissatisfaction, as to forbear acting up to the heighth of his own Perswasion, about what may be judged convictive of a Crime, whose Nature shall be so abstruse and obscure, as to raise much Disputation. Tho' he may not do what he should leave undone, yet he may leave undone something that else he could do, when the Publick Safety makes an *Exigency*.

§ VII.

I was going to make one Venture more; that is, to offer some safe Rules, for the finding out of the Witches, which are at this day our accursed Troublers: but this were a Venture too *Presumptuous* and *Icarian* for me to make; I leave that unto those Excellent and Judicious Persons, with whom I am not worthy to be numbred: All that I shall do, shall be to lay before my Readers, a brief *Synopsis* of what has been written on that Subject, by a Triumvirate of as Eminent Persons as have ever handled it. I will begin with,

AN ABSTRACT OF MR. PERKINS'S WAY FOR THE DISCOVERY OF WITCHES.

I. There are *Presumptions*, which do at least probably and conjecturally note one to be a *Witch*. These give occasion to Examine, yet they are no sufficient Causes of Conviction.

II. If any Man or Woman be notoriously defamed for a *Witch*, this yields a strong Suspition. Yet the Judge ought carefully to look, that the Report be made by *Men* of Honesty and Credit.

III. If a *Fellow-Witch*, or *Magician*, give Testimony of any Person to be a *Witch*; this indeed is not sufficient for Condemnation; but it is a fit Presumption to cause a strait Examination.

IV. If after Cursing there follow Death, or at least some mischief: for *Witches* are wont to practise their mischievous Facts, by Cursing and Banning: This also is a sufficient matter of Examination, tho' not of Conviction.

V. If after Enmity, Quarrelling, or Threatning, a present mischief does follow; that also is a great Presumption.

VI. If the Party suspected be the Son or Daughter, the man-servant or maid-servant, the Familiar Friend, near Neighbor, or old Companion, of a known and convicted Witch; this may be likewise a Presumption; for Witchcraft is an Art that may be learned, and conveyed from man to man.

VII. Some add this for a Presumption: If the Party suspected be found to have the Devil's mark; for it is commonly thought, when the Devil makes his Covenant with them, he alwaies leaves his mark behind them, whereby he knows them for his own:—a mark whereof no evident Reason in Nature can be given.

VIII. Lastly, If the party examined be Unconstant, or contrary to himself, in his deliberate Answers, it argueth a Guilty Conscience, which stops the freedom of Utterance. And yet there are causes of Astonishment, which may befal the Good, as well as the Bad.

IX. But then there is a *Conviction*, discovering the *Witch*, which must proceed from just and sufficient proofs, and not from bare presumptions.

X. Scratching of the suspected party, and Recovery thereupon, with several other such weak Proofs; as also, the fleeting of the suspected Party, thrown upon the Water; these Proofs are so far from being sufficient, that some of them are, after a sort, practices of Witchcraft.

XI. The Testimony of some Wizzard, tho' offering to shew the Witches Face in a Glass: This, I grant, may be a good Presumption, to cause a strait Examination; but a sufficient Proof of Conviction it cannot be. If the Devil tell the Grand Jury, that the person in question is a Witch, and offers withal to confirm the same by Oath, should the Inquest receive his Oath or Accusation to condemn the man? Assuredly no. And yet, that is as much as the Testimony of another Wizzard, who only by the Devil's help reveals the Witch.

XII. If a man, being dangerously sick, and like to dye, upon Suspicion, will take it on his Death, that such a one hath bewitched him, it is an Allegation of the same nature, which may move the Judge to examine the Party, but it is of no moment for Conviction.

XIII. Among the sufficient means of Conviction, the first is, the free and voluntary Confession of the Crime, made by the party suspected and accused, after Examination. I say not, that a bare confession is sufficient, but a Confession after due Examination, taken upon pregnant presumptions. What needs now more witness or further Enquiry?

XIV. There is a second sufficient Conviction, by the Testimony of two Witnesses, of good and honest Report, avouching before the Magistrate, upon their own Knowledge, these two things: either that the party accused hath made a League with the Devil, or hath done some known practice of witchcraft. And, *all Arguments that do necessarily prove either of these,* being brought by two sufficient Witnesses, are of force fully to convince the party suspected.

XV. If it can be proved, that the party suspected hath called upon the *Devil,* or desired his Help, this is a pregnant proof of a League formerly made between them.

XVI. If it can be proved, that the party hath entertained a Familiar Spirit, and had Conference with it, in the likeness of some visible Creatures; here is Evidence of witchcraft.

XVII. If the witnesses affirm upon Oath, that the suspected person hath done any action or work which necessarily infers a Covenant made, as, that he hath used Enchantments, divined things before they come to pass, and that peremptorily, raised Tempests, caused the Form of a dead man to appear; it proveth sufficiently, that he or she is a *Witch. This is the Substance of Mr.* Perkins.

Take next the Sum of Mr. *Gaules* Judgment about the Detection of Witches. '1. Some Tokens for the Trial of Witches, are altogether unwarrantable. Such are the old

Paganish Sign, the Witches *Long Eyes*; the Tradition of Witches not weeping; the casting of the Witch into the Water, with Thumbs and Toes ty'd a-cross. And many more such Marks, which if they are to know a Witch by, certainly 'tis no other Witch, but the User of them. 2. There are some Tokens for the Trial of Witches, more probable, and yet not so certain as to afford Conviction. Such are strong and long Suspicion: Suspected Ancestors, some appearance of Fact, the Corps bleeding upon the Witches touch, the Testimony of the Party bewitched, the supposed Witches unusual Bodily marks, the Witches usual Cursing and Banning, the Witches lewd and naughty kind of Life. 3. Some Signs there are of a Witch, more certain and infallible. As, *firstly*, Declining of Judicature, or faultering, faulty, unconstant, and contrary Answers, upon judicial and deliberate examination. *Secondly*, When upon due Enquiry into a person's Faith and Manners, there are found *all* or *most* of the Causes which produce Witchcraft, namely, *God* forsaking, *Satan* invading, particular *Sins* disposing; and lastly, a compact compleating all. *Thirdly*, The Witches free Confession, together with full Evidence of the Fact. *Confession* without *Fact* may be a meer Delusion, and *Fact* without *Confession* may be a meer Accident. *4thly*, The semblable Gestures and Actions of suspected Witches, with the comparable Expressions of Affections, which in all Witches have been observ'd and found very much alike. *Fifthly*, The Testimony of the Party bewitched, whether pining or dying, together with the joynt Oaths of sufficient persons, that have seen certain prodigious Pranks or Feats, wrought by the Party accused. 4. Among the most unhappy circumstances to convict a Witch, one is, a maligning and oppugning the Word, Work, and Worship of God, and by any extraordinary sign seeking to seduce any from it. See *Deut. 13.1, 2., Mat. 24.24., Act. 13.8, 10., 2 Tim. 3.8*. Do but mark well the places, and for this very Property (of thus opposing and perverting) they are all there concluded arrant and absolute Witches. 5. It is not requisite, that so *palpable Evidence of Conviction* should here come in, as in other more sensible matters; 'tis enough, if there be but so much *circumstantial* Proof or Evidence, as the Substance, Matter, and Nature of such an abstruse Mystery of Iniquity will well admit. But I could heartily wish, that the Juries were empanell'd of the most eminent Physicians, Lawyers, and Divines that a Country could afford. In the mean time 'tis not to be called a Toleration, if Witches escape, where Conviction is wanting.' To this purpose our *Gaule*.

I will transcribe a little from one Author more, 'tis the Judicious *Bernard* of *Batcomb*, who in his *Guide to grand Jurymen*, after he has mention'd several things that are shrewd Presumptions of a Witch, proceeds to such things as are the *Convictions* of such an one. And he says, '*A witch in league with the* Devil *is convicted by these Evidences*; I. By a witches *Mark*; which is upon the Baser sort of Witches; and this, by the Devils either Sucking or Touching of them. *Tertullian* says, *It is the Devils custome to mark his*. And note, That this mark is *Insensible*, and being prick'd it will not Bleed. Sometimes, its like a *Teate*; sometimes but a *Blewish Spot*, sometimes a *Red* one; and sometimes the *flesh Sunk*: but the Witches do sometimes cover them. II. By the Witches *Words*. As when they have been heard calling on, speaking to, or Talking of their *Familiars*; or, when they have been heard *Telling* of *Hurt* they have done to man or beast: Or when they have been heard *Threatning* of such Hurt; Or if they have been heard Relating their *Transportations*. III. By the Witches *Deeds*. As when they have been *seen* with their Spirits, or seen secretly Feeding any of their *Imps*. Or, when there can be found their Pictures, Poppets, and other Hellish Compositions. IV. By the Witches *Extasies*: With the Delight whereof, Witches are so taken, that they will hardly conceal the same: Or, however at some time or other, they may be found in them. V. By one or more *Fellow-Witches*, Confessing their own Witchcraft, and bearing Witness against others; if they can make good the Truth of their Witness, and give sufficient proof of it. As, that they have seen them with their Spirits or, that they have Received Spirits from them; or that they can tell, when they used Witchery-Tricks to Do Harm; or, that they told them what Harm they had done; or that they can show the mark upon them; or, that they have been together in their Meetings; and such like. VI. By some *Witness of God* Himself, happening upon the Execrable Curses of Witches upon themselves, Praying of God to show some Token, if they be Guilty. VII. By the Witches own *Confession*, of Giving their Souls to the Devil. It is no Rare thing, for Witches to Confess.'

They are Considerable Things, which I have thus Recited; and yet it must be with *Open Eyes*, kept upon *Open Rules*, that we are to follow these things,

S. 8. But *Juries* are not the only Instruments to be imploy'd in such a Work; all *Christians* are to be concerned with daily and fervent *Prayers*, for the assisting of it. In the Days of *Athanasius*, the Devils were found unable to stand before, that Prayer, however then used perhaps with too much of Ceremony, *Let God Arise, Let his Enemies be Scattered. Let them also that Hate Him, flee before Him.*

O that instead of letting our Hearts *Rise* against one another, our Prayers might *Rise* unto an high pitch of Importunity, for such a *Rising* of the Lord! Especially, Let them that are *Suffering* by *Witchcraft*, be sure to *stay* and *pray*, and *Beseech the Lord thrice*, even as much as ever they can, before they complain of any Neighbour for afflicting them. Let them also that are *accused* of *Witchcraft*, set themselves to *Fast* and *Pray*, and so shake off the *Dæmons* that would like *Vipers* fasten upon them; and get the *Waters of Jealousie* made profitable to them.

And Now, O Thou Hope of *New-England*, and the Saviour thereof in the Time of Trouble; Do thou look mercifully down upon us, & Rescue us, out of the Trouble which at this time do's threaten to swallow us up. Let Satan be shortly bruised under our Feet, and Let the Covenanted Vassals of Satan, which have Traiterously brought him in upon us, be Gloriously Conquered, by thy Powerful and Gracious Presence in the midst of us. Abhor us not, O God, but cleanse us, but heal us, but save us, for the sake of thy Glory. Enwrapped in our Salvations. By thy Spirit, Lift up a standard against our infernal adversaries, Let us quickly find thee making of us glad, according to the Days wherein we have been afflicted. Accept of all our Endeavours to glorify thee, in the Fires that are upon us; and among the rest, Let these my poor and weak essays, composed with what Tears, what Cares, what Prayers, thou *only* knowest, not want the Acceptance of the Lord.

A DISCOURSE ON THE WONDERS OF THE INVISIBLE WORLD.

UTTERED (IN PART) ON AUG. 4, 1692.

Ecclesiastical History has Reported it unto us, That a Renowned Martyr at the Stake, seeing the Book of the Revelation thrown by his no less Profane than Bloody Persecutors, to be Burn'd in the same Fire with himself, he cryed out, *O Beata Apocalypsis; quam bene mecum agitur, qui tecum Comburar!* Blessed Revelation! said he, *How Blessed am I in this Fire, while I have Thee to bear me Company.* As for our selves this Day, 'tis a Fire of sore Affliction and Confusion, wherein we are Embroiled; but it is no inconsiderable Advantage unto us, that we have the Company of this Glorious and Sacred Book the Revelation to assist us in our Exercises. From that Book there is one Text, which I would single out at this time to lay before you; 'tis that in

Revel. XII. 12.

Wo to the Inhabitants of the Earth, and of the Sea; for the Devil is come down unto you, having great Wrath; because he knoweth, that he hath but a short time.

he Text is Like the Cloudy and Fiery Pillar, vouchsafed unto *Israel*, in the Wilderness of old; there is a very *dark side* of it in the Intimation, that, *The Devil is come down having great Wrath*; but it has also a *bright side*, when it assures us, that, *He has but a short time*; Unto the Contemplation of *both*, I do this Day Invite you.

We have in our Hands a Letter from our Ascended Lord in Heaven, to Advise us of his being still alive, and of his Purpose e're long, to give us a Visit, wherein we shall see our Living *Redeemer, stand at the latter day upon the Earth.* 'Tis the last Advice that we have had from Heaven, for now sixteen Hundred years; and the scope of it, is, to represent how the Lord Jesus Christ having begun to set up his Kingdom in the World, by the preaching of the Gospel, he would from time to time utterly break to pieces all Powers that should make Head against it, until, *The Kingdoms of this World are become the Kingdomes of our Lord, and of his Christ, and he shall Reign for ever and ever.* 'Tis a Commentary on what had been written by *Daniel*, about, *The fourth Monarchy*; with some Touches upon, *The Fifth*; wherein, *The greatness of the Kingdom under the whole Heaven, shall be given to the people of the Saints of the most High*: And altho' it have, as 'tis expressed by one of the Ancients, *Tot Sacramenta quot verba*, a Mystery in every Syllable, yet it is not altogether to be neglected with such a Despair, as that, *I cannot Read, for the Book is Sealed*. It is a Revelation, and a singular, and notable *Blessing* is pronounc'd upon them that humbly study it.

The Divine Oracles, have with a most admirable Artifice and Carefulness, drawn, as the very pious *Beverley*, has laboriously Evinced, an exact Line of Time, from the first Sabbath at the *Creation* of the World, unto the great Sabbatism at the *Restitution* of all Things. In that famous *Line of Time*, from the Decree for the Restoring of

Jerusalem, after the *Babylonish* Captivity, there seem to remain a matter of *Two Thousand and Three Hundred Years*, unto that *New Jerusalem*, whereto the Church is to be advanced, when the Mystical *Babylon* shall be *fallen*. At the Resurrection of our Lord, there were seventeen or eighteen Hundred of those Years, yet upon the Line, to run unto, *The rest which remains for the People of God*; and this Remnant in the *Line of Time*, is here in our *Apocalypse*, variously Embossed, Adorned, and Signalized with such Distinguishing Events, if we mind them, will help us escape that Censure, *Can ye not Discern the Signs of the Times?*

The Apostle *John*, for the View of these Things, had laid before him, as I conceive, a *Book*, with leaves, or folds; which *Volumn* was written both on the *Backside*, and on the *Inside*, and Roll'd up in a Cylindriacal Form, under seven *Labels*, fastned with so many *Seals*. The first *Seal* being opened, and the first *Label* removed, under the first *Label* the Apostle saw what he saw, of a first *Rider* Pourtray'd, and so on, till the last *Seal* was broken up; each of the Sculptures being enlarged with agreeable *Visions* and *Voices*, to illustrate it. The Book being now Unrolled, there were *Trumpets*, with wonderful Concomitants, Exhibited successively on the Expanding *Backside* of it. Whereupon the Book was *Eaten*, as it were to be Hidden, from Interpretations; till afterwards, in the *Inside* of it, the Kingdom of Anti-christ came to be Exposed. Thus, the Judgments of God on the *Roman Empire*, first unto the Downfal of *Paganism*, and then, unto the Downfal of *Popery*, which is but Revived *Paganism*, are in these Displayes, with Lively Colours and Features made sensible unto us.

Accordingly, in the Twelfth Chapter of this Book, we have an August Preface, to the Description of that Horrid *Kingdom*, which our Lord Christ refused, but Antichrist accepted, from the Devils Hands; a Kingdom, which for *Twelve Hundred and Sixty* Years together, was to be a continual oppression upon the People of God, and opposition unto his Interests; until the Arrival of that Illustrious Day, wherein, *The Kingdom shall be the Lords, and he shall be Governour among the Nations.* The Chapter is (as an Excellent Person calls it) an *Extravasated Account* of the Circumstances, which befell the *Primitive Church*, during the first Four or Five Hundred Years of Christianity: It shows us the Face of the Church, first in *Rome* Heathenish, and then in *Rome* Converted, before the *Man of Sin* was yet come to *Mans Estate.* Our Text contains the Acclamations made upon the most Glorious Revolution that ever yet happened upon the Roman Empire; namely, That wherein the Travailing Church brought forth a Christian Emperour. This was a most Eminent *Victory* over the Devil, and *Resemblance* of the State, wherein the World, ere long shall see, *The Kingdom of our God, and the Power of his Christ.* It is here noted,

First, As a matter of *Triumph.* 'Tis said, *Rejoyce, ye Heavens, and ye that dwell in them.* The Saints in both Worlds, took the Comfort of this Revolution; the Devout Ones that had outlived the late Persecutions, were filled with Transporting Joys, when they saw the *Christian* become the *Imperial* Religion, and when they saw Good Men come to give Law unto the rest of Mankind; the Deceased Ones also, whose Blood had been Sacrificed in the Ten Persecutions, doubtless made the Light Regions to ring with *Hallelujahs* unto God, when there were brought unto them, the Tidings of the Advances now given to the *Christian* Religion, for which they had suffered *Martyrdom.*

Secondly, As a matter of *Horror.* 'Tis said, *Wo to the Inhabiters of the Earth and of the Sea.* The *Earth* still means the *False Church*, the *Sea* means the *Wide World*, in Prophetical Phrasæology. There was yet left a vast party of Men that were Enemies to the Christian Religion, in the power of it; a vast party left for the Devil to work upon: Unto these is a *Wo* denounced; and why so? 'Tis added, *For the Devil is come down unto you, having great Wrath, because he knows, that he has but a short time.* These were, it seems, to have some desperate and peculiar Attempts of the Devil made upon them. In the mean time, we may Entertain this for our Doctrine,

Great Wo proceeds from the Great *WRATH*, with which the *DEVIL*, towards the end of his *TIME*, will make a *DESCENT* upon a miserable World.

I have now Published a most awful and solemn Warning for our selves at this day; which has four *Propositions*, comprehended in it.

Proposition I. That there is a *Devil*, is a thing Doubted by none but such as are under the Influences of the *Devil*. For any to deny the Being of a *Devil* must be from an Ignorance or Profaneness, worse than *Diabolical. A Devil.* What is *that*? We have a Definition of the Monster, in *Eph. 6.12. A Spiritual Wickedness,* that is, *A wicked Spirit.* A Devil is a *Fallen Angel*, an Angel *Fallen* from the Fear and Love of God, and from all Celestial Glories; but *Fallen* to all manner of Wretchedness and Cursedness. He was once in that Order of Heavenly Creatures, which God in the Beginning made *Ministering Spirits,* for his own peculiar Service and Honour, in the management of the Universe; but we may now write that Epitaph upon him, *How art thou fallen from Heaven! thou hast said in thine Heart, I will Exalt my Throne above the Stars of God; but thou art brought down to Hell!* A Devil is a *Spiritual* and *Rational* Substance, by his *Apostacy* from God, inclined unto all that is Vicious, and for that *Apostacy* confined unto the Atmosphere of this Earth, *in Chains under Darkness, unto the Judgment of the Great Day.* This is a *Devil*; and the *Experience* of Mankind as well as the *Testimony* of Scripture, does abundantly prove the Existence of such a Devil.

About this *Devil*, there are many things, whereof we may reasonably and profitably be Inquisitive; such things, I mean, as are in our Bibles Reveal'd unto us; according to which if we do not speak, on so *dark* a Subject, but according to our own uncertain, and perhaps humoursome Conjectures, *There is no Light in us.* I will carry you with me, but unto one Paragraph of the Bible, to be informed of three Things, relating to the *Devil*; 'tis the Story of the *Gadaren Energumen*, in the fifth Chapter of *Mark*.

First, then, 'Tis to be granted; the *Devils* are so many, that some Thousands, can sometimes at once apply themselves to vex one Child of Man. It is said, in *Mark 5.15. He that was Possessed with the Devil, had the Legion.* Dreadful to be spoken! A *Legion* consisted of Twelve Thousand Five Hundred People: And we see that in one Man or two, so many *Devils* can be spared for a Garrison. As the Prophet cryed out, *Multitudes, Multitudes, in the Valley of Decision!* So I say, *There are multitudes, multitudes, in the valley of Destruction, where the Devils are!* When we speak of, *The Devil*, 'tis, *A name of Multitude*; it means not *One* Individual Devil, so Potent and Scient, as perhaps a *Manichee* would imagine; but it means a *Kind*, which a *Multitude* belongs unto. Alas, the *Devils*, they swarm about us, like the *Frogs of Egypt*, in the most Retired of our Chambers. Are we at our *Boards?* There will be Devils to Tempt us unto Sensuality: Are we in our *Beds?* There will be Devils to Tempt us unto Carnality; Are we in our *Shops?* There will be Devils to Tempt us into Dishonesty. Yea, Tho' we get into the Church of God, there will be Devils to Haunt us in the very *Temple* it self, and there tempt us to manifold Misbehaviours. I am verily perswaded, That there are very few Humane Affairs whereinto some Devils are not

Insinuated; There is not so much as a *Journey* intended, but *Satan* will have an hand in *hindering* or *furthering* of it.

Secondly, 'Tis to be supposed, That there is a sort of Arbitrary, even Military *Government*, among the *Devils*. This is intimated, when in *Mar. 5.9. The unclean Spirit said, My Name is Legion:* they are such a Discipline as *Legions* use to be. Hence we read about, *The Prince of the power of the Air*. Our *Air* has a *power*? or an Army of Devils in the *High Places* of it; and these Devils have a *Prince* over them, who is *King over the Children of Pride*. 'Tis probable, That the Devil, who was the Ringleader of that mutinous and rebellious Crew, which first shook off the Authority of God, is now the General of those Hellish Armies; Our Lord, that Conquered him, has told us the Name of him; 'tis *Belzebub*; 'tis he that is *the Devil*, and the rest are *his Angels*, or his Souldiers. Think on vast Regiments of cruel and bloody *French Dragoons*, with an *Intendant* over them, overrunning a pillaged Neighbourhood, and you will think a little, what the Constitution among the *Devils* is.

Thirdly, 'tis to be supposed, that some *Devils* are more peculiarly *Commission'd*, and perhaps *Qualify'd*, for some Countries, while others are for others. This is intimated when in *Mar. 5.10. The Devils besought our Lord much, that he would not send them away out of the Countrey.* Why was that? But in all probability, because *these Devils* were more able to *do the works of the Devil*, in such a Countrey, than in another. It is not likely that every Devil does know every *Language*; or that every Devil can do every *Mischief*. 'Tis possible, that the *Experience*, or, if I may call it so, the *Education* of all Devils is not alike, and that there may be some difference in their *Abilities*. If one might make an Inference from what the Devils *do*, to what they *are*, One cannot forbear dreaming, that there are *degrees* of Devils. Who can allow, that such Trifling *Dæmons*, as that of *Mascon*, or those that once infested our *New berry*, are of so much Grandeur, as those *Dæmons*, whose Games are mighty Kingdoms? Yea, 'tis certain, that all Devils do not make a like Figure in the *Invisible World*. Nor does it look agreeably, That the *Dæmons*, which were the Familiars of such a Man as the old *Apollonius*, differ not from those baser Goblins that chuse to Nest in the filthy and loathsom Rags of a beastly Sorceress. Accordingly, why may not some Devils be more accomplished for what is to be done in such and such places, when others must be *detach'd* for other Territories? Each Devil, as he sees his advantage, cries out, *Let me be in this Countrey, rather than another*.

But *Enough*, if not *too much*, of these things.

Proposition II. There is a Devilish *Wrath* against *Mankind*, with which the *Devil* is for *God's sake* Inspired. The Devil is himself broiling under the intollerable and interminable *Wrath* of God; and a fiery *Wrath* at God, is, that which the Devil is for that cause Enflamed. Methinks I see the posture of the Devils in *Isa. 8.21. They fret themselves, and Curse their God, and look upward.* The first and chief *Wrath* of the Devil, is at the Almighty God himself; he knows, *The God that made him, will not have mercy on him, and the God that formed him, will shew him no favour;* and so he can have no *Kindness* for that God, who has no *Mercy*, nor *Favour* for him. Hence 'tis, that he cannot bear the *Name* of God should be acknowledged in the World: Every Acknowledgement paid unto *God*, is a fresh drop of the burning Brimstone falling upon the Devil; he does make his Insolent, tho Impotent Batteries, even upon the *Throne* of God himself: and foolishly affects to have himself exalted unto that *Glorious High Throne*, by all people, as he sometimes is, by Execrable *Witches*. This horrible Dragon does not only with his Tayl strike at the *Stars of God*, but at the God himself, who made the *Stars*, being desirous to out-shine them all. God and the Devil are sworn Enemies to each other; the Terms between them, are those, in *Zech. 11.18. My Soul loathed them, and their Soul also abhorred me.* And from this Furious *wrath*, or Displeasure and Prejudice at God, proceeds the Devils *wrath* at us, the poor Children of Men. Our doing the *Service* of God, is one thing that exposes us to the *wrath* of the Devil. We are the *High Priests* of the World; when all Creatures are called upon, *Praise ye the Lord*, they bring to us those demanded *Praises* of God, saying, *do you offer them for us*. Hence 'tis, that the Devil has a Quarrel with us, as he had with the *High-Priest* in the Vision of Old. Our bearing the Image of God is another thing that brings the *wrath* of the Devil upon us. As a *Tyger*, thro his Hatred at man will tear the very Picture of him, if it come in his way; such a *Tyger* the Devil is; because God said of old, *Let us make Man in our Image*, the Devil is ever saying, *Let us pull this man to pieces*. But the envious *Pride* of the Devil, is one thing more that gives an Edge unto his Furious *Wrath* against us. The Apostle has given us an hint, as if *Pride* had been the *Condemnation of the Devil*. 'Tis not unlikely, that the Devil's *Affectation* to be above that Condition which he might learn that Mankind was to be preferr'd unto, might be the occasion of his taking up Arms against the *Immortal King*. However, the Devil now sees *Man* lying in the Bosom of God, but *himself* damned in the bottom of Hell; and this enrages him exceedingly; *O*, says he, *I cannot bear it, that man should not be as miserable as my self*.

Proposition III. The *Devil*, in the prosecution, and the execution of his *wrath* upon them, often gets a *Liberty* to make a *Descent* upon the Children of men. When the Devil *does hurt* unto us, he *comes down* unto us; for the Rendezvouze of the *Infernal Troops*, is indeed in the *supernal parts* of our Air. But as 'tis said, *A sparrow of the Air does not fall down without the will of God*; so I may say, *Not a Devil in the Air, can come down without the leave of God*. Of this we have a famous Instance in that Arabian Prince, of whom the Devil was not able so much as to *Touch* any thing, till the most high God gave him a permission, to *go down*. The Devil stands with all the Instruments of death, aiming at us, and begging of the Lord, as that King ask'd for the Hood-wink'd *Syrians* of old, *Shall I smite 'em, shall I smite 'em?* He cannot strike a blow, till the Lord say, *Go down and smite,* but sometimes he *does* obtain from the *high possessor of Heaven and Earth,* a License for the doing of it. The Devil sometimes does make most rueful Havock among us; but still we may say to him, as our Lord said unto a great Servant of his, *Thou couldest have no power against me, except it were given thee from above.* The Devil is called in *1 Pet. 5.8. Your Adversary.* This is a Law-term; and it notes *An Adversary at Law.* The Devil cannot come at us, except in some sence according to *Law*; but sometimes he does procure sad things to be inflicted, according to the *Law* of the eternal King upon us. The Devil first *goes up* as an *Accuser* against us. He is therefore styled *The Accuser*; and it is on this account, that his proper Name does belong unto him. There is a Court somewhere kept; a Court of Spirits, where the Devil enters all sorts of Complaints against us all; he charges us with manifold *sins* against the Lord our God: *There* he loads us with heavy *Imputations* of Hypocrysie, Iniquity, Disobedience; whereupon he urges, *Lord, let 'em now have the death, which is their wages, paid unto 'em!* If our *Advocate* in the Heavens do not now take off his Libels; the Devil, then, with a Concession of God, *comes down,* as a *destroyer* upon us. Having first been an *Attorney,* to bespeak that the Judgments of Heaven may be ordered for us, he then also pleads, that he may be the *Executioner* of those Judgments; and the God of Heaven sometimes after a sort, signs a Warrant, for this *destroying Angel,* to do what has been *desired* to be done for the *destroying of men.* But such a *permission* from God, for the Devil to *come down,* and *break in* upon mankind, oftentimes must be accompany'd with a *Commission* from some wretches of mankind it self. Every man is, as 'tis hinted in *Gen. 4.9. His brother's keeper.* We are to *keep* one another from the Inroads of the Devil, by mutual and cordial Wishes of prosperity to one another. When ungodly people give their *Consents* in *witchcrafts* diabolically performed, for the Devil to annoy their Neighbours, he finds a breach made in the Hedge about us, whereat he Rushes in upon us, with grievous molestations. Yea, when the impious people, that never saw the Devil, do but utter their *Curses* against their Neighbours, those are so many *watch words*, whereby the Mastives of Hell are animated presently to fall upon us. 'Tis thus, that the Devil gets *leave* to worry us.

Proposition IV. Most horrible *woes* come to be inflicted upon Mankind, when the *Devil* does in *great wrath*, make a *descent* upon them. The *Devil* is a *Do-Evil*, and wholly set upon mischief. When our Lord once was going to *Muzzel* him, that he might not mischief others, he cry'd out, *Art thou come to torment me?* He is, it seems, himself *Tormented*, if he be but *Restrained* from the tormenting of Men. If upon the sounding of the Three last *Apocalyptical Angels*, it was an outcry made in Heaven, *Wo, wo, wo, to the inhabitants of the Earth by reason of the voice of the Trumpet.* I am sure, a *descent* made by the Angel of *death*, would give cause for the like Exclamation: *Wo to the world, by reason of the wrath of the Devil!* what a *woful* plight, mankind would by the descent of the Devil be brought into, may be gathered from the *woful* pains, and wounds, and hideous desolations which the Devil brings upon them, with whom he has with a *bodily Possession* made a Seisure. You may both in Sacred and Profane History, read many a direful Account of the *woes*, which they that are possessed by the Devil, do undergo: And from thence conclude, *What must the Children of Men hope from such a Devil!* Moreover, the *Tyrannical Ceremonies*, whereto the Devil uses to subjugate such *Woful* Nations or Orders of Men, as are more Entirely under his Dominion, do declare what *woful* Work the Devil would make where he comes. The very Devotions of those forlorn *Pagans*, to whom the Devil is a Leader, are most bloody *Penances*; and what *Woes* indeed must we expect from such a Devil of a *Moloch*, as relishes no Sacrifices like those of Humane Heart-blood, and unto whom there is no Musick like the bitter, dying, doleful Groans, ejaculated by the Roasting Children of Men.

Furthermore, the servile, abject, needy circumstances wherein the Devil keeps the Slaves, that are under his more sensible Vassalage, do suggest unto us, how *woful* the Devil would render all our Lives. We that live in a Province, which affords unto us all that may be necessary or comfortable for us, found the Province fill'd with vast Herds of Salvages, that never saw so much as a *Knife*, or a *Nail*, or a *Board*, or a Grain of *Salt*, in all their Days. No better would the Devil have the World provided for. Nor should we, or any else, have one convenient thing about us, but be as indigent as *usually* our most *Ragged Witches* are; if *the Devil's Malice* were not over-ruled by a *compassionate God*, who *preserves Man and Beast*. Hence 'tis, that *the Devil*, even like a *Dragon*, keeping a Guard upon such *Fruits* as would *refresh* a languishing World, has hindred Mankind for many Ages, from hitting those *useful Inventions*, which yet *were so obvious* and *facil*, that it is every bodies wonder, they were no sooner hit upon. The *bemisted World*, must jog on for thousands of Years, without the knowledg of *the Loadstone*, till a *Neapolitan* stumbled upon it, about *three hundred years* ago. Nor must the World be *blest* with such a *matchless Engine* of *Learning* and *Vertue*, as that of *Printing*, till about *the middle of the Fifteenth Century*. Nor could *One Old Man, all over the Face of the whole Earth*, have the *benefit* of such a *Little*, tho most *needful* thing, as a pair of *Spectacles*, till a *Dutch-Man*, a *little while* ago accommodated us.

Indeed, as the Devil does begrutch us all manner of *Good*, so he does annoy us with all manner of *Wo*, as often as he finds himself capable of doing it. But shall we mention some of the *special woes* with which the Devil does usually infest the World! Briefly then; *Plagues* are some of those *woes* with which the Devil troubles us. It is said of the *Israelites*, in *1 Cor. 10.10. They were destroyed of the destroyer.* That is, they had the *Plague* among them. 'Tis the *Destroyer*, or *the Devil*, that scatters *Plagues* about the World. Pestilential and Contagious Diseases, 'tis the Devil who does oftentimes invade us with them. 'Tis no uneasy thing for the Devil to impregnate the Air about us, with such Malignant *Salts*, as meeting with *the Salt* of our *Microcosm*, shall immediately cast us into that Fermentation and Putrefaction, which will utterly dissolve all the Vital Tyes within us; Ev'n as an *Aqua-Fortis*, made with a conjunction of *Nitre* and *Vitriol*, Corrodes what it Seizes upon. And when the Devil has raised those *Arsenical Fumes*, which become *Venemous Quivers* full of *Terrible Arrows*, how easily can he shoot the deleterious *Miasms* into those Juices or Bowels of Mens Bodies, which will soon Enflame them with a Mortal Fire! Hence come such *Plagues*, as that *Beesom of Destruction*, which within our memory swept away such a Throng of People from one *English* City in one Visitation; And hence those Infectious Fevers, which are but so many *Disguised Plagues* among us, causing Epidemical Desolations. Again, *Wars* are also some of those *Woes*, with which the Devil causes our Trouble. It is said in *Rev. 12.17. The Dragon was Wrath, and he went to make War*; and there is in truth scarce any *War*, but what is of the *Dragon's* kindling. The Devil is that *Vulcan*, out of whose Forge come the instruments of our *Wars*, and it is he that finds us Employments for those Instruments. We read concerning *Dæmoniacks*, or People in whom the Devil was, that they would cut and wound themselves; and so, when the Devil is in Men, he puts 'em upon dealing in that barbarous fashion with one another.

Wars do often furnish him with some Thousands of Souls in one Morning from one Acre of Ground; and for the sake of such *Thyestæan* Banquets, he will push us upon as many *Wars* as he can.

Once more, why may not *Storms* be reckoned among those *Woes*, with which the Devil does disturb us? It is not improbable that *Natural Storms* on the World are often of the Devils raising. We are told in *Job 1.11, 12, 19.* that the Devil made a *Storm*, which hurricano'd the House of *Job*, upon the Heads of them that were Feasting in it. *Paracelsus* could have informed the Devil, if he had not been informed, as besure he was before, That if much *Aluminious* matter, with *Salt Petre* not throughly prepared, be mixed, they will send up a cloud of Smoke, which *will* come down in Rain. But undoubtedly the *Devil* understands as *well* the way to make a *Tempest* as to turn the *Winds* at the *Solicitation* of a *Laplander*; whence perhaps it is, that Thunders are observed oftner to break upon *Churches* than upon any other *Buildings*; and besides many a Man, yea many a Ship, yea, many a Town has miscarried, when the Devil has been permitted from above to make an horrible Tempest. However that the Devil has raised many *Metaphorical Storms* upon the Church, is a thing, than which there is nothing more notorious. It was said unto Believers in *Rev. 2.10. The Devil shall cast some of you into Prison.* The Devil was he that at first set *Cain upon Abel* to butcher him, as the Apostle seems to suggest, for his Faith in God, as a *Rewarder*. And in how many *Persecutions*, as well as *Heresies* has the Devil been ever since Engaging all the Children of *Cain*! That Serpent the Devil has acted his cursed Seed in unwearied endeavours to have them, *Of whom the World is not worthy*, treated as those who are *not worthy to live in the World*. By the impulse of the Devil, 'tis that first the old *Heathens*, and then the mad *Arians* were *pricking Briars* to the true Servants of God; and that the *Papists* that came after them, have out done them all for

Slaughters, upon those that have been *accounted as the Sheep for the Slaughters*. The late *French* Persecution is perhaps the horriblest that ever was in the World: And as the Devil of *Mascon* seems before to have meant it in his out-cries upon *the Miseries preparing for the poor Hugonots*! Thus it has been all acted by a singular Fury of the old Dragon inspiring of his Emissaries.

But in reality, *Spiritual Woes* are the *principal Woes* among all those that the Devil would have us undone withal. *Sins* are the worst of *Woes*, and the Devil seeks nothing so much as to plunge us into Sins. When men do commit a Crime for which they are to be Indicted, they are usually *mov'd by the Instigation of the Devil*. The Devil will put *ill men upon being worse*. Was it not he that said in *1 King. 22.22. I will go forth, and be a lying Spirit in the Mouth of all the Prophets?* Even so the Devil becomes an *Unclean Spirit, a Drinking Spirit, a Swearing Spirit, a Worldly Spirit, a Passionate Spirit, a Revengeful Spirit*, and the like in the Hearts of those that are already too much of such a Spirit; and thus they become improv'd in Sinfulness. Yea, the Devil will put *good men upon doing ill*. Thus we read in *1 Chron. 21.1. Satan provoked David to number Israel*. And so the *Devil provokes* men that are Eminent in Holiness unto such things as may become eminently Pernicious; he *provokes* them especially unto *Pride*, and unto many unsuitable Emulations. There are likewise most lamentable Impressions which the *Devil* makes upon the *Souls of Men* by way of punishment upon them for their *Sins*. 'Tis thus when an Offended God puts the Souls of Men over into the Hands of that Officer *who has the power of Death, that is, the Devil*. It is the woful Misery of Unbelievers in *2 Cor. 4.4. The god of this World has blinded their minds*. And thus it may be said of those woful Wretches whom the *Devil* is a God unto, *the Devil so muffles them that they cannot see the things of their peace*. And *the Devil so hardens them, that nothing will awaken their cares about their Souls:* How come so many to be *Seared* in their Sins? 'Tis the Devil that with a red hot Iron fetcht from his Hell does *cauterise* them. Thus 'tis, till perhaps at last they come to have a *Wounded Conscience* in them, and the Devil has often a share in their Torturing and confounding Anguishes. The *Devil* who Terrified *Cain*, and *Saul*, and *Judas* into Desperation, still becomes a *King of Terrors* to many Sinners, and frights them from laying hold on the Mercy of God in the Lord Jesus Christ. In these regards, *Wo to us, when the Devil comes down upon us.*

Proposition V. Toward the *End* of his *Time* the *Descent* of the Devil in *Wrath* upon the World will produce more *woful Effects*, than what have been *in former Ages.* The dying Dragon, will bite more cruelly and sting more bloodily than ever he did before: The Death-pangs of the Devil will make him to be more of a *Devil* than ever he was; and the Furnace of this *Nebuchadnezzar* will be heated *seven times* hotter, just before its putting out.

We are in the first place to apprehend that there is a time fixed and stated by God for the Devil to enjoy a dominion over our sinful and therefore woful World. The *Devil* once exclaimed in *Mat. 8.29. Jesus, thou Son of God, art thou come hither to Torment us before our Time?* It is plain, that until the second coming of our Lord the *Devil* must have a time of plagueing the World, which he was afraid would have Expired at his first. The *Devil* is *by the wrath of God the Prince of this World*; and the time of his Reign is to continue until the time when our Lord himself shall *take to himself his great Power and Reign.* Then 'tis that the *Devil* shall hear the Son of God swearing with loud Thunders against him, *Thy time shall now be no more!* Then shall the *Devil* with his Angels receive their doom, which will be, *depart into the everlasting Fire prepared for you.*

We are also to apprehend, that in the *mean time*, the Devil can give a shrewd guess, when he draws near to the *End of his Time*. When he saw Christianity enthron'd among the *Romans*, it is here said, in our *Rev. 12.12. He knows he hath but a short time.* And how does he *know* it? Why *Reason* will make the Devil to *know* that God won't suffer him to have *the Everlasting Dominion*; and that when God has once begun to rescue the World out of his hands, he'll go through with it, until *the Captives of the mighty shall be taken away and the prey of the terrible shall be delivered.* But the Devil will have *Scripture* also, to make him *know*, that when his Antichristian *Vicar*, the *seven-headed Beast* on the *seven-hilled* City, shall have spent his determined years, he with his *Vicar* must unavoidably go down into the *bottomless Pit*. It is not improbable, that the Devil often hears the *Scripture* expounded in our Congregations; yea that we never assemble without a *Satan* among us. As there are some Divines, who do with more uncertainty conjecture, from a certain place in the Epistle to the *Ephesians*, That the Angels do sometimes come into our Churches, to gain some advantage from our Ministry. But be sure our *Demonstrable Interpretations* may give Repeated Notices to the Devil, *That his time is almost out*; and what the Preacher says unto the *Young Man, Know thou, that God will bring thee into Judgment!* That may our Sermons tell unto the *Old Wretch, Know thou, that thy Judgment is at hand.*

But we must now, likewise, apprehend, that in *such a time*, the *woes* of the World will be heightened, beyond what they were at *any time* yet from the foundation of the World. Hence 'tis, that the Apostle has forewarned us, in *2 Tim. 3.1. this know, that in the last days, perillous times shall come.* Truly, when the Devil *knows*, that he is got into his *Last days*, he will make *perillous times* for us; the times will grow more full of *Devils*, and therefore more full of *Perils*, than ever they were before. Of this, if we would *know*, what cause is to be assigned; It is not only, because the Devil grows more *able*, and more *eager* to vex the World; but also, and chiefly, because the World is more *worthy* to be vexed by the Devil, than ever heretofore. The *Sins* of men in this Generation, will be more *mighty Sins*, than those of the former Ages; men will be more Accurate and Exquisite and Refined in the arts of *Sinning*, than they use to be. And besides, their own sins, the sins of all the former Ages will also lie upon the sinners of this generation. Do we ask why the *mischievous powers of darkness* are to prevail more in our days, than they did in those that are past and gone! 'Tis because that men by sinning over again the sins of the former days, have a *Fellowship with all those unfruitful works of darkness*. As 'twas said in *Matth. 23.36. All these things shall come upon this generation*; so, the men of the last Generation, will find themselves involved in the gulf of all that went before them. Of Sinners 'tis said, *They heap up wrath*; and the sinners of the Last Generations do not only add unto the *heap* of sin that has been pileing up ever since the Fall of man, but they Interest themselves in every sin of that enormous heap. There has been a *Cry* of all former ages going up to God, *That the Devil may come down!* and the sinners of the Last Generations, do sharpen and louden that *cry*, till the thing do come to pass, as Destructively as Irremediably. From whence it follows, that the Thrice Holy God, with his Holy Angels, will now after a sort more *abandon* the World, than in the former ages. The roaring Impieties of *the old World*, at last gave mankind such a distast in the Heart of the Just God, that he came to say, *It Repents me that I have made such a Creature!* And however, it may be but a witty Fancy, in a late Learned Writer, that the *Earth* before the Flood was nearer to the Sun, than it is at this Day; and that Gods Hurling down the *Earth* to a further distance from the *Sun*, were the cause of that Flood; yet we may fitly enough say, that men perished by a *Rejection* from the God of Heaven. Thus the enhanc'd Impieties of this *our World*, will Exasperate the Displeasure of God, at such a rate, as that he will more *cast us off*, than heretofore; until at last, he do with a more than ordinary Indignation say, *Go Devils; do you take them, and make them beyond all former measures miserable!*

If Lastly, We are inquisitive after Instances of those aggravated *woes*, with which the Devil will towards the *End* of his *Time* assault us; let it be remembred, That all the Extremities which were foretold by the *Trumpets* and *Vials* in the Apocalyptick Schemes of these things, to come upon the World, were the *woes* to come from the *wrath* of the Devil, upon the *shortning* of his *Time*. The horrendous desolations that have come upon mankind, by the Irruptions of the old *Barbarians* upon the *Roman* World, and then of the *Saracens*, and since, of the *Turks*, were such *woes* as men had never seen before. The Infandous *Blindness* and *Vileness* which then came upon mankind, and the Monstrous *Croisadoes* which thereupon carried the *Roman* World by Millions together unto the Shambles; were also such *woes* as had never yet had a Parallel. And yet these were some of the things here intended, when it was said, *Wo! For the Devil is come down in great Wrath, having but a short time.*

But besides all these things, and besides the increase of *Plagues* and *Wars*, and *Storms*, and *Internal Maladies* now in our days, there are especially two most extraordinary *Woes*, one would fear, will in these days become very ordinary. One *Woe* that may be look'd for is, A frequent Repetition of *Earthquakes*, and this perhaps by the energy of the Devil in the *Earth*. The Devil will be clap't up, as a Prisoner in or near the Bowels of the earth, when once that *Conflagration* shall be dispatched, which will make, *The New Earth wherein shall dwell Righteousness*; and that *Conflagration* will doubtless be much promoted, by the Subterraneous *Fires*, which are a cause of the *Earthquakes* in our Dayes. Accordingly, we read, *Great Earthquakes in divers places*, enumerated among the Tokens of the *Time* approaching, when the Devil shall have no longer *Time*. I suspect, That we shall now be visited with more Usual and yet more Fatal *Earthquakes*, than were our Ancestors; in asmuch as the *Fires* that are shortly to *Burn unto the Lowest Hell, and set on Fire the Foundations of the Mountains*, will now get more Head than they use to do; and it is not impossible, that the Devil, who is ere long to be punished in those *Fires*, may aforehand augment his Desert of it, by having an hand in using some of those *Fires*, for our Detriment. Learned Men have made no scruple to charge the Devil with it; *Deo permittente, Terræ motus causat*. The Devil surely, was a party in the *Earthquake*, whereby the Vengeance of God, in one black Night sunk Twelve considerable Cities of *Asia*, in the Reign of *Tiberious*. But there will be more such Catastrophes in our Dayes; *Italy* has lately been *Shaking*, till its *Earthquakes* have brought Ruines at once upon more than thirty Towns; but it will within a little while, *shake* again, and *shake* till the Fire of God have made an Entire *Etna* of it. And behold, This very Morning, when I was intending to utter among you such Things as these, we are cast into an *Heartquake* by Tidings of an *Earthquake* that has lately happened at *Jamaica*: an horrible *Earthquake*, whereby the *Tyrus* of the English *America*, was at once pull'd into the Jaws of the Gaping and Groaning Earth, and many Hundreds of the Inhabitants buried alive. The Lord sanctifie so dismal a Dispensation of his Providence, unto all the *American* Plantations! But be assured, my Neighbours, the *Earthquakes* are not over yet! We have not yet seen *the last*. And then, Another *Wo* that may be Look'd for is, The Devils being now let Loose in *preternatural Operations* more than formerly; and perhaps in *Possessions* and *Obsessions* that shall be very marvellous. You are not Ignorant, That just before our Lords *First Coming*, there were most observable Outrages committed by the Devil upon the

Children of Men: And I am suspicious, That there will again be an unusual Range of the Devil among us, a little before the *Second Coming* of our Lord, which will be, to give the last stroke, in *Destroying the works of the Devil*. The *Evening Wolves* will be much abroad, when we are near the *Evening* of the World. The Devil is going to be Dislodged of the *Air*, where his present Quarters are; God will with flashes of hot *Lightning* upon him, cause him to *fall as Lightning* from his Ancient Habitations: And the *Raised Saints* will there have a *New Heaven*, which We *expect according to the Promise of God*. Now a little before this thing, you be like to see the Devil more *sensible* and *visibly* Busy upon *Earth* perhaps, than ever he was before. You shall oftner hear about *Apparitions* of the Devil, and about poor people strangely Bewitched, *Possessed* and *Obsessed*, by Infernal Fiends. When our Lord is going to set up His Kingdom, in the most *sensible* and *visible* manner, that ever was, and in a manner answering *the Transfiguration* in *the Mount*, it is a Thousand to One, but *the Devil* will in sundry *parts of the world*, assay *the like* for Himself, with a most Apish Imitation: and Men, at least in *some* Corners of the World, and perhaps in *such* as God may have some special Designs upon, will to their Cost, be more Familiarized *with the World of Spirits*, than they had been formerly.

So that, in fine, if just before *the End*, when [the times of the Jews](#) were to be finished, a man then ran about every where, crying, *Wo to the Nation! Wo to the City! Wo to the Temple! Wo! Wo! Wo!* Much more may the descent of the Devil, just before his *End*, when also *the times of the Gentiles* will be finished, cause us to cry out, *Wo! Wo! Wo! because of the black things that threaten us!*

But it is now Time to make our Improvement of what has been said. And, first, we shall entertain our selves with a few *Corollaries*, deduced from what has been thus asserted.

Corollary I.

What cause have we to bless God, for our preservation from the *Devils wrath*, in this which may too reasonably be called the *Devils World!* While we are in *this present evil world*, We are continually surrounded with swarms of those Devils, who make this *present world*, become so *evil*. What a wonder of Mercy is it, that no *Devil* could ever yet make a prey of us! We can set our foot no where but we shall tread in the midst of most Hellish *Rattle-Snakes*; and one of those *Rattle-Snakes* once thro' the mouth of a Man, on whom he had Seized, hissed out such a Truth as this, *If God would let me loose upon you, I should find enough in the Best of you all, to make you all mine.* What shall I say? The *Wilderness* thro' which we are passing to the *Promised Land*, is all over fill'd with *Fiery flying serpents.* But, blessed be God; None of them have hitherto so fastned upon us, as to confound us utterly! All our way to Heaven, lies by the *Dens of Lions*, and the *Mounts of Leopards*; there are incredible Droves of Devils in our way. But have we safely got on our way thus far? O let us be thankful to our Eternal preserver for it. It is said in *Psal. 76.10. Surely the wrath of Man shall praise thee, and the Remainder of wrath shalt thou restrain*; But *surely* it becomes us to praise God, in that we have yet sustain'd no more Damage by the *wrath of the Devil*, and in that he has restrain'd that Overwhelming *wrath*. We are poor, Travellers in a World, which is as well the Devils *Field*, as the Devils *Gaol*; a World in every Nook whereof, the Devil is encamped, with *Bands of Robbers*, to pester all that have their *Face looking Zion-ward*: And are we all this while preserved from the undoing Snares of the *Devil?* it is, *Thou, O keeper of Israel, that hast hitherto been our Keeper!* And therefore, *Bless the Lord, O my soul, Bless his Holy Name, who has redeemed thy Life from the Destroyer!*

Corollary II.

We may see the rise of those multiply'd, magnify'd, and Singularly-stinged Afflictions, with which *aged*, or *dying* Saints frequently have their *Death* Prefaced, and their *Age* embittered. When the Saints of God are going to leave the World, it is usually a more *Stormy World* with them, than ever it was; and they find more *Vanity*, and more *Vexation* in the world than ever they did before. It is true, *That many are the afflictions of the Righteous;* but a little before they bid adieu to all those many *Afflictions*, they often have greater, harder, Sorer, Loads thereof laid upon them, than they had yet endured. It is true, *That thro' much Tribulation we must enter in the Kingdom of God;* but a little before our *Entrance* thereinto, our *Tribulation* may have some sharper accents of Sorrow, than ever were yet upon it. And what is the cause of this? It is indeed the *Faithfulness of our God unto us,* that we should find the *Earth* more full of *Thorns* and *Briars* than ever, just before he fetches us from *Earth* to *Heaven;* that so we may go away the more willingly, the more easily, and with less Convulsion, at his calling for us. O there are *ugly Ties*, by which we are fastned unto this world; but God will by *Thorns and Briars* tear those *Ties* asunder. But, *is not the Hand of Joab here?* Sure, There is the *wrath* of the *Devil* also in it. A little before we step into Heaven, the *Devil* thinks with himself, *My time to abuse that Saint is now but short; what Mischief I am to do that Saint, must be done quickly, if at all; he'l shortly be out of my Reach for ever.* And for this cause he will now fly upon us with the Fiercest Efforts and Furies of his *Wrath*. It was allowed unto the *Serpent*, in *Gen. 2.15. To Bruise the Heel.* Why, at the *Heel*, or at the *Close*, of our Lives, the *Serpent* will be nibbling, more than ever in our Lives before: and it is, *Because now he has but a short time.* He knows, That we shall very shortly be, *Where the wicked cease from Troubling, and where the Weary are at Rest;* wherefore that *Wicked* one will now *Trouble* us, more than ever he did, and we shall have so much *Disrest,* as will make us more *weary* than ever we were, of things here below.

Corollary III.

What a Reasonable Thing then is it, that they whose *Time* is but *short,* should make as great *Use* of their *Time,* as ever they can! pray, let us learn some *good,* even from the *wicked One* himself. It has been advised, *Be wise as Serpents:* why, there is a piece of *Wisdom,* whereto that old *Serpent,* the Devil himself, may be our Moniter. When the Devil perceives his *Time* is but *short,* it puts him upon *Great Wrath.* But how should it be with *us,* when we perceive that our *Time* is but *short?* why, it should put us upon *Great Work.* The motive which makes the Devil to be more full of *wrath;* should make us more full of *warmth,* more full of *watch,* and more full of *All Diligence to make our Vocation, and Election sure.* Our *Pace* in our Journey *Heaven-ward,* must be Quickened, if our *space* for that Journey be shortned, even as *Israel* went further the *two last* years of their Journey *Canaan-ward,* than they did in 38 years before. The Apostle brings this, as a *spur* to the Devotions of Christians, in *1 Cor. 7.29. This I say, Brethren, the time is short.* Even so, I *say* this; some things I lay before you, which I do only *think,* or *guess,* but here is a thing which I venture to *say* with all the freedom imaginable. You have now a *Time* to *Get* good, even a *Time* to make sure of *Grace and Glory, and every good thing,* by true Repentance: But, *This I say, the time is but short.* You have now *Time* to *Do* good, even to *serve out your generation,* as by the *Will,* so for the *Praise* of God; but, *This I say, the time is but short.* And what I say thus to *All* People, I say to *Old* People, with a peculiar Vehemency: Sirs, It cannot be long before your *Time* is out; there are but a few sands left in the glass of your *Time:* And it is of all things the saddest, for a man to say, *My Time is done, but my work undone!* O then, *To work* as fast as you can; and of Soul-work, and Church-work, dispatch as much as ever you can. Say to all *Hindrances*, as the gracious *Jeremiah Burrows* would sometimes to *Visitants*: *You'll excuse me if I ask you to be short with me, for my work is great, and my time is but short.* Methinks every *time* we hear a Clock, or see a Watch, we have an admonition given us, that our *Time* is upon the *wing*, and it will all be gone within a little while. I remember I have read of a famous man, who having a *Clock-watch* long lying by him, out of Kilture in his Trunk, it unaccountably struck Eleven just before he died. Why, there are many of you, for whom I am to do that office this day: I am to tell you *You are come to your* Eleventh *hour*; there is no more than a *twelfth part* at most, of your life yet behind. But if we neglect our business, till our *short Time* shall be reduced into *none*, then, *woe to us, for the great wrath of God will send us down from whence there is no Redemption.*

Corollary IV.

How welcome should a *Death in the Lord* be unto them that belong not unto the Devil, but unto the Lord! While we are sojourning in this World, we are in what may upon too many accounts be called *The Devils Country*: We are where the Devil may come upon us in *great wrath* continually. The day when God shall take us out of this World, will be, *The day when the Lord will deliver us from the hand of all our Enemies, and from the hand of Satan.* In such a day, why should not our song be that of the Psalmist, *Blessed be my Rock, and let the God of my Salvation be exalted!* While we are here, we are in *the valley of the shadow of death*; and what is it that makes it so? 'Tis because the *wild Beasts of Hell* are lurking on every side of us, and every minute ready to salley forth upon us. But our *Death* will fetch us out of that *Valley*, and carry us where we shall be *for ever with the Lord*. We are now under the daily *Buffetings* of the Devil, and he does molest us with such *Fiery Darts*, as cause us even to cry out, *I am weary of my Life.* Yea, but are we as *willing to die,* as, *weary of Life?* Our Death will then soon set us where we cannot be reach'd by the *Fist of Wickedness*; and where the *Perfect cannot be shotten at.* It is said in *Rev. 14.13. Blessed are the Dead which die in the Lord, they rest from their labours.* But we may say, *Blessed are the Dead in the Lord, inasmuch as they rest from the Devils!* Our *dying* will be but our *taking wing*: When attended with a Convoy of winged Angels, we shall be convey'd into that Heaven, from whence the Devil having been thrown he shall never more come thither after us. What if God should now say to us, as to *Moses, Go up and die!* As long as we *go up,* when we *die,* let us receive the Message with a joyful Soul; we shall soon be there, where the Devil can't *come down* upon us. If the *God of our Life* should now send that Order to us, which he gave to *Hezekiah, Set thy house in order, for thou shalt die, and not live;* we need not be cast into such deadly Agonies thereupon, as *Hezekiah* was: We are but going to that *House,* the Golden Doors whereof, cannot be entred by the Devil that here did use to persecute us. Methinks I see the Departed *Spirit* of a Believer, triumphantly carried thro' the Devils *Territories,* in such a stately and Fiery Chariot, as the *Spiritualizing Body of Elias* had; methink I see the Devil, with whole Flocks of *Harpies,* grinning at this Child of God, but unable to fasten any of their griping Talons upon him: And then, upon the utmost edge of our *Atmosphære,* methinks I overhear the holy Soul, with a most heavenly Gallantry, deriding the defeated Fiend, and saying, *Ah! Satan! Return to thy Dungeons again; I am going where thou canst not come for ever!* O 'tis a brave thing so to die! and especially so to die, *in our time.* For, tho' when we call to mind, *That the Devils time is now but short,* it may almost make us wish to *live* unto the *end* of it; and to say with the Psalmist, *Because the Lord will shortly appear in his Glory, to build up Zion. O my God! Take me not away in the midst of my days.* Yet when we bear in mind, *that the Devils Wrath is now most great,* it would make one willing to be *out of the way.* Inasmuch as now is the time for the doing of those things in the prospect whereof *Balaam* long ago cry'd out *Who shall live when such things are done!* We should not be inordinately loth to *die* at such a time. In a word, the *Times* are so *bad*, that we may well count it, as *good* a *time* to die in, as ever we saw.

Corollary V.

Good News for the *Israel* of God, and particularly for his *New-English Israel.* If the Devils *Time* were above a *thousand years ago*, pronounced *short*, what may we suppose it now in *our* Time? Surely we are not a *thousand years* distant from those happy *thousand years* of rest and peace, and *Holiness* reserved for the People of God in the latter days; and if we are not a *thousand years* yet short of that Golden Age, there is cause to think, that we are not an *hundred.* That the blessed *Thousand years* are not yet begun, is abundantly clear from this, *We do not see the Devil bound*; No, the Devil was never more let *loose* than in our Days; and it is very much that any should imagine otherwise: But the same thing that proves the *Thousand Years* of prosperity for the Church of God, under the whole Heaven, to be not yet *begun*, does also prove, that it is not very *far off;* and that is the prodigious *wrath* with which the Devil does in our days Persecute, yea, desolate the World. Let us cast our Eyes almost where we will, and we shall see the *Devils* domineering at such a rate as may justly fill us with astonishment; it is questionable whether *Iniquity* ever were so rampant, or whether *Calamity* were ever so pungent, as in this Lamentable *time*; We may truly say, *'Tis the Hour and the Power of Darkness.* But, tho the *wrath* be so *great*, the *time* is but *short*: when we are perplexed with the *wrath* of the Devil, the *Word* of our God at the same time unto us, is that in *Rom. 16.20. The God of Peace shall bruise Satan under your feet Shortly.* Shortly, didst thou say, dearest Lord! O gladsome word! Amen, *Even so, come Lord! Lord Jesus, come quickly! We shall never be rid of this troublesome Devil, till thou do come to Chain him up!*

But because the people of God, would willingly be told *whereabouts* we are, with reference to the *wrath and the time* of the Devil, you shall give me leave humbly to set before you a few *Conjectures*.

The first Conjecture.

The Devils *Eldest Son* seems to be towards the *End* of his last *Half-time*; and if it be so, the Devils *Whole-time*, cannot but be very near its *End*. It is a very scandalous thing that any *Protestant*, should be at a loss where to find *the Anti-Christ*. But, we have a sufficient assurance, that the Duration of *Anti-Christ*, is to be but for a *Time*, and for *Times*, and for *Half a time*; that is for *Twelve hundred and Sixty Years*. And indeed, those *Twelve Hundred and Sixty Years*, were the very Spott of *Time* left for the *Devil*, and meant when 'tis here said, *He has but a short time*. Now, I should have an *easie time* of it, if I were never put upon an *Harder Task*, than to produce what might render it extreamly probable, that Antichrist entred his last *Half-time*, or the last *Hundred* and *Fourscore* years of his Reign, *at* or soon *after* the celebrated *Reformation* which began at the year 1517 in the former century. Indeed, it is very agreeable to see how Antichrist then lost *Half* of his Empire; and how that *half* which then became *Reformed*, have been upon many accounts little more than *Half-reformed*. But by this computation, we must needs be within a very few years of such a *Mortification* to befal the See of *Rome*, as that Antichrist, who has lately been planting (what proves no more lasting than) a *Tabernacle in the Glorious Holy Mountain between the Seas*, must quickly, *Come to his End and none shall help him*. So then, within a very little while, we shall see the Devil stript of the grand, yea, the last, *Vehicle*, wherein he will be capable to abuse our World. The *Fires*, with which, *That Beast* is to be consumed, will so singe the Wings of the *Devil* too, that he shall no more set the Affairs of *this* world on *Fire*. Yea, they shall both go into the same *Fire*, to be *tormented for ever and ever.*

The Second Conjecture.

That which is, perhaps, the greatest Effect of the *Devils Wrath*, seems to be in a manner at an *end*: and this would make one hope that the *Devils time* cannot be far from its *end.* It is in Persecution, that the *wrath* of the Devil uses to break forth, with its greatest fury. Now there want not probabilities, that the *last Persecution* intended for the Church of God, before the Advent of our Lord, has been upon it. When we see the *second Woe passing away*, we have a fair signal given unto us, *That the last slaughter of our Lord's Witnesses is over;* and then what Quickly follows? The next thing is, *The Kingdoms of this World, are become the Kingdoms of Our Lord, and of His Christ:* and then *down* goes the Kingdom of the Devil, so that he cannot any more *come down* upon us. Now, the Irrecoverable and Irretrievable Humiliations that have lately befallen the *Turkish Power*, are but so many Declarations of the *second Woe passing away.* And the dealings of God with the *European* parts of the world, at this day, do further strengthen this our expectation. We *do* see, *at this hour a great Earth-quake all Europe over:* and we *shall* see, that this *great Earth-quake*, and these great Commotions, will but contribute unto the advancement of our Lords hitherto-depressed Interests. 'Tis also to be remark'd that, a disposition to recognize the *Empire* of God over the *Conscience* of man, does now prevail more in the world than formerly; and God from on High more touches the Hearts of Princes and Rulers with an averseness to Persecution. 'Tis particularly the unspeakable happiness of the English Nation, to be under the Influences of that excellent Queen, who could say, *In as much as a man cannot make himself believe what he will, why should we Persecute men for not believing as we do! I wish I could see all good men of one mind; but in the mean time I pray, let them however love one another.* Words worthy to be written in Letters of Gold! and by *us* the more to be considered, because to one of *Ours* did that royal Person express Her self so excellently, so obligingly. When the late King *James* published his Declaration for *Liberty of Conscience,* a worthy Divine in the Church of *England,* then studying the *Revelation,* saw cause upon *Revelational* Grounds, to declare himself in such words as these, *Whatsoever others may intend or design by this Liberty of Conscience, I cannot believe, that it will ever be recalled in* England, *as long as the World stands.* And you know how miraculously the *Earth-quake* which then immediately came upon the Kingdom, has established that *Liberty*! But that which exceeds all the tendencies this way, is, the dispensation of God at this Day, towards the blessed *Vaudois.* Those renowned *Waldenses,* which were a sort of *Root* unto all Protestant Churches, were never dissipated, by all the Persecutions of many Ages, till within these few years, the *French* King and the Duke of *Savoy* leagued for their dissipation. But just *Three years and a half after* the *scattering* of that holy people, to the surprise of all the World, *Spirit of life from God* is come into them; and having with a thousand Miracles repossessed themselves of their antient Seats, their hot *Persecutor* is become their great *Protector.* Whereupon the reflection of the worthy person, that writes the story is, The Churches of Piemont, *being the Root of the Protestant Churches, they have been the first established; the Churches of other places, being but the Branches, shall be established in due time, God will deliver them speedily, He has already delivered the Mother, and He will not long leave the Daughter behind: He will finish what he has gloriously begun!*

The Third Conjecture.

There is a *little room* for hope, that the *great wrath* of the Devil, will not prove the present ruine of our poor *New-England* in particular. I believe, there never was a poor Plantation, more pursued by the *wrath* of the *Devil*, than our poor *New-England*; and that which makes our condition very much the more deplorable is, that the *wrath* of the *great God* Himself, at the same time also presses hard upon us. It was a rousing *alarm* to the Devil, when a great Company of English *Protestants* and *Puritans*, came to erect Evangelical Churches, in a corner of the World, where he had reign'd without any controul for many Ages; and it is a vexing *Eye-sore* to the Devil, that our Lord Christ should be known, and own'd, and preached in this *howling Wilderness*. Wherefor he has left no *Stone unturned*, that so he might undermine his Plantation, and force us out of our Country.

First, The Indian *Powawes*, used all their Sorceries to molest the first Planters here; but God said unto them, *Touch them not!* Then, *Seducing Spirits* came to *root* in this Vineyard, but God so rated them off, that they have not prevail'd much farther than the Edges of our Land. After this, we have had a continual *blast* upon some of our principal Grain, annually diminishing a vast part of our *ordinary Food*. Herewithal, wasting *Sicknesses*, especially Burning and Mortal Agues, have Shot the Arrows of Death in at our Windows. Next, we have had many Adversaries of our own Language, who have been perpetually assaying to deprive us of those *English Liberties*, in the encouragement whereof these Territories have been settled. As if this had not been enough; The *Tawnies* among whom we came, have watered our Soil with the Blood of many Hundreds of our Inhabitants. Desolating *Fires* also have many times laid the chief Treasure of the whole Province in Ashes. As for *Losses* by

Sea, *they* have been multiply'd upon us: and particularly in the present *French War*, the whole English Nation have observ'd that no part of the Nation has proportionably had so many Vessels taken, as our poor *New-England.* Besides all which, now at last the Devils are (if I may so speak) *in Person* come down upon us with such a *Wrath,* as is justly *much,* and will quickly be *more,* the Astonishment of the World. Alas, I may sigh over *this* Wilderness, as *Moses* did over *his,* in *Psal. 90.7, 9. We are consumed by thine Anger, and by thy Wrath we are troubled: All our days are passed away in thy Wrath.* And I may add this unto it, *The Wrath of the Devil too has been troubling and spending of us, all our days.*

But what will become of this poor *New-England* after all? Shall we sink, expire, perish, before the *short time* of the Devil shall be finished? I must confess, That when I consider the lamentable *Unfruitfulness* of men, among us, under as powerful and perspicuous Dispensations of the Gospel, as are in the World; and when I consider the declining state of the *Power of Godliness* in our Churches, with the most horrible Indisposition that perhaps ever was, to recover out of this declension; I cannot but *Fear* lest it comes to this, and lest an *Asiatic* Removal of Candlesticks come upon us. But upon some other Accounts, I would fain *hope* otherwise; and I will give *you* therefore the opportunity to try what Inferences may be drawn from these probable Prognostications.

I say, *First,* That surely, *America's* Fate, must at the long run include *New-Englands* in it. What was the design of our God, in bringing over so many *Europæans* hither of later years? Of what use or state will *America* be, when the *Kingdom of God* shall come? If it must all be the Devils propriety, while the *saved Nations* of the other Hæmisphere shall be *Walking in the Light of the New Jerusalem,* Our *New-England* has then, 'tis likely, done all that it was erected for. But if God have a purpose to make here a seat for any of *those glorious things which are spoken of thee, O thou City of God*; then even thou, *O New-England*, art within a very little while of better days than ever yet have dawn'd upon thee.

I say, *Secondly,* That tho' there be very *Threatning* Symptoms on *America*, yet there are some *hopeful* ones. I confess, when one thinks upon the crying Barbarities with which the most of those *Europæans* that have Peopled this New world, became the Masters of it; it looks but *Ominously.* When one also thinks how much the way of living in many parts of *America,* is utterly inconsistent with the very Essentials of *Christianity*; yea, how much Injury and Violence is therein done to *Humanity* it self; it is enough to damp the Hopes of the most Sanguine Complexion. And the *Frown* of Heaven which has hitherto been upon Attempts of better Gospellizing the Plantations, considered, will but increase the *Damp.* Nevertheless, on the other side, what shall be said of all the *Promises,* That *our Lord Jesus Christ shall have the uttermost parts of the Earth for his Possession?* and of all the *Prophecies,* That *All the ends of the Earth shall remember and turn unto the Lord?* Or does it look *agreeably,* That such a rich quarter of the World, equal in some regards to all the rest, should never be out of the *Devils* hands, from the first Inhabitation unto the last Dissolution of it? No sure; why may not the *last* be the *first?* and the *Sun of Righteousness* come to shine *brightest,* in Climates which it rose *latest* upon!

I say, *Thirdly,* That *as* it fares with *Old England,* so it will be most likely to fare with *New-England.* For which cause, by the way, there may be more of the Divine Favour in the present Circumstances of our dependence on *England,* than we are well aware of. This is very sure, if matters *go ill* with our *Mother,* her poor American *Daughter* here, must feel it; nor could our former Happy Settlement have hindred our sympathy in that Unhappiness. But if matters *go Well* in the Three Kingdoms; as long as God shall bless the English Nation, with Rulers that shall encourage *Piety, Honesty, Industry,* in their Subjects, and that shall cast a Benign Aspect upon the Interests of our Glorious Gospel, *Abroad* as well as at *Home*; so long, *New-England* will at least keep its head above water: and so much the more, for our comfortable Settlement in such a Form as we are now cast into. Unless there should be any singular, destroying, *Topical Plagues,* whereby an offended God should at last make us *Rise*; But, *Alas, O Lord, what other Hive hast thou provided for us!*

I say, *Fourthly,* That the *Elder England* will certainly and speedily be Visited with the *ancient loving kindness* of God. When one sees, how strangely the Curse of our *Joshua,* has fallen upon the Persons and Houses of them that have attempted the Rebuilding of the *Old* Romish *Jericho,* which has there been so far demolished, they cannot but say, That the *Reformation* there, shall not only be maintained, but also pursued, proceeded, perfected; and that God will shortly there have a *New Jerusalem.* Or, Let a Man in his thoughts run over but the series of amazing Providences towards the English Nation for the last *Thirty Years*: Let him reflect, how many *Plots* for the ruine of the Nation, have been strangely discovered? yea, how very unaccountably those very *Persons,* yea, I may also say, and those very *Methods* which were intended for the tools of that ruine, have become the instruments or occasions of Deliverances? A man cannot but say upon these Reflections, as the Wife of *Manoah* once prudently expressed her self, *If the Lord were pleased to have Destroyed us, He would not have shew'd us all these things.* Indeed, It is not unlikely, that the Enemies of the English Nation, may yet provoke such a *Shake* unto it, as may perhaps exceed any that has hitherto been undergone: the Lord prevent the Machinations of his Adversaries! But that *shake* will usher in the most *glorious Times* that ever arose upon the English *Horizon*. As for the *French* Cloud which hangs over *England*, tho' it be like to Rain showers of *Blood* upon a Nation, where the *Blood* of the Blessed Jesus has been too much treated as an *Unholy Thing*; yet I believe God will shortly scatter it: and my belief is grounded upon a bottom that will bear it. If that overgrown *French Leviathan* should accomplish any thing like a Conquest of *England*, what could there be to hinder him from the Universal Empire of the *West*? But the *Visions* of the Western World, in the *Views* both of *Daniel* and of *John*, do assure us, that whatever Monarch, shall while the *Papacy* continues go to swallow up the *Ten Kings* which received *their Power* upon the Fall of the Western Empire, he must miscarry in the Attempt. The *French Phaetons* Epitaph seems written in that, *Sure Word of Prophecy*.

Now, *In the Salvation of* England, the Plantations cannot but *Rejoyce*, and *New-England* also will *be Glad*.

But so much for our *Corollaries*, I hasten to the main thing designed for your entertainment. And that is,

AN HORTATORY AND NECESSARY ADDRESS,
TO A COUNTRY NOW EXTRAORDINARILY ALARUM'D BY THE WRATH OF THE DEVIL.
TIS THIS,

Let us now make a good and a right use of the prodigious *descent* which the *Devil* in *Great Wrath* is at this day making upon our Land. Upon the Death of a Great Man once, an Orator call'd the Town together, crying out, *Concurrite Cives, Dilapsa sunt vestra Mœnia!* that is, *Come together, Neighbours, your Town-Walls are fallen down!* But such is the descent of the Devil at this day upon our selves, that I may truly tell you, *The Walls of the whole World are broken down!* The usual *Walls* of defence about mankind have such a Gap made in them, that the very *Devils* are broke in upon us, to seduce the *Souls*, torment the *Bodies*, sully the *Credits*, and consume the *Estates* of our Neighbours, with Impressions both as *real* and as *furious*, as if the *Invisible* World were becoming *Incarnate*, on purpose for the vexing of us. And what use ought now to be made of so tremendous a dispensation? We are engaged in a *Fast* this day; but shall we try to fetch *Meat out of the Eater*, and make the *Lion* to afford some *Hony* for our *Souls*?

That the Devil is *come down unto us with great Wrath*, we find, we feel, we now deplore. In many ways, for many years hath the Devil been assaying to Extirpate the Kingdom of our Lord Jesus here. *New-England* may complain of the Devil, as in *Psal. 129.1, 2. Many a time have they afflicted me, from my Youth,* may New-England *now say; many a time have they afflicted me from my Youth; yet they have not prevailed against me.* But now there is a more than ordinary *affliction*, with which the *Devil* is Galling of us: and such an one as is indeed Unparallelable. The things confessed by *Witches*, and the things endured by *Others*, laid together, amount unto this account of our *Affliction*. The *Devil*, Exhibiting himself ordinarily as a small *Black man*, has decoy'd a fearful knot of proud, froward, ignorant, envious and malicious creatures, to lift themselves in his horrid Service, by entring their Names in a *Book* by him tendred unto them. These *Witches*, whereof above a Score have now *Confessed, and shown their Deeds*, and some are now tormented by the Devils, for *Confessing*, have met in Hellish *Randezvouzes*, wherein the Confessors do say, they have had their diabolical Sacraments, imitating the *Baptism* and the *Supper* of our Lord. In these hellish meetings, these Monsters have associated themselves to do no less a thing than, *To destroy the Kingdom of our Lord Jesus Christ, in these parts of the World*; and in order hereunto, First they each of them have their *Spectres*, or Devils, commission'd by them, & representing of them, to be the Engines of their Malice. By these wicked *Spectres*, they seize poor people about the Country, with various & bloudy *Torments*; and of those evidently Preternatural torments there are some have dy'd. They have bewitched some, even so far as to make *Self-destroyers*: and others are in many Towns here and there languishing under their *Evil hands*. The people thus afflicted, are miserably scratched and bitten, so that the Marks are most visible to all the World, but the causes utterly invisible; and the same Invisible Furies do most visibly stick Pins into the bodies of the afflicted, and *scale* them, and hideously distort, and disjoint all their members, besides a thousand other sorts of Plagues beyond these of any natural diseases which they give unto them. Yea, they sometimes drag the poor people out of their chambers, and carry them over Trees and Hills, for divers miles together. A large part of the persons tortured by these Diabolical *Spectres*, are horribly tempted by them, sometimes with fair promises, and sometimes with hard threatnings, but always with felt miseries, to sign the

Devils Laws in a Spectral Book laid before them; which two or three of these poor Sufferers, being by their tiresome sufferings overcome to do, they have immediately been released from all their miseries and they appear'd in *Spectre* then to Torture those that were before their Fellow-Sufferers. The *Witches* which by their covenant with the Devil, are become Owners of *Spectres*, are oftentimes by their own *Spectres* required and compelled to give their consent, for the molestation of some, which they had no mind otherwise to fall upon; and cruel depredations are then made upon the Vicinage. In the Prosecution of these Witchcrafts, among a thousand other unaccountable things, the *Spectres* have an odd faculty of cloathing the most substantial and corporeal Instruments of Torture, with Invisibility, while the wounds thereby given have been the most palpable things in the World; so that the Sufferers assaulted with Instruments of Iron, wholly unseen to the standers by, though, to their cost, seen by themselves, have, upon snatching, wrested the Instruments out of the *Spectres* hands, and every one has then immediately not only *beheld*, but *handled*, an Iron Instrument taken by a Devil from a Neighbour. These wicked *Spectres* have proceeded so far, as to steal several quantities of Mony from divers people, part of which Money, has, before sufficient Spectators, been dropt out of the Air into the Hands of the Sufferers, while the *Spectres* have been urging them to subscribe their *Covenant with Death*. In such extravagant ways have these Wretches propounded, the *Dragooning* of as many as they can, in their own Combination, and the *Destroying* of others, with lingring, spreading, deadly diseases; till our Countrey should at last become too hot for us. Among the Ghastly Instances of the *success* which those Bloody Witches have had, we have seen even some of their own Children, so dedicated unto the Devil, that in their Infancy, it is found, the *Imps* have sucked them, and rendred them Venemous to a Prodigy. We have also seen the Devils first batteries upon the Town, where the first Church of our Lord in this Colony was gathered, producing those distractions, which have almost ruin'd the Town. We have seen likewise the *Plague* reaching afterwards into other Towns far and near, where the Houses of good Men have the Devils filling of them with terrible Vexations!

This is the Descent, which, it seems, the Devil has now made upon us. But that which makes this Descent the more formidable, is; The *multitude* and *quality* of Persons accused of an interest in this *Witchcraft*, by the Efficacy of the *Spectres* which take their Name and shape upon them; causing very many good and wise Men to fear, That many *innocent*, yea, and some *vertuous* persons, are by the Devils in this matter, imposed upon; That the Devils have obtain'd the power, to take on them the likeness of harmless people, and in that likeness to afflict other people, and be so abused by Præstigious *Dæmons*, that upon their look or touch, the afflicted shall be odly affected. Arguments from the *Providence of God*, on the one side, and from our *Charity* towards *Man* on the other side, have made this now to become a most agitated Controversie among us. There is an *Agony* produced in the Minds of Men, lest the Devil should sham us with *Devices*, of perhaps a finer Thred, than was ever yet practised upon the World. The whole business is become hereupon so *Snarled*, and the determination of the Question one way or another, so *dismal*, that our Honourable Judges have a Room for *Jehoshaphat's* Exclamation, *We know not what to do!* They have used, as Judges have heretofore done, the *Spectral Evidences*, to introduce their further Enquiries into the *Lives* of the persons accused; and they have thereupon, by the wonderful Providence of God, been so strengthened with *other evidences*, that some of the *Witch Gang* have been fairly Executed. But what shall be done, as to those against whom the *evidence* is chiefly founded in the *dark world*? Here they do solemnly demand our Addresses to the *Father of Lights*, on their behalf. But in the mean time, the Devil improves the *Darkness* of this Affair, to push us into a *Blind Mans Buffet*, and we are even ready to be *sinfully*, yea, hotly, and madly, mauling one another in the *dark*.

The consequence of these things, every *considerate* Man trembles at; and the more, because the frequent cheats of Passion, and Rumour, do precipitate so many, that I wish I could say, The most were *considerate*.

But that which carries on the formidableness of our Trials, unto that which may be called, *A wrath unto the uttermost*, is this: It is not without the *wrath* of the Almighty *God* himself, that the *Devil* is permitted thus to come down upon us in *wrath*. It was said, in *Isa. 9.19. Through the wrath of the Lord of Hosts, the Land is darkned*. Our Land is *darkned* indeed; since the *Powers of Darkness* are turned in upon us: 'tis a *dark time*, yea a black night indeed, now the *Ty-dogs* of the Pit are abroad among us: but, *It is through the wrath of the Lord of Hosts!* Inasmuch as the *Fire-brands* of *Hell* it self are used for the scorching of us, with cause enough may we cry out, *What means the heat of this anger?* Blessed Lord! Are all the other Instruments of thy Vengeance, too good for the chastisement of such transgressors as we are? Must the very *Devils* be sent out of *Their own place*, to be our Troublers: Must we be lash'd with *Scorpions*, fetch'd from the *Place of Torment?* Must this *Wilderness* be made a Receptacle for the *Dragons of the Wilderness?* If a *Lapland* should nourish in it vast numbers, the successors of the old *Biarmi*, who can with looks or words bewitch other people, or sell Winds to Marriners, and have their *Familiar Spirits* which they bequeath to their Children when they die, and by their Enchanted Kettle-Drums can learn things done a Thousand Leagues off; If a *Swedeland* should afford a Village, where some scores of Haggs, may not only have their Meetings with

Familiar Spirits, but also by their Enchantments drag many scores of poor children out of their Bed-chambers, to be spoiled at those Meetings; This, were not altogether a matter of so much wonder! But that *New-England* should this way be harassed! They are not *Chaldeans*, that *Bitter and Hasty Nation*, but they are, *Bitter and Burning Devils*; They are not *Swarthy Indians*, but they are *Sooty Devils*; that are let loose upon us. Ah, Poor *New-England!* Must the plague of *Old Ægypt* come upon thee? Whereof we read in *Psal. 78.49. He cast upon them the fierceness of his Anger, Wrath, and Indignation, and Trouble, by sending Evil Angels among them.* What, O what must next be looked for? Must that which is there next mentioned, be next encountered? *He spared not their soul from death, but gave their life over to the Pestilence.* For my part, when I consider what *Melancthon* says, in one of his Epistles, *That these Diabolical Spectacles are often Prodigies;* and when I consider, how often people have been by *Spectres* called upon, just before their Deaths; I am verily afraid, lest some wasting *Mortality* be among the things, which this Plague is the *Forerunner* of. I pray God prevent it!

But now, *What shall we do?*

I. Let the Devils *coming down* in *great wrath* upon us, cause us to *come down* in *great grief* before the Lord. We may truly and sadly say, *We are brought very low! Low* indeed, when the Serpents of the dust, are crawling and coyling about us, and Insulting over us. May we not say, *We are in the very belly of Hell,* when *Hell* it self is feeding upon us? But how *Low* is that! O let us then most penitently lay our selves very *Low* before the God of Heaven, who has thus Abased us. When a Truculent *Nero*, a *Devil* of a Man, was turned in upon the World, it was said, in *1 Pet. 5.6. Humble your selves under the mighty hand of God.* How much more now ought we to *humble our selves* under that *Mighty Hand* of that God who indeed has the *Devil* in a *Chain*, but has horribly lengthened out the *Chain*! When the old people of God heard any *Blasphemies*, tearing of his Ever-Blessed Name to pieces, they were to *Rend their Cloaths* at what they heard. I am sure that we have cause to *Rend our Hearts* this Day, when we see what an High Treason has been committed against the most high God, by the Witchcrafts in our Neighbourhood. We may say; and shall we not be *humbled* when we say it? *We have seen an horrible thing done in our Land!* O 'tis a most humbling thing, to think, that ever there should be such an abomination among us, as for a crue of humane race, to renounce their *Maker*, and to unite with the *Devil*, for the troubling of mankind, and for People to be, (as is by some confess'd) *Baptized* by a *Fiend* using this form upon them, *Thou art mine, and I have a full power over thee!* afterwards communicating in an Hellish *Bread* and *Wine*, by that Fiend administred unto them. It was said in *Deut. 18.10, 11, 12. There shall not be found among you an Inchanter, or a Witch, or a Charmer, or a Consulter with Familiar Spirits, or a Wizzard, or a Necromancer; For all that do these things are an Abomination to the Lord, and because of these Abominations, the Lord thy God doth drive them out before thee.* That *New-England* now should have these *Abominations* in it, yea, that some of no mean *Profession*, should be found guilty of them: Alas, what *Humiliations* are we all hereby oblig'd unto? O 'tis a *Defiled Land*, wherein we live; Let us be humbled for these *Defiling Abominations*, lest we be driven out of our Land. It's a very *humbling* thing to think, what reproaches will be cast upon us, for this matter, among *The Daughters of the Philistines.* Indeed, enough might easily be said for the vindication of *this* Country from the *Singularity* of this matter, by ripping up, what has been discovered in *others*. *Great Brittain* alone, and this also in our days of *Greatest Light*, has had that in it, which may divert the Calumnies of an ill-natured World, from centring here. They are words of the Devout Bishop *Hall*, *Satans prevalency in this Age, is most clear in the marvellous*

Number of Witches, abounding in all places. Now Hundreds are discovered in one Shire; and, if Fame Deceives us not, in a Village of Fourteen Houses in the North, are found so many of this Damned Brood. Yea, and those of both Sexes, who have Professed much Knowledge, Holiness, and Devotion, are drawn into this Damnable Practice. I suppose the Doctor in the first of those Passages, may refer to what happened in the Year 1645. When so many Vassals of the Devil were Detected, that there were *Thirty* try'd at one time, whereas about *fourteen* were Hang'd, and an Hundred more detained in the Prisons of *Suffolk* and *Essex*. Among other things which many of these Acknowledged, one was, That they were to undergo certain *Punishments*, if they did not such and such *Hurts*, as were appointed them. And, among the rest that were then Executed, there was an Old Parson, called *Lowis*, who confessed, That he had a couple of *Imps*, whereof *one* was always putting him upon the doing of Mischief; Once particularly, that *Imp* calling for his Consent so to do, went immediately and Sunk a *Ship*, then under Sail. I pray, let not *New-England* become of an Unsavoury and a Sulphurous Resentment in the Opinion of the World abroad, for the Doleful things which are now fallen out among us, while there are such *Histories* of other places abroad in the World. Nevertheless, I am sure that *we*, the People of *New-England*, have cause enough to *Humble* our selves under our most *Humbling* Circumstances. We must no more be *Haughty, because of the Lords Holy Mountain among us*; No it becomes us rather to be, *Humble, because we have been such an Habitation of Unholy Devils!*

II. Since the Devil is *come down in great wrath* upon us, let not us in our *great wrath* against one another provide a *Lodging* for him. It was a most wholesome caution, in *Eph.* 4.26, 27. *Let not the Sun go down upon your wrath: Neither give place to the Devil.* The Devil is come down to see what *Quarter* he shall find among us: And if his coming down, do now fill us with *wrath* against one another, and if between the cause of the *Sufferers* on one hand, and the cause of the *Suspected* on t'other, we carry things to such extreams of *Passion* as are now gaining upon us, the Devil will Bless himself, to find such a convenient *Lodging* as we shall therein afford unto him. And it may be that the *wrath* which we have had against one another has had more than a little influence upon the coming down of the Devil in that *wrath* which now amazes us. Have not many of us been *Devils* one unto another for Slanderings, for Backbitings, for Animosities? For *this*, among other causes, perhaps, God has permitted the Devils to be worrying, as they now are, among us. But it is high time to leave off all *Devilism*, when the *Devil* himself is falling upon us: And it is *no time* for us to be Censuring and Reviling one another, with a *Devilish wrath*, when the *wrath* of the *Devil* is annoying of us. The way for us to outwit the Devil, in the *Wiles* with which he now *Vexes* us, would be for us to joyn as one man in our cries to God, for the Directing, and Issuing of this Thorny Business; but if we do not *Lift up* our Hands to Heaven, *without Wrath*, we cannot then do it *without Doubt*, of speeding in it. I am ashamed when I read French Authors giving this Character of Englishmen *They hate one another, and are always Quarrelling one with another.* And I shall be much more ashamed, if it become the Character of *New-Englanders*; which is indeed what the Devil would have. *Satan* would make us *bruise* one another, by breaking of the *Peace* among us; but O let us disappoint him. We read of a thing that sometimes happens to the *Devil*, when he is foaming with his *Wrath*, in *Mar. 12.43. The unclean Spirit seeks rest, and finds none.* But we give *rest* unto the Devil, by *wrath* one against another. If we would lay aside all fierceness, and keenness, in the disputes which the Devil has raised among us; and if we would use to one another none but the *soft Answers, which turn away wrath*: I should hope that we might light upon such Counsels, as would quickly Extricate us out of our *Labyrinths*. But the old *Incendiary* of the world, is come from Hell, with *Sparks* of Hell-Fire flashing on every side of him; and we make our selves *Tynder* to the Sparks. When the Emperour *Henry* III. kept the Feast of *Pentecost*, at the City *Mentz*, there arose a dissension among some of the people there, which came from words to blows, and at last it passed on to the shedding of Blood. After the Tumult was over, when they came to that clause in their Devotions, *Thou hast made this day Glorious;* the Devil to the unexpressible Terrour of that vast Assembly, made the Temple Ring with that Outcry *But I have made this Day Quarrelsome!* We are truly come into a day, which by being well managed might be very *Glorious*, for the exterminating of those *Accursed things*, which have hitherto been the Clogs of our Prosperity; but if we make this day *Quarrelsome*, thro' any *Raging Confidences*, Alas, O Lord, *my Flesh Trembles for Fear of thee, and I am afraid of thy Judgments. Erasmus*, among other Historians, tells us, that at a Town in *Germany*, a Witch or Devil, appeared on the Top of a Chimney, Threatning to set the Town on *Fire*: And at length, Scattering a Pot of Ashes abroad, the Town was presently and horribly Burnt unto the Ground. Methinks, I see the *Spectres*, from the Top of the Chimneys to the Northward, threatning to scatter *Fire*, about the Countrey; but let us quench that *Fire*, by the most amicable Correspondencies: Lest, as the *Spectres*, have, they say, already most Literally burnt some of our Dwellings there do come forth a further *Fire* from the *Brambles* of Hell, which may more terribly *Devour* us. Let us not be like a *Troubled House*, altho' we are so much haunted by the *Devils*. Let our *Long suffering* be a well-placed piece of *Armour*, about us, against the *Fiery Darts* of the wicked ones. History informs us, That so long ago, as the year, 858, a certain Pestilent and Malignant sort of a *Dæmon*, molested *Caumont* in *Germany* with all sorts of methods to stir up strife among the Citizens. He uttered Prophecies, he detected Villanies, he branded people with all kind of Infamies. He incensed the Neighbourhood against one Man particularly, as the cause of all the mischiefs: who yet proved himself innocent. He threw stones at the Inhabitants, and at length burnt their Habitations, till the Commission of the *Dæmon* could go no further. I say, Let us be well aware lest such *Dæmons* do *Come hither also.*

III. Inasmuch as the Devil is come down in *Great Wrath*, we had need Labour, with all the Care and Speed we can to Divert the *Great Wrath* of Heaven from coming at the same time upon us. The God of Heaven has with long and loud Admonitions, been calling us to *a Reformation of our Provoking Evils,* as the only way to avoid that *Wrath* of His, which does not only *Threaten* but *Consume* us. 'Tis because we have been Deaf to those *Calls* that we are now by a provoked God, laid open to the *Wrath* of the Devil himself. It is said in *Pr. 16.17. When a mans ways please the Lord, he maketh even his Enemies to be at peace with him.* The Devil is our grand *Enemy*; and tho' we would not be at peace *with* him, yet we would be at peace from him, that is, we would have him unable to disquiet our *peace.* But inasmuch as the *wrath* which we endure from this *Enemy,* will allow us no *peace*, we may be sure, *our ways have not pleased the Lord.* It is because we have *broken the hedge* of Gods *Precepts*, that the hedge of Gods *Providence* is not so entire as it uses to be about us; but *Serpents* are *biting* of us. O let us then set our selves to make our *peace* with our God, whom we have *displeased* by our iniquities: and let us not imagine that we can encounter the *Wrath* of the Devil, while there is the *Wrath* of God Almighty to set that Mastiff upon us. Reformation! Reformation! has been the repeated *Cry* of all the Judgments that have hitherto been upon us; because we have been as *deaf Adders* thereunto, the *Adders* of the Infernal Pit are now hissing about us. At length, as it was of old said, *Luke 16.30. If one went unto them from the dead, they will repent;* even so, there are some come unto us from the *Damned*. The great God has loosed the Bars of the Pit, so that many *damned Spirits* are come in among us, to make us *repent* of our Misdemeanours. The means which the Lord had formerly employ'd for our *awakening*, were such, that he might well have said, *What could I have done more?* and yet after all, he has done *more*, in some regards, than was ever done for the awakening of any People in the World. The things now done to awaken our Enquiries after our *provoking Evils*, and our endeavours to Reform those Evils, are most *extraordinary* things; for which cause I would freely speak it, if we now do not some *extraordinary* things in returning to God; we are the most *incurable*, and I wish it be not quickly said, the most *miserable* People under the Sun. Believe me, 'tis a time for all people to do something *extraordinary, in searching and trying of their ways, and in turning to the Lord*. It is at an *extraordinary* rate of *Circumspection* and *Spiritual mindedness*, that we should all now maintain a *walk with God*. At such a time as this ought *Magistrates* to do something *extraordinary* in promoting of what is laudable, and in restraining and chastising of *Evil Doers*. At such a time as this ought *Ministers* to do something *extraordinary* in pulling the Souls of men out of the *Snares* of the Devil, not only by publick Preaching, but by personal Visits and Counsels, *from house to house*. At such a time as this ought *Churches* to do something *extraordinary*, in *renewing* of their Covenants, and in *remembring*, and *reviving* the Obligations of what they have renewed. Some admirable Designs about the *Reformation* of Manners, have lately been on foot in the English Nation, in pursuance of the most excellent Admonitions which have been given for it, by the Letters of Their Majesties. Besides the vigorous Agreements of the *Justices* here and there in the Kingdom, assisted by godly Gentlemen and Informers, to Execute the *Laws* upon prophane Offenders; there has been started a *Proposal* for the well-affected people in every Parish, to enter into orderly *Societies*, whereof every Member shall bind himself, not only to *avoid* Prophaneness in himself, but also according unto to their Place, to do their utmost in first *Reproving*; and, if it must be so, then *Exposing*, and so *Punishing*, as the Law directs, for others that shall be guilty. It has been observed, that the English Nation has had some of its greatest Successes, upon some special and signal *Actions* this way; and a discouragement given under Legal Proceedings of this kind, must needs be very exercising to the *Wise that observe these things.* But, O why should not *New-England* be the most forward part of the English Nation in such *Reformations*? Methinks I hear the Lord from Heaven saying over us, *O that my People had hearkened unto me; then I should soon have subdued the Devils, as well as their other Enemies!* There have been some feeble Essays towards *Reformation* of late in our *Churches*; but, I pray what comes of them? Do we stay till the *Storm* of his *Wrath* be over? Nay, let us be doing what we can, as fast as we can, to divert the *Storm.* The Devils having broke in upon our World, there is great asking, *Who is it that has brought them in?* And many do by *Spectral* Exhibitions come to be *cry'd out* upon. I hope in Gods time it will be found, that among those that are thus *cry'd out* upon, there are persons yet *Clear from the great Transgression*; but indeed, all the *Unreformed* among us, may justly be *cry'd out* upon, as having too much of an hand in letting of the Devils into our Borders; 'tis *our* Worldliness, *our* Formality, *our* Sensuality, and *our* Iniquity that has help'd this letting of the Devils in. O let us then at last, *consider our ways.* 'Tis a strange passage recorded by Mr. *Clark* in the Life of his Father, That the People of his Parish, refusing to be Reclaimed from their *Sabbath breaking*, by all the zealous Testimonies which that good Man bore against it; at last, on a night after the people had retired home from a Revelling Prophanation of the *Lords Day*, there was heard a great Noise, with rattling of Chains up and down the Town, and an horrid Scent of Brimstone fill'd the Neighbourhood. Upon which the *guilty Consciences* of the

Wretches told them, the Devil was come to fetch them away; and it so terrifi'd them, that an Eminent *Reformation* follow'd the Sermons which that Man of God Preached thereupon. Behold, Sinners, behold and *wonder*, lest you *perish*: the very *Devils* are walking about our Streets, with lengthened *Chains*, making a dreadful Noise in our Ears, and *Brimstone* even without a Metaphor, is making an hellish and horrid stench in our Nostrils. I pray leave off all those things whereof your *guilty Consciences* may now accuse you, lest these Devils do yet more direfully fall upon you. *Reformation* is at this time our only *Preservation*.

IV. When the Devil is come down in *great Wrath*, let every great *Vice* which may have a more particular tendency to make us a Prey unto that *Wrath*, come into a due discredit with us. It is the general Concession of all men, who are not become too *Unreasonable* for common Conversation, that the Invitation of *Witchcrafts* is the thing that has now introduced the Devil into the midst of us. I say then, let not only all *Witchcrafts* be duly abominated with us, but also let us be duly watchful against all the *Steps* leading thereunto. There are lesser *Sorceries* which they say, are too frequent in our Land. As it was said in *2 King. 17.9. The Children of* Israel *did secretly those things that were not right, against the Lord their God.* So 'tis to be feared, the Children of *New-England* have *secretly* done many things that have been pleasing to the Devil. They say, that in some Towns it has been an usual thing for People to cure Hurts with *Spells*, or to use detestable Conjurations, with *Sieves*, *Keys*, and *Pease*, and *Nails*, and *Horse-shoes*, and I know not what other Implements, to learn the things for which they have a forbidden, and an impious *Curiosity*. 'Tis in the Devils Name, that such things are done; and in Gods Name I do this day charge them, as vile Impieties. By these Courses 'tis, that People play upon *The Hole of the Asp*, till that cruelly venemous *Asp* has pull'd many of them into the deep *Hole* of *Witchcraft* it self. It has been acknowledged by some who have sunk the deepest into this *horrible Pit*, that they began at these little *Witchcrafts*; on which 'tis pity but the Laws of the English Nation, whereby the incorrigible repetition of those *Tricks*, is made *Felony*, were severely Executed. From the like sinful *Curiosity* it is, that the Prognostications of *Judicial Astrology*, are so injudiciously regarded by multitudes among us; and altho' the Jugling *Astrologers* do scarce ever hit right, except it be in such *Weighty Judgments*, forsooth, as that many *Old Men* will die such a year, and that there will be many *Losses* felt by some that venture to Sea, and that there will be much *Lying* and *Cheating* in the World; yet their foolish Admirers will not be perswaded but that the Innocent *Stars* have been concern'd in these Events. It is a disgrace to the English Nation, that the Pamphlets of such idle, futil, trifling *Stargazers* are so much considered; and the Countenance hereby given to a Study, wherein at last, all is done by *Impulse*, if any thing be done to any purpose at all, is not a little perillous to the Souls of Men. It is (*a Science*, I dare not call it, but) a *Juggle*, whereof the Learned *Hall* well says, *It is presumptuous and unwarrantable, and cry'd ever down by Councils and Fathers, as unlawful, as that which lies in the mid-way between Magick and Imposture, and partakes not a little of both.* Men consult the Aspects of Planets, whose Northern or Southern motions receive denominations from a *Cælestial Dragon*, till the *Infernal Dragon* at length insinuate into them, with a *Poison* of *Witchcraft* that can't be cured. Has there not also been a world of *discontent* in our Borders? 'Tis no wonder, that the *fiery Serpents* are so Stinging of us; We have been a most *Murmuring Generation.* It is not Irrational, to ascribe the late Stupendious growth of *Witches* among us, partly to the bitter *discontents*, which Affliction and Poverty has fill'd us with: it is inconceivable, what advantage the Devil gains over men, by *discontent.* Moreover, the Sin of *Unbelief* may be reckoned as perhaps the chief *Crime* of our Land. We are told, *God swears in wrath, against them that believe not;* and what follows then but this, *That the Devil comes unto them in wrath?* Never were the offers of the *Gospel,* more freely tendered, or more basely despised, among any People under the whole Cope of Heaven, than in this *N. E.* Seems it at all marvellous unto us, that the *Devil* should get such footing in our Country? Why, 'tis because the *Saviour* has been slighted here, perhaps more than any where. The Blessed Lord Jesus Christ has been profering to us, *Grace, and Glory, and every good thing,* and been alluring of us to Accept of Him, with such Terms as these, *Undone Sinner, I am All; Art thou willing that I should be thy All?* But, as a proof of that Contempt which this Unbelief has cast upon these proffers, I would seriously ask of the so many Hundreds above a Thousand People within these Walls; which of you all, O how few of you, can indeed say, *Christ is mine, and I am his, and he is the Beloved of my Soul?* I would only say thus much: When the precious and glorious Jesus, is Entreating of us to Receive *Him,* in all His *Offices,* with all His *Benefits;* the Devil minds what Respect we pay unto that Heavenly Lord; if we *Refuse Him that speaks from Heaven,* then he that, *Comes from Hell,* does with a sort of claim set in, and cry out, *Lord, since this Wretch is not willing that thou shouldst have him, I pray, let me have him.* And thus, by the just vengeance of Heaven, the Devil becomes a *Master,* a *Prince,* a *God,* unto the miserable Unbelievers: but O what are many of them then hurried unto! All of these Evil Things, do I now set before you, as *Branded* with the Mark of the Devil upon them.

V. With *Great Regard,* with *Great Pity,* should we Lay to Heart the Condition of those, who are cast into Affliction, by the *Great Wrath* of the Devil. There is a Number of our Good Neighbours, and some of them very particularly noted for Goodness and Vertue, of whom we may say, *Lord, They are vexed with Devils.* Their Tortures being primarily Inflicted on their *Spirits,* may indeed cause the Impressions thereof upon their Bodies to be the less

Durable, tho' rather the more *Sensible*: but they Endure Horrible Things, and many have been actually Murdered. Hard *Censures* now bestow'd upon these poor Sufferers, cannot but be very Displeasing unto our Lord, who, as He said, about some that had been Butchered by a *Pilate,* in Luc. 13.2, 3. *Think ye that these were Sinners above others, because they suffered such Things? I tell you No, But except ye Repent, ye shall all likewise Perish:* Even so, he now says, *Think ye that they who now suffer by the Devil, have been greater Sinners than their Neighbours?* No, Do you Repent of your *own Sins,* Lest the Devil come to fall foul of *you,* as he has done to *them.* And if this be so, How *Rash* a thing would it be, if such of the poor Sufferers, as carry it with a Becoming Piety, Seriousness, and Humiliation under their present Suffering, should be unjustly *Censured*; or have their very *Calamity* imputed unto them as a *Crime?* It is an easie thing, for us to fall into the Fault of, *Adding Affliction to the Afflicted,* and of, *Talking to the Grief of those that are already wounded.* Nor can it be wisdom to slight the Dangers of such a Fault. In the mean time, We have no Bowels in us, if we do not Compassionate the Distressed County of *Essex,* now crying to all these Colonies, *Have pity on me, O ye my Friends, Have pity on me, for the Hand of the Lord has Touched me, and the Wrath of the Devil has been therewithal turned upon me.* But indeed, if an hearty *pity* be due to any, I am sure, the Difficulties which attend our Honourable *Judges,* do demand no Inconsiderable share in that *Pity.* What a Difficult, what an Arduous Task, have those Worthy Personages now upon their Hands? To carry the *Knife* so exactly, that on the one side, there may be no Innocent Blood Shed, by too unseeing a *Zeal for the Children of Israel*; and that on the other side, there may be no Shelter given to those Diabolical *Works of Darkness,* without the Removal whereof we never shall have *Peace*; or to those *Furies* whereof several have kill'd *more people* perhaps than would serve to make a Village: *Hic Labor, Hoc Opus est!* O what need have we, to be concerned, that the Sins of our *Israel*, may not provoke the God of Heaven to leave his *Davids*, unto a wrong Step, in a matter of such Consequence, as is now before them! Our Disingenuous, Uncharitable, Unchristian Reproaching of such *Faithful Men*, after all, *The Prayers and Supplications, with strong Crying and Tears*, with which we are daily plying the Throne of Grace, that they may be kept, from what *They Fear*, is none of the way for our preventing of what *We Fear*. Nor all this while, ought our *Pity* to forget such *Accused* ones, as call for indeed our most Compassionate *Pity*, till there be fuller Evidences that they are less worthy of it. If *Satan* have any where maliciously brought upon the *Stage*, those that have hitherto had a just and good stock of Reputation, for their just and good Living, among us; If the *Evil One* have obtained a permission to *Appear*, in the Figure of such as we have cause to think, have hitherto *Abstained*, even from the *Appearance of Evil*: It is in Truth, such an Invasion upon *Mankind*, as may well Raise an Horror in us all: But, O what Compassions are due to such as may come under such Misrepresentations, of the *Great Accuser*! Who of us can say, what may be shewn in the *Glasses* of the Great *Lying Spirit?* Altho' the *Usual Providence* of God keeps us from such a Mishap; yet where have we an *Absolute Promise*, that we shall every one always be kept from it? As long as *Charity* is bound to Think *no Evil*, it will not Hurt us that are *Private Persons*, to forbear the *Judgment* which belongs not unto us. Let it rather be our Wish, May the Lord help them to Learn the *Lessons*, for which they are now put unto so hard a School.

VI. With a *Great Zeal*, we should lay hold on the *Covenant* of God, that we may secure *Us* and *Ours*, from the *Great Wrath*, with which the Devil Rages. Let us come into the *Covenant of Grace*, and then we shall not be hook'd into a *Covenant with the Devil*, nor be altogether unfurnished with Armour, against the Wretches that are in that *Covenant*. The way to come under the Saving Influences of the *New*

Covenant, is, to close with the Lord Jesus Christ, who is the All-sufficient *Mediator* of it: Let us therefore do, *that,* by Resigning up our selves unto the Saving, Teaching, and Ruling Hands of this Blessed *Mediator.* Then we shall be, what we read in *Jude 1. Preserved in Christ Jesus*: That is, as the *Destroying Angel,* could not meddle with such as had been distinguished, by the Blood of the *Passeover* on their Houses: Thus the Blood of the Lord Jesus Christ, Sprinkled on our Souls, will *Preserve* us from the Devil. The *Birds of prey* (and indeed the *Devils* most literally in the shape of great *Birds*!) are flying about. Would we find a Covert from these *Vultures*? Let us then Hear our Lord Jesus from Heaven Clocquing unto us, *O that you would be gathered under my wings!* Well; When this is done, Then let us own the *Covenant,* which we are now come into, by joining our selves to a Particular *Church,* walking in the Order of the Gospel; at the doing whereof, according to that *Covenant* of God, We give up Our selves unto the Lord, and in Him unto One Another. While others have had their Names Entred in the *Devils Book*; let our Names be found in the *Church Book,* and let us be *Written among the Living in Jerusalem.* By no means let, *Church work* sink and fail in the midst of us; but let the Tragical Accidents which now happen, exceedingly Quicken that *work.* So many of the *Rising Generation,* utterly forgetting the Errand of our Fathers to build Churches in this Wilderness, and so many of our *Cottages* being allow'd to Live, where they do not, and perhaps cannot, wait upon God with the Churches of His People; 'tis as likely as any one thing to procure the swarmings of *Witch crafts* among us. But it becomes us, with a like Ardour, to bring our poor *Children* with us, as we shall do, when we come our selves, into the *Covenant* of God. It would break an heart of Stone, to have seen, what I have lately seen; Even poor Children of several Ages, even from seven to twenty, more or less, *Confessing* their Familiarity with Devils; but at the same time, in Doleful bitter Lamentations, that made a little Pourtraiture of *Hell* it self, Expostulating with their execrable Parents, for *Devoting* them to the Devil in their Infancy, and so *Entailing* of Devillism upon them! Now, as the Psalmist could say, *My Zeal hath consumed me, because my Enemies have forgotten thy words:* Even so, let the Nefarious wickedness of those that have Explicitly dedicated their Children to the Devil, even with Devilish Symbols, of such a Dedication, Provoke our *Zeal* to have our Children, Sincerely, Signally, and openly *Consecrated* unto God; with an *Education* afterwards assuring and confirming that Consecration.

VII. Let our *Prayer* go up with great Faith, against the Devil, that comes down in great Wrath. Such is the Antipathy of the Devil to our *Prayer*, that he cannot bear to stay long where much of it is: Indeed it is *Diaboli Flagellum*, as well as, *Miseriæ Remedium*; the Devil will soon be Scourg'd out of the Lord's Temple, by a *Whip*, made and used, with the *effectual fervent Prayer of Righteous Men.* When the Devil by Afflicting of us, drives us to our Prayers, he is *The Fool making a Whip for his own Back.* Our Lord said of the Devil in *Matt. 17.21. This Kind goes not out, but by Prayer and Fasting.* But, *Prayer and Fasting* will soon make the Devil be gone. Here are *Charms* indeed! Sacred and Blessed *Charms*, which the Devil cannot stand before. A Promise of God, being well managed in the *Hands* of them that are much upon their Knees, will so resist the Devil, that he will *Flee from us.* At every other Weapon the Devils will be too hard for us; the *Spiritual Wickednesses in High Places*, have manifestly the Upper hand of us; that *Old Serpent* will be too old for us, too cunning, too subtil; they will soon *out wit* us, if we think to Encounter them with any *Wit* of our own. But when we come to *Prayers*, Incessant and Vehement *Prayers* before the Lord, there we shall be too hard for them. When well-directed *Prayers*, that great Artillery of Heaven, are brought into the Field, *There* methinks I see, *There are these workers of Iniquity fallen, all of them!* And who can tell, how much the most *Obscure Christian* among you all, may do towards the Deliverance of our Land from the Molestations which the Devil is now giving to us. I have Read, That on a day of Prayer kept by some good People for and with a Possessed Person, the Devil at last flew out of the Window, and referring to a Devout, plain, mean Woman then in the Room, he cry'd out, *O the Woman behind the Door! 'Tis that Woman that forces me away!* Thus the Devil that now troubles us, may be forced within a while to forsake us; and it shall be said, *He was driven away by the Prayers of some Obscure and Retired Souls, which the World has taken but little notice of!* The Great God is about a *Great Work* at this day among us: Now, there is extream Hazard, lest the Devil by Compulsion must submit to that *Great Work*, may also by *Permission*, come to Confound that *Work*; both in the Detections of some, and in the Confessions of others, whose Ungodly deeds may be brought forth, by a *Great Work* of God; there is great Hazard lest the Devil intertwist some of his Delusions. 'Tis Prayer, I say, 'tis Prayer, that must carry us well through the strange things that are now upon us. Only that Prayer must then be the Prayer of Faith: O where is our Faith in him, Who *hath spoiled these Principalities and Powers, on his Cross, Triumphing over them*!

VIII. Lastly, Shake off, every Soul, shake off the *hard Yoak* of the Devil. Where 'tis said, *The whole World lyes in Wickedness;* 'tis by some of the Ancients rendred, *The whole World lyes in the Devil.* The Devil is a Prince, yea, the Devil is a God unto all the Unregenerate; and alas, there is *A whole World of them.* Desolate Sinners, consider what an horrid Lord it is that you are Enslav'd unto; and Oh shake off your Slavery to such a Lord. Instead of *him,* now make your Choice of the Eternal God in Jesus Christ; Chuse him with a most unalterable Resolution, and unto him say, with *Thomas, My Lord, and my God!* Say with the Church,

Lord, other Lords have had the Dominion over us, but now thou alone shalt be our Lord for ever. Then instead of your Perishing under the wrath of the Devils, God will fetch you to a place among those that fill up the Room of the Devils, left by their Fall from the Ethereal Regions. It was a most awful Speech made by the Devil, Possessing a young Woman, at a Village in *Germany, By the command of God, I am come to Torment the Body of this young Woman, tho I cannot hurt her Soul; and it is that I may warn Men, to take heed of sinning against God. Indeed* (said he) *'tis very sore against my will that I do it; but the command of God forces me to declare what I do; however I know that at the Last Day, I shall have more Souls than God himself.* So spoke that horrible Devil! But O that none of our Souls may be found among the Prizes of the Devil, in the Day of God! O that what the Devil has been forced to declare, of his Kingdom among us, may prejudice our Hearts against him for ever!

My Text says, *The Devil is come down in great Wrath, for he has but a short time.* Yea, but if you do not by a speedy and through Conversion to God, escape the Wrath of the Devil, you will your selves go down, where the Devil is to be, and you will there be sweltring under the Devils Wrath, not for a *short Time*, but, *World without end*; not for a *Short Time*, but for *Infinite Millions of Ages.* The smoak of your Torment under that Wrath, will *Ascend for ever and ever*! Indeed, the Devil's time for his Wrath upon you in this World, can be but short, but his time for you to do his Work, or, which is all one, to delay your turning to God, that is a *Long Time.* When the Devil was going to be Dispossessed of a Man, he Roar'd out, *Am I to be Tormented before my time?* You will *Torment* the Devil, if you Rescue your Souls out of his hands, by true Repentance: If once you begin to look that way, he'll Cry out, *O this is before my Time, I must have more Time, yet in the Service of such a guilty Soul.* But, I beseech you, let us join thus to torment the Devil, in an holy Revenge upon him, for all the Injuries which he has done unto us; let us tell him, *Satan, thy time with me is but short, Nay, thy time with me shall be no more; I am unutterably sorry that it has been so much; Depart from me thou Evil-Doer, that would'st have me to be an Evil Doer like thy self; I will now for ever keep the Commandments of that God, in whom I Live and Move, and have my Being!* The Devil has plaid a fine Game for himself indeed, if by his troubling of our Land, the Souls of many People should come to *think upon their ways, till even they turn their Feet into the Testimonies of the Lord.* Now that the Devil may be thus outshot in his own Bow, is the desire of all that love the Salvation of God among us, as well as of him, who has thus Addressed you. *Amen.*

Having thus discoursed on the *Wonders of the Invisible World,* I shall now, with God's help, go on to relate some Remarkable and Memorable Instances of *Wonders* which that *World* has given to ourselves. And altho the chief Entertainment which my Readers do expect, and shall receive, will be a true History of what has occurred, respecting the Witchcrafts wherewith we are at this day Persecuted; yet I shall choose to usher in the mention of those things, with

A NARRATIVE OF AN APPARITION WHICH
A GENTLEMAN IN BOSTON, HAD OF HIS BROTHER, JUST THEN MURTHERED IN LONDON.

It was on the Second of *May* in the Year 1687, that a most ingenious, accomplished and well-disposed Gentleman, Mr. *Joseph Beacon,* by Name, about Five a Clock in the Morning, as he lay, whether Sleeping or Waking he could not say, (but judged the latter of them) had a View of his Brother then at *London,* altho he was now himself at Our *Boston,* distanced from him a thousand Leagues. This his Brother appear'd unto him, in the Morning about Five a Clock at *Boston,* having on him a *Bengal* Gown, which he usually wore, with a Napkin tyed about his Head; his Countenance was very Pale, Gastly, Deadly, and he had a bloody Wound on one side of his Fore-head. *Brother!* says the Affrighted *Joseph. Brother!* Answered the Apparition. Said *Joseph, What's the matter Brother? How came you here!* The Apparition replied, *Brother, I have been most barbarously and injuriously Butchered, by a Debauched Drunken Fellow, to whom I never did any wrong in my Life.* Whereupon he gave a particular Description of the Murderer; adding, *Brother, This Fellow changing his Name, is attempting to come over unto* New-England, *in* Foy, *or* Wild; *I would pray you on the first Arrival of either of these, to get an Order from the Governor, to Seize the Person, whom I have now described; and then do you Indict him for the Murder of me your Brother: I'll stand by you and prove the Indictment.* And so he Vanished. Mr. *Beacon* was extreamly astonished at what he had seen and hear'd; and the People of the Family not only observed an extraordinary Alteration upon him, for the Week following, but have also given me under their Hands a full Testimony, that he then gave them an Account of this Apparition.

All this while, Mr. *Beacon* had no advice of any thing amiss attending his Brother then in *England*; but about the latter end of *June* following, he understood by the common ways of Communication, that the *April* before, his Brother going in haste by Night to call a Coach for a Lady, met a Fellow then in Drink, with his *Doxy* in his Hand: Some way or other the Fellow thought himself Affronted with the hasty passage of this *Beacon*, and immediately ran into the Fire-side of a Neighbouring Tavern, from whence he fetch'd out a Fire-fork, wherewith he grievously wounded *Beacon* in the Skull; even in that very part where the Apparition show'd his Wound. Of this Wound he Languished until he Dyed on the Second of *May*, about five of the Clock in the Morning at *London*. The Murderer it seems was endeavouring to Escape, as the Apparition affirm'd, but the

Friends of the Deceased *Beacon*, Seized him; and Prosecuting him at Law, he found the help of such Friends as brought him off without the loss of his Life; since which, there has no more been heard of the Business.

This History I received of Mr. *Joseph Beacon* himself; who a little before his own Pious and hopeful Death, which follow'd not long after, gave me the Story written and signed with his own Hand, and attested with the Circumstances I have already mentioned.

But I shall no longer detain my Reader, from his expected Entertainment, in a brief account of the Tryals which have passed upon some of the Malefactors lately Executed at *Salem*, for the *Witchcrafts* whereof they stood Convicted. For my own part, I was not present at any of them; nor ever had I any Personal prejudice at the Persons thus brought upon the Stage; much less at the Surviving Relations of those Persons, with and for whom I would be as hearty a Mourner as any Man living in the World: *The Lord Comfort them!* But having received a Command so to do, I can do no other than shortly relate the chief *Matters of Fact*, which occurr'd in the Tryals of some that were Executed, in an Abridgment Collected out of the *Court-Papers*, on this occasion put into my hands. You are to take the *Truth*, just as it was; and the Truth will hurt no good Man. There might have been more of these, if my Book would not thereby have swollen too big; and if some other worthy hands did not perhaps intend something further in these *Collections*; for which cause I have only singled out Four or Five, which may serve to illustrate the way of Dealing, wherein *Witchcrafts* use to be concerned; and I report matters not as an *Advocate*, but as an *Historian*.

They were some of the Gracious Words inserted in the Advice, which many of the Neighbouring Ministers, did this Summer humbly lay before our Honorable Judges, *We cannot but with all thankfulness, acknowledge the success which the Merciful God has given unto the Sedulous and Assiduous endeavours of Our Honourable Rulers, to detect the abominable Witchcrafts which have been committed in the Country; Humbly Praying, that the discovery of those mysterious and mischievous wickednesses, may be Perfected.* If in the midst of the many Dissatisfactions among us, the Publication of these Tryals, may promote such a Pious Thankfulness unto God, for Justice being so far executed among us, I shall Rejoice that God is Glorified; and pray, that no wrong steps of ours may ever sully any of his Glorious Works. But we will begin with,

A MODERN INSTANCE OF WITCHES,
DISCOVERED AND CONDEMNED IN A TRYAL, BEFORE THAT CELEBRATED JUDGE, SIR MATTHEW HALE.

It may cast some Light upon the Dark things now in *America*, if we just give a glance upon the *like things* lately happening in *Europe*. We may see the *Witchcrafts* here most exactly resemble the *Witchcrafts* there; and we may learn what sort of Devils do trouble the World.

The Venerable *Baxter* very truly says, *Judge* Hale *was a Person, than whom, no Man was more Backward to Condemn a Witch, without full Evidence.*

Now, one of the latest Printed Accounts about a *Tryal of Witches,* is of what was before him, and it ran on this wise. And it is here the rather mentioned, because it was a Tryal, much considered by the Judges of *New England*.

I. *Rose Cullender* and *Amy Duny,* were severally Indicted, for Bewitching *Elizabeth Durent, Ann Durent, Jane Bocking,*

Susan Chandler, William Durent, Elizabeth and *Deborah Pacy*. And the Evidence whereon they were Convicted, stood upon divers particular Circumstances.

II. *Ann Durent, Susan Chandler,* and *Elizabeth Pacy*, when they came into the Hall, to give Instructions for the drawing the Bills of Indictments, they fell into strange and violent Fits, so that they were unable to give in their Depositions, not only then, but also during the whole Assizes. *William Durent* being an Infant, his Mother Swore, That *Amy Duny* looking after her Child one Day in her absence, did at her return confess, that she had *given suck to the Child*: (tho' she were an Old Woman:) Whereat, when *Durent* expressed her displeasure, *Duny* went away with Discontents and Menaces.

The Night after, the Child fell into strange and sad Fits, wherein it continued for Divers Weeks. One Doctor *Jacob* advised her to hang up the Childs Blanket, in the Chimney Corner all Day, and at Night, when she went to put the Child into it, if she found any Thing in it then to throw it without fear into the Fire. Accordingly, at Night, there fell a great Toad out of the Blanket, which ran up and down the Hearth. A Boy catch't it, and held it in the Fire with the Tongs: where it made an horrible Noise, and Flash'd like to Gun-Powder, with a report like that of a Pistol: Whereupon the Toad was no more to be seen. The next Day a Kinswoman of *Duny's*, told the Deponent, that her Aunt was all grievously scorch'd with the Fire, and the Deponent going to her House, found her in such a Condition. *Duny* told her, she might thank her for it; but she should live to see some of her Children Dead, and her self upon Crutches. But after the Burning of the Toad, this Child Recovered.

This Deponent further Testifi'd, That Her Daughter *Elizabeth*, being about the Age of Ten Years, was taken in like manner, as her first Child was, and in her Fits complained much of *Amy Duny*, and said, that she did appear to Her, and afflict her in such manner as the former. One Day she found *Amy Duny* in her House, and thrusting her out of Doors, *Duny* said, *You need not be so Angry, your Child won't live long.* And within three Days the Child Died. The Deponent added, that she was Her self, not long after taken with such a Lameness, in both her Legs, that she was forced to go upon Crutches; and she was now in Court upon them.

III. As for *Elizabeth* and *Deborah Pacy*, one Aged Eleven Years, the other Nine; the elder, being in Court, was made utterly senseless, during all the time of the Trial: or at least speechless. By the direction of the Judg, *Duny* was privately brought to *Elizabeth Pacy*, and she touched her Hand: whereupon the Child, without so much as seeing her, suddenly leap'd up and flew upon the Prisoner; the younger was too ill, to be brought unto the Assizes. But *Samuel Pacy*, their Father, testifi'd, that his Daughter *Deborah* was taken with a sudden Lameness; and upon the grumbling of *Amy Duny*, for being denied something, where this Child was then sitting, the Child was taken with an extream pain in her stomach, like the pricking of Pins; and shrieking at a dreadful manner, like a Whelp, rather than a Rational Creature. The Physicians could not conjecture the cause of the Distemper; but *Amy Duny* being a Woman of ill Fame, and the Child in Fits crying out of *Amy Duny*, as affrighting her with the Apparition of her Person, the Deponent suspected her, and procured her to be set in the stocks. While she was there, she said in the hearing of Two Witnesses, *Mr.* Pacy *keeps a great stir about his Child, but let him stay till he has done as much by his Children, as I have done by mine:* And being Asked, What she had done to her Children, she Answered, *She had been fain to open her Childs Mouth with a Tap to give it Victuals.* The Deponent added, that within Two Days, the Fits of his

Daughters were such, that they could not preserve either Life or Breath, without the help of a Tap. And that the Children Cry'd out of *Amy Duny*, and of *Rose Cullender*, as afflicting them with their Apparitions.

IV. The Fits of the Children were various. They would sometimes be Lame on one side; sometimes on t'other. Sometimes very sore; sometimes restored unto their Limbs, and then Deaf, or Blind, or Dumb, for a long while together. Upon the Recovery of their Speech, they would Cough extreamly; and with much Flegm, they would bring up Crooked Pins; and one time, a Two-penny Nail, with a very broad Head. Commonly at the end of every Fit, they would cast up a Pin. When the Children Read, they could not pronounce the Name of, *Lord*, or *Jesus*, or *Christ*, but would fall into Fits; and say, Amy Duny *says, I must not use that Name*. When they came to the Name of *Satan*, or *Devil*, they would clap their Fingers on the Book, crying out, *This bites, but it makes me speak right well!* The Children in their Fits would often Cry out, *There stands* Amy Duny, or *Rose Cullender*; and they would afterwards relate, *That these Witches appearing before them, threatned them, that if they told what they saw or heard, they would Torment them ten times more than ever they did before.*

V. Margaret Arnold, the Sister of Mr. *Pacy*, Testifi'd unto the like Sufferings being upon the Children, at her House, whither her Brother had Removed them. And that sometimes, the Children (*only*) would see things like Mice, run about the House; and one of them suddenly snap'd one with the Tongs, and threw it into the Fire, where it screeched out like a Rat. At another time, a thing like a Bee, flew at the Face of the younger Child; the Child fell into a Fit; and at last Vomited up a *Two-penny Nail*, with a Broad Head; affirming, *That the Bee brought this Nail, and forced it into her Mouth*. The Child would in like manner be assaulted with Flies, which brought Crooked Pins, unto her, and made her first swallow them, and then Vomit them. She one Day caught an Invisible *Mouse*, and throwing it into the Fire, it Flash'd like to Gun-Powder. None besides the Child saw the *Mouse*, but every one saw the *Flash*. She also declared, out of her Fits, that in them, *Amy Duny* much tempted her to destroy her self.

VI. As for *Ann Durent*, her Father Testified, That upon a Discontent of *Rose Cullender*, his Daughter was taken with much Illness in her Stomach and great and sore Pains, like the Pricking of Pins: and then Swooning Fits, from which Recovering, she declared, *She had seen the Apparition of* Rose Cullender, *Threatning to Torment her*. She likewise Vomited up diverse Pins. The Maid was Present at Court, but when *Cullender* look'd upon her, she fell into such Fits, as made her utterly unable to declare any thing.

Ann Baldwin deposed the same.

VII. Jane Bocking, was too weak to be at the Assizes. But her Mother Testifi'd, that her Daughter having formerly been Afflicted with Swooning Fits, and Recovered of them; was now taken with a great Pain in her Stomach; and New Swooning Fits. That she took little Food, but every Day Vomited Crooked Pins. In her first Fits, she would Extend her Arms, and use Postures, as if she catched at something, and when her Clutched Hands were forced open, they would find several Pins diversely Crooked, unaccountably lodged there. She would also maintain a Discourse with some that were Invisibly present, when casting abroad her Arms, she would often say, *I will not have it!* but at last say, *Then I will have it!* and closing her Hand, which when they presently after opened, a Lath-Nail was found in it. But her great Complaints were of being Visited by the shapes of *Amy Duny*, and *Rose Cullender*.

VIII. As for *Susan Chandler*, her Mother Testified, That being at the search of *Rose Cullender*, they found on her Belly a thing like a Teat, of an Inch long; which the *said Rose* ascribed to a strain. But near her Privy-parts, they found Three more, that were smaller than the former. At the end of the long Teat, there was a little Hole, which appeared, as if newly Sucked; and upon straining it, a white Milky matter issued out. The Deponent further said, That her Daughter being one Day concerned at *Rose Cullenders* taking her by the Hand, she fell very sick, and at Night cry'd out, *That* Rose Cullender *would come to Bed unto her*. Her Fits grew violent, and in the Intervals of them, she declared, *That she saw* Rose Cullender *in them, and once having of a great Dog with her*. She also Vomited up Crooked Pins; and when she was brought into Court, she fell into her Fits. She Recovered her self in some Time, and was asked by the Court, whether she was in a Condition to take an Oath, and give Evidence. She said, she could; but having been Sworn, she fell into her Fits again, and, *Burn her! Burn her!* were all the words that she could obtain power to speak. Her Father likewise gave the same Testimony with her Mother; as to all but the Search.

IX. Here was the Sum of the Evidence: Which Mr. Serjeant *Keeling*, thought not sufficient to Convict the Prisoners. For admitting the Children were Bewitched, yet, said he, it can never be Apply'd unto the Prisoners, upon the Imagination only of the Parties Afflicted; inasmuch as no person whatsoever could then be in Safety.

Dr. *Brown*, a very Learned Person then present, gave his Opinion, that these Persons were Bewitched. He added, That in *Denmark*, there had been lately a great Discovery of Witches; who used the very same way of Afflicting people, by Conveying Pins and Nails into them. His Opinion was, that the Devil in Witchcrafts, did Work upon the Bodies of Men and Women, upon a *Natural*

Foundation; and that he did Extraordinarily afflict them, with such Distempers as their Bodies were most subject unto.

X. The Experiment about the *Usefulness*, yea, or *Lawfulness* whereof Good Men have sometimes disputed, was divers Times made, That tho' the Afflicted were utterly deprived of all sense in their Fits, yet upon the *Touch* of the Accused, they would so screech out, and fly up, as not upon any other persons. And yet it was also found that once upon the touch of an innocent person, the like effect follow'd, which put the whole Court unto a stand: altho' a small Reason was at length attempted to be given for it.

XI. However, to strengthen the Credit of what had been already produced against the Prisoners, One *John Soam* Testifi'd, That bringing home his Hay in Three Carts, one of the Carts wrenched the Window of *Rose Cullenders* House, whereupon she flew out, with violent Threatenings against the Deponent. The other Two Carts, passed by Twice, Loaded, that Day afterwards; but the Cart which touched *Cullenders* House, was Twice or Thrice that Day overturned. Having again Loaded it, as they brought it thro' the Gate which Leads out of the Field, the Cart stuck so fast in the Gates Head, that they could not possibly get it thro', but were forced to cut down the Post of the Gate, to make the Cart pass thro', altho' they could not perceive that the Cart did of either side touch the Gate-Post. They afterwards, did with much Difficulty get it home to the Yard; but could not for their Lives get the Cart near the place, where they should unload. They were fain to unload at a great Distance; and when they were Tired, the Noses of them that came to Assist them, would burst forth a Bleeding; so they were fain to give over till next morning; and then they unloaded without any difficulty.

XII. Robert Sherringham also Testifi'd, That the Axle-Tree of his Cart, happening in passing, to break some part of *Rose Cullenders* House, in her Anger at it, she vehemently threatned him, *His Horses should suffer for it.* And within a short time, all his Four Horses dy'd; after which he sustained many other Losses in the sudden Dying of his Cattle. He was also taken with a Lameness in his Limbs; and so vexed with Lice of an extraordinary Number and Bigness, that no Art could hinder the Swarming of them, till he burnt up two Suits of Apparel.

XIII. As for *Amy Duny*, 'twas Testifi'd by one *Richard Spencer* that he heard her say, *The Devil would not let her Rest; until she were Revenged on the Wife of* Cornelius Sandswel. And that *Sandswel* testifi'd, that her Poultry dy'd suddenly, upon *Amy Dunys* threatning of them; and that her Husbands Chimney fell, quickly after *Duny* had spoken of such a disaster. And a Firkin of Fish could not be kept from falling into the Water, upon suspicious words of *Duny's*.

XIV. The Judg told the Jury, they were to inquire now, first, whether these Children were Bewitched; and secondly, Whether the Prisoners at the Bar were guilty of it. He made no doubt, there were such Creatures as Witches; for the Scriptures affirmed it; and the Wisdom of all Nations had provided Laws against such persons. He pray'd the God of Heaven to direct their Hearts in the weighty thing they had in hand; for, *To Condemn the Innocent, and let the Guilty go free, were both an Abomination to the Lord.*

The Jury in half an hour brought them in *Guilty* upon their several Indictments, which were Nineteen in Number.

The next Morning, the Children with their Parents, came to the Lodgings of the Lord Chief Justice, and were in as good health as ever in their Lives; being Restored within half an Hour after the Witches were Convicted.

The Witches were Executed; and *Confessed* nothing; which indeed will not be wondred by them, who Consider and Entertain the Judgment of a Judicious Writer, *That the Unpardonable Sin, is most usually Committed by Professors of the Christian Religion, falling into Witchcraft.*

We will now proceed unto several of the like Tryals among our selves.

I.

THE TRYAL OF G. B. AT A COURT OF OYER AND TERMINER,
HELD IN SALEM, 1692.

Glad should I have been, if I had never known the Name of this Man; or never had this occasion to mention so much as the first Letters of his Name. But the Government requiring some Account of his Trial to be inserted in this Book, it becomes me with all Obedience to submit unto the Order.

I. This *G. B.* Was Indicted for Witch-craft, and in the prosecution of the Charge against him, he was Accused by five or six of the Bewitched, as the Author of their Miseries; he was Accused by Eight of the Confessing Witches, as being an head Actor at some of their Hellish Randezvouzes, and one who had the promise of being a King in Satan's Kingdom, now going to be Erected: He was accused by Nine Persons for extraordinary Lifting, and such feats of Strength, as could not be done without a Diabolical Assistance. And for other such things he was Accused, until about thirty Testimonies were brought in against him; nor were these judg'd the half of what might have been considered for his Conviction: However they were enough to fix the Character of a Witch upon him according to the Rules of Reasoning, by the Judicious *Gaule*, in that Case directed.

II. The Court being sensible, that the Testimonies of the Parties Bewitched, use to have a Room among the *Suspicions* or *Presumptions*, brought in against one Indicted for Witch-craft; there were now heard the Testimonies of several Persons, who were most notoriously Bewitched, and every day Tortured by Invisible Hands, and these now all charged the Spectres of *G. B.* to have a share in their Torments. At the Examination of this *G. B.* the Bewitched People were grievously harrassed with Preternatural Mischiefs, which could not possibly be Dissembled; and they still ascribed it unto the endeavours of *G. B.* to Kill them. And now upon the Tryal of one of the Bewitched Persons, testified, that in her Agonies, a little black Hair'd Man came to her, saying his Name was *B.* and bidding her set her hand to a Book which he shewed unto her; and bragging that he was a *Conjurer*, above the ordinary Rank of Witches; That he often Persecuted her with the offer of that Book, saying, *She should be well, and need fear nobody, if she would but Sign it*; But he inflicted cruel Pains and Hurts upon her, because of her denying so to do. The Testimonies of the other Sufferers concurred with these; and it was remarkable, that whereas *Biting* was one of the ways which the Witches used for the vexing of the Sufferers; when they cry'd out of *G. B.* Biting them, the print of the Teeth would be seen on the Flesh of the Complainers, and just such a Set of Teeth as *G. B's* would then appear upon them, which could be distinguished from those of some other Mens. Others of them testified, That in their Torments, *G. B.* tempted them to go unto a Sacrament, unto which they perceived him with a Sound of Trumpet, Summoning of other Witches, who quickly after the Sound, would come from all Quarters unto the Rendezvouz. One of them falling into a kind of Trance, affirmed, that *G. B.* had carried her away into a very high Mountain, where he shewed her mighty and glorious Kingdoms, and said, *He would give them all to her, if she would write in his Book;* but she told him, *They were none of his to give;* and refused the Motions; enduring of much Misery for that refusal.

It cost the Court a wonderful deal of Trouble, to hear the Testimonies of the Sufferers; for when they were going to give in their Depositions, they would for a long time be taken with Fits, that made them uncapable of saying any thing. The Chief Judg asked the Prisoner, who he thought hindred these Witnesses from giving their *Testimonies?* And he answered, *He supposed it was the Devil.* That Honourable Person replied, *How comes the Devil then to be so loath to have any Testimony born against you?* Which cast him into very great Confusion.

III. It has been a frequent thing for the Bewitched People to be entertained with Apparitions of *Ghosts* of Murdered People, at the same time that the *Spectres* of the Witches trouble them. These Ghosts do always affright the Beholders more than all the other spectral Representations; and when they exhibit themselves, they cry out, of being Murthered by the Witch-crafts or other Violences of the Persons who are then in Spectre present. It is further considered, that once or twice, these *Apparitions* have been seen by others, at the very same time they have shewn themselves to the Bewitched; and seldom have there been these *Apparitions,* but when something unusual or suspected, have attended the Death of the Party thus Appearing. Some that have been accused by these *Apparitions* accosting of the Bewitched People, who had never heard a word of any such Persons ever being in the World, have upon a fair Examination, freely and fully confessed the Murthers of those very Persons, altho' these also did not know how the Apparitions had complained of them. Accordingly several of the Bewitched, had given in their Testimony, that they had been troubled with the Apparitions of two Women, who said, that they were *G. B's* two Wives, and that he had been the Death of them; and that the Magistrates must be told of it, before whom if *B.* upon his Tryal denied it, they did not know but that they should appear again in Court. Now, *G. B.* had been Infamous for the Barbarous usage of his two late Wives, all the Country over. Moreover, it was testified, the Spectre of *G. B.* threatning of the Sufferers, told them, he had Killed (besides others) Mrs. *Lawson* and her Daughter *Ann.* And it was noted, that these were the Vertuous Wife and Daughter of one at whom this *G. B.* might have a prejudice for his being serviceable at *Salem Village*, from whence himself had in ill Terms removed some Years before: And that when they dy'd, which was long since, there were some odd Circumstances about them, which made some of the Attendents there suspect something of Witch-craft, tho none Imagined from what Quarter it should come.

Well, *G. B.* being now upon his Tryal, one of the Bewitched Persons was cast into Horror at the Ghost of *B's* two Deceased Wives then appearing before him, and crying for *Vengeance* against him. Hereupon several of the Bewitched Persons were successively called in, who all not knowing what the former had seen and said, concurred in their Horror of the Apparition, which they affirmed that he had before him. But he, tho much appalled, utterly deny'd that he discerned any thing of it; nor was it any part of his *Conviction.*

IV. Judicious Writers have assigned it a great place in the Conviction of *Witches, when Persons are Impeached by other notorious Witches, to be as ill as themselves; especially, if the*

Persons have been much noted for neglecting the Worship of God. Now, as there might have been Testimonies enough of *G. B's* Antipathy to *Prayer*, and the other Ordinances of God, tho by his Profession, singularly Obliged thereunto; so, there now came in against the Prisoner, the Testimonies of several Persons, who confessed their own having been horrible *Witches*, and ever since their Confessions, had been themselves terribly Tortured by the Devils and other Witches, even like the other Sufferers; and therein undergone the Pains of many *Deaths* for their Confessions.

These now testified, that *G. B.* had been at Witch-meetings with them; and that he was the Person who had Seduc'd, and Compell'd them into the snares of Witchcraft; That he promised them *Fine Cloaths*, for doing it; that he brought Poppets to them, and Thorns to stick into those Poppets, for the Afflicting of other People; and that he exhorted them with the rest of the Crew, to Bewitch all *Salem Village*, but besure to do it Gradually, if they would prevail in what they did.

When the *Lancashire Witches* were Condemn'd I don't remember that there was any considerable further Evidence, than that of the Bewitched, and than that of some that confessed. We see so much already against *G. B.* But this being indeed not enough, there were other things to render what had been already produced *credible*.

V. A famous Divine recites this among the Convictions of a Witch; *The Testimony of the party Bewitched, whether Pining or Dying; together with the joint Oaths of sufficient Persons that have seen certain Prodigious Pranks or Feats wrought by the Party Accused.* Now, God had been pleased so to leave this *G. B.* that he had ensnared himself by several Instances, which he had formerly given of a Preternatural Strength, and which were now produced against him. He was a very Puny Man, yet he had often done things beyond the strength of a Giant. A Gun of about seven foot Barrel, and so heavy that strong Men could not steadily hold it out with both hands; there were several Testimonies, given in by Persons of Credit and Honor, that he made nothing of taking up such a Gun behind the Lock, with but one hand, and holding it out like a Pistol, at Arms-end. *G. B.* in his Vindication, was so foolish as to say, That *an* Indian *was there, and held it out at the same time:* Whereas none of the Spectators ever saw any such *Indian*; but they supposed, the *Black Man*, (as the Witches call the Devil; and they generally say he resembles an *Indian*) might give him that Assistance. There was Evidence likewise brought in, that he made nothing of taking up whole Barrels fill'd with *Malasses* or *Cider*, in very disadvantageous Postures, and Carrying of them through the difficultest Places out of a Canoo to the Shore.

Yea, there were two Testimonies, that *G. B.* with only putting the Fore Finger of his Right hand into the Muzzle of an heavy Gun, a Fowling-piece of about six or seven foot Barrel, did lift up the Gun, and hold it out at Arms-end; a Gun which the Deponents thought strong Men could not with both hands lift up, and hold out at the But-end, as is usual. Indeed, one of these Witnesses was over-perswaded by some Persons, to be out of the way upon *G. B's* Tryal; but he came afterwards with Sorrow for his withdraw, and gave in his Testimony: Nor were either of these Witnesses made use of as Evidences in the Trial.

VI. There came in several Testimonies relating to the Domestick Affairs of *G. B.* which had a very hard Aspect upon him; and not only prov'd him a very ill Man; but also confirmed the belief of the Character, which had been already fastned on him.

'Twas testified, that keeping his two Successive Wives in a strange kind of Slavery, he would when he came home from abroad, pretend to tell the Talk which any had with them; That he has brought them to the point of Death, by his harsh Dealings with his Wives, and then made the People about him, to promise that in case Death should happen, they would say nothing of it; That he used all means to make his Wives Write, Sign, Seal, and Swear a Covenant, never to reveal any of his Secrets; That his Wives had privately complained unto the Neighbours about frightful Apparitions of Evil Spirits, with which their House was sometimes infested; and that many such things have been whispered among the Neighbourhood. There were also some other Testimonies relating to the Death of People whereby the Consciences of an Impartial Jury were convinced that *G. B.* had Bewitched the Persons mentioned in the Complaints. But I am forced to omit several passages, in this as well as in all the succeeding Tryals, because the Scribes who took notice of them, have not supplyed me.

VII. One Mr. *Ruck*, Brother-in-Law to this *G. B.* testified, that *G. B.* and himself, and his Sister, who was *G. B's* Wife, going out for two or three Miles to gather Straw-berries, *Ruck* with his Sister, the Wife of *G. B.* Rode home very Softly, with *G. B.* on Foot in their Company, *G. B.* stept aside a little into the Bushes; whereupon they halted and Halloo'd for him. He not answering, they went away homewards, with a quickened pace, without expectation of seeing him in a considerable while; and yet when they were got near home, to their Astonishment, they found him on foot with them, having a Basket of Straw-berries. *G. B.* immediately then fell to Chiding his Wife, on the account of what she had been speaking to her Brother, of him, on the Road: which when they wondred at, he said, *He knew their thoughts. Ruck* being startled at that, made some Reply, intimating, that the Devil himself did not know so far; but *G. B.* answered, *My God makes known your Thoughts unto me.* The Prisoner now at the Bar had nothing to answer, unto what was thus witnessed against him, that was worth considering. Only he said, *Ruck, and his Wife left a Man with him, when they left him.* Which *Ruck* now affirm'd to be false; and when the Court asked *G. B. What the Man's Name was?* his Countenance was much altered; nor could he say, who 'twas. But the Court began to think, that he then step'd aside, only that by the assistance of the *Black Man*, he might put on his *Invisibility*, and in that *Fascinating Mist*, gratifie his own Jealous Humour, to hear what they said of him. Which trick of rendring themselves *Invisible*, our Witches do in their Confessions pretend, that they sometimes are Masters of; and it is the more credible, because there is Demonstration, that they often render many other things utterly *Invisible*.

VIII. *Faltring, faulty, unconstant, and contrary Answers upon judicial and deliberate Examination,* are counted some unlucky Symptoms of Guilt, in all Crimes, especially in Witchcrafts. Now there never was a Prisoner more eminent for them, than *G. B.* both at his Examination and on his Trial. His *Tergiversations, Contradictions,* and *Falshoods*, were very sensible: he had little to say, but that he had heard some things that he could not prove, Reflecting upon the Reputation of some of the Witnesses. Only he gave in a Paper to the Jury; wherein, altho' he had many times before, granted, not only that there are *Witches*, but also, that the present Sufferings of the Country are the effects of *horrible Witchcrafts*, yet he now goes to evince it, *That there neither are, nor ever were Witches, that having made a Compact with the Devil, can send a Devil to Torment other people at a distance.* This Paper was Transcribed out of *Ady*; which the Court presently knew, as soon as they heard it. But he said, he had taken none of it out of any Book; for which, his Evasion afterwards, was,

That a Gentleman gave him the Discourse in a Manuscript, from whence he Transcribed it.

IX. The Jury brought him in *Guilty*: But when he came to Die, he utterly deni'd the Fact, whereof he had been thus convicted.

II.
THE TRYAL OF BRIDGET BISHOP, ALIAS
OLIVER, AT THE COURT OF OYER AND TERMINER, HELD AT SALEM, JUNE 2. 1692.

I.

She was Indicted for Bewitching of several Persons in the Neighbourhood, the Indictment being drawn up, according to the *Form* in such Cases usual. And pleading, *Not Guilty*, there were brought in several persons, who had long undergone many kinds of Miseries, which were preternaturally inflicted, and generally ascribed unto an *horrible Witchcraft*. There was little occasion to prove the *Witchcraft*, it being evident and notorious to all beholders. Now to fix the *Witchcraft* on the Prisoner at the Bar, the first thing used, was the Testimony of the *Bewitched*; whereof several testifi'd, That the *Shape* of the Prisoner did oftentimes very grievously Pinch them, Choak them, Bite them, and Afflict them; urging them to write their Names in a *Book*, which the said Spectre called, *Ours*. One of them did further testifie, that it was the *Shape* of this Prisoner, with another, which one day took her from her Wheel, and carrying her to the Riverside, threatned there to Drown her, if she did not Sign to the *Book* mentioned: which yet she refused. Others of them did also testifie, that the said *Shape* did in her Threats brag to them that she had been the Death of sundry Persons, then by her named; that she had *Ridden* a Man then likewise named. Another testifi'd, the Apparition of *Ghosts* unto the Spectre of

Bishop, crying out, *You Murdered us!* About the Truth whereof, there was in the Matter of Fact but too much suspicion.

II. It was testifi'd, That at the Examination of the Prisoner before the Magistrates, the Bewitched were extreamly tortured. If she did but cast her Eyes on them, they were presently struck down; and this in such a manner as there could be no Collusion in the Business. But upon the Touch of her Hand upon them, when they lay in their Swoons, they would immediately Revive; and not upon the Touch of any ones else. Moreover, Upon some Special Actions of her Body, as the shaking of her Head, or the turning of her Eyes, they presently and painfully fell into the like postures. And many of the like Accidents now fell out, while she was at the Bar. One at the same time testifying, That she said, *She could not be troubled to see the afflicted thus tormented.*

III. There was Testimony likewise brought in, that a Man striking once at the place, where a bewitched person said, the *Shape* of this *Bishop* stood, the bewitched cried out, *That he had tore her Coat*, in the place then particularly specifi'd; and the Woman's Coat was found to be Torn in that very place.

IV. One *Deliverance Hobbs*, who had confessed her being a Witch, was now tormented by the Spectres, for her Confession. And she now testifi'd, That this *Bishop* tempted her to Sign the *Book* again, and to deny what she had confess'd. She affirm'd, That it was the Shape of this Prisoner, which whipped her with Iron Rods, to compel her thereunto. And she affirmed, that this *Bishop* was at a General Meeting of the Witches, in a Field at *Salem-*Village, and there partook of a Diabolical Sacrament in Bread and Wine then administred.

V. To render it further unquestionable, that the Prisoner at the Bar, was the Person truly charged in THIS *Witchcraft*, there were produced many Evidences of OTHER *Witchcrafts*, by her perpetrated. For Instance, *John Cook* testifi'd, That about five or six Years ago, one Morning, about Sun-Rise, he was in his Chamber assaulted by the *Shape* of this Prisoner: which look'd on him, grinn'd at him, and very much hurt him with a Blow on the side of the Head: and that on the same day, about Noon, the same *Shape* walked in the Room where he was, and an Apple strangely flew out of his Hand, into the Lap of his Mother, six or eight Foot from him.

VI. *Samuel Gray* testifi'd, That about fourteen Years ago, he wak'd on a Night, and saw the Room where he lay full of Light; and that he then saw plainly a Woman between the Cradle, and the Bed-side, which look'd upon him. He rose, and it vanished; tho' he found the Doors all fast. Looking out at the Entry-door, he saw the same Woman, in the same Garb again; and said, *In God's Name, what do you come for?* He went to Bed, and had the same Woman again assaulting him. The Child in the Cradle gave a great Screech, and the Woman disappeared. It was long before the Child could be quieted; and tho' it were a very likely thriving Child, yet from this time it pined away, and, after divers Months, died in a sad Condition. He knew not *Bishop*, nor her Name; but when he saw her after this, he knew by her Countenance, and Apparel, and all Circumstances, that it was the Apparition of this *Bishop*, which had thus troubled him.

VII. *John Bly* and his Wife testifi'd, That he bought a Sow of *Edward Bishop*, the Husband of the Prisoner; and was to pay the Price agreed, unto another person. This Prisoner being angry that she was thus hindred from fingring the Mony, quarrell'd with *Bly*. Soon after which, the Sow was taken with strange Fits; Jumping, Leaping, and Knocking her Head against the Fence; she seem'd Blind and Deaf, and would neither Eat nor be Suck'd. Whereupon a Neighbour said, she believed the Creature was *Over-looked*; and sundry other Circumstances concurred, which made the Deponents believe that *Bishop* had bewitched it.

VIII. *Richard Coman* testifi'd, That eight Years ago, as he lay awake in his Bed, with a Light burning in the Room, he was annoy'd with the Apparition of this *Bishop*, and of two more that were strangers to him, who came and oppressed him so, that he could neither stir himself, nor wake any one else, and that he was the Night after, molested again in the like manner; the said *Bishop*, taking him by the Throat, and pulling him almost out of the Bed. His Kinsman offered for this cause to lodge with him; and that Night, as they were awake, discoursing together, this *Coman* was once more visited by the Guests which had formerly been so troublesom; his Kinsman being at the same time struck speechless, and unable to move Hand or Foot. He had laid his Sword by him, which these unhappy Spectres did strive much to wrest from him; only he held too fast for them. He then grew able to call the People of his House; but altho' they heard him, yet they had not power to speak or stir; until at last, one of the People crying out, *What's the matter?* The Spectres all vanished.

IX. *Samuel Shattock* testify'd, That in the Year, 1680, this *Bridget Bishop*, often came to his House upon such frivolous and foolish Errands, that they suspected she came indeed with a purpose of mischief. Presently, whereupon, his eldest Child, which was of as promising Health and Sense, as any Child of its Age, began to droop exceedingly; and the oftner that *Bishop* came to the House, the worse grew the Child. As the Child would be standing at the Door, he would be thrown and bruised against the Stones, by an invisible Hand, and in like sort knock his Face against the sides of the House, and bruise it after a miserable manner. Afterwards this *Bishop* would bring him things to Dye, whereof he could not imagin any use; and when she paid him a piece of Mony, the Purse and Mony were unaccountably conveyed out of a lock'd Box, and never seen any more. The Child was immediately, hereupon, taken with terrible Fits, whereof his Friends thought he would have dyed: Indeed he did almost nothing but Cry and Sleep for several Months together; and at length his Understanding was utterly taken away. Among other Symptoms of an Inchantment upon him, one was, That there was a Board in the Garden, whereon he would walk; and all the Invitations in the World could never fetch him off. About 17 or 18 years after, there came a Stranger to *Shattock's* House, who seeing the Child, said, *This poor Child is Bewitched; and you have a Neighbour living not far off, who is a Witch.* He added, *Your Neighbour has had a falling out with your Wife; and she said, in her Heart, your Wife is a proud Woman, and she would bring down her Pride in this Child.* He then remembred, that *Bishop* had parted from his Wife in muttering and menacing Terms, a little before the Child was taken Ill. The abovesaid Stranger would needs carry the bewitched Boy with him, to *Bishop's* House, on pretence of buying a pot of Cyder. The Woman entertained him in furious manner; and flew also upon the Boy, scratching his Face till the Blood came; and saying, *Thou Rogue, what dost thou bring this Fellow here to plague me?* Now it seems the Man had said, before he went, That he would fetch Blood of *her*. Ever after the Boy was follow'd with grievous Fits, which the Doctors themselves generally ascribed unto *Witchcraft*; and wherein he would be thrown still into the *Fire* or the *Water*, if he were not constantly look'd after; and it was verily believed that *Bishop* was the cause of it.

X. *John Louder* testify'd, That upon some little Controversy with *Bishop* about her Fowls, going well to Bed, he did awake in the Night by Moonlight, and did see clearly the likeness of this Woman grievously oppressing him; in which miserable condition she held him, unable to help himself, till near Day. He told *Bishop* of this; but she deny'd it, and threatned him very much. Quickly after this, being at home on a Lords day, with the doors shut about him, he saw a black Pig approach him; at which, he going to kick, it vanished away. Immediately after, sitting down, he saw a black Thing jump in at the Window, and come and stand before him. The Body was like that of a Monkey, the Feet like a Cocks, but the Face much like a Mans. He being so extreamly affrighted, that he could not speak; this Monster spoke to him, and said, *I am a Messenger sent unto you, for I understand that you are in some Trouble of Mind, and if you will be ruled by me, you shall want for nothing in this World.* Whereupon he endeavoured to clap his Hands upon it; but he could feel no substance; and it jumped out of the Window again; but immediately came in by the Porch, tho' the Doors were shut, and said, *You had better take my Counsel!* He then struck at it with a Stick, but struck only the Ground, and broke the Stick: The Arm with which he struck was presently Disenabled, and it vanished away. He presently went out at the Back-door, and spied this *Bishop*, in her Orchard, going toward her House; but he had not power to set one foot forward unto her. Whereupon, returning into the House, he was immediately accosted by the Monster he had seen before; which Goblin was now going to fly at him; whereat he cry'd out, *The whole Armour of God be between me and you!* So it sprang back, and flew over the Apple-tree; shaking many Apples off the Tree, in its flying over. At its leap, it flung Dirt with its Feet against the Stomack of the Man; whereon he was then struck Dumb, and so continued for three Days together. Upon the producing of this Testimony, *Bishop* deny'd that she knew this Deponent: Yet their two Orchards joined; and they had often had their little Quarrels for some years together.

XI. *William Stacy* testify'd, That receiving Mony of this *Bishop*, for work done by him; he was gone but a matter of three Rods from her, and looking for his Mony, found it unaccountably gone from him. Some time after, *Bishop* asked him, whether her Father would grind her Grist for her? He demanded why? She reply'd, *Because Folks count me a Witch*. He answered, *No question but he will grind it for you*. Being then gone about six Rods from her, with a small Load in his Cart, suddenly the Off-wheel stump'd, and sunk down into an hole, upon plain Ground; so that the Deponent was forced to get help for the recovering of the Wheel: But stepping back to look for the hole, which might give him this Disaster, there was none at all to be found. Some time after, he was waked in the Night; but it seem'd as light as day; and he perfectly saw the shape of this *Bishop* in the Room, troubling of him; but upon her going out, all was dark again. He charg'd *Bishop* afterwards with it, and she deny'd it not; but was very angry. Quickly after, this Deponent having been threatned by *Bishop*, as he was in a dark Night going to the Barn, he was very suddenly taken or lifted from the Ground, and thrown against a Stone-wall: After that, he was again hoisted up and thrown down a Bank, at the end of his House. After this again, passing by this *Bishop*, his Horse with a small Load, striving to draw, all his Gears flew to pieces, and the Cart fell down; and this Deponent going then to lift a Bag of Corn, of about two Bushels, could not budge it with all his Might.

Many other Pranks of this *Bishop's* this Deponent was ready to testify. He also testify'd, That he verily believ'd, the said *Bishop* was the Instrument of his Daughter *Priscilla's* Death; of which suspicion, pregnant Reasons were assigned.

XII. To crown all, *John Bly* and *William Bly* testify'd, That being employ'd by *Bridget Bishop*, to help to take down the

Cellar-wall of the old House wherein she formerly lived, they did in holes of the said old Wall, find several *Poppets*, made up of Rags and Hogs-bristles, with headless Pins in them, the Points being outward; whereof she could give no Account unto the Court, that was reasonable or tolerable.

XIII. One thing that made against the Prisoner was, her being evidently convicted of *gross Lying* in the Court, several times, while she was making her Plea; but besides this, a Jury of Women found a preternatural Teat upon her Body: But upon a second search, within 3 or 4 hours, there was no such thing to be seen. There was also an Account of other People whom this Woman had Afflicted; and there might have been many more, if they had been enquired for; but there was no need of them.

XIV. There was one very strange thing more, with which the Court was newly entertained. As this Woman was under a Guard, passing by the great and spacious Meeting-house of *Salem*, she gave a look towards the House: And immediately a *Dæmon* invisibly entring the Meeting-house, tore down a part of it; so that tho' there was no Person to be seen there, yet the People, at the noise, running in, found a Board, which was strongly fastned with several Nails, transported unto another quarter of the House.

III.
THE TRYAL OF SUSANNA MARTIN, AT THE
COURT OF OYER AND TERMINER, HELD BY ADJOURNMENT AT SALEM, JUNE 29. 1692.

I.

Susanna Martin, pleading *Not Guilty* to the Indictment of *Witchcraft*, brought in against her, there were produced the Evidences of many Persons very sensibly and grievously Bewitched; who all complained of the Prisoner at the Bar, as the Person whom they believed the cause of their Miseries. And now, as well as in the other Trials, there was an extraordinary Endeavour by *Witchcrafts*, with Cruel and frequent Fits, to hinder the poor Sufferers from giving in their Complaints, which the Court was forced with much Patience to obtain, by much waiting and watching for it.

II. There was now also an account given of what passed at her first Examination before the Magistrates. The Cast of her *Eye*, then striking the afflicted People to the Ground, whether they saw that Cast or no; there were these among other Passages between the Magistrates and the Examinate.

Magistrate. Pray, what ails these People?

Martin. I don't know.

Magistrate. But what do you think ails them?

Martin. I don't desire to spend my Judgment upon it.

Magistrate. Don't you think they are bewitch'd?

Martin. No, I do not think they are.

Magistrate. Tell us your Thoughts about them then.

Martin. No, my thoughts are my own, when they are in, but when they are out they are anothers. Their Master.—
—

Magistrate. Their Master? who do you think is their Master?

Martin. If they be dealing in the Black Art, you may know as well as I.

Magistrate. Well, what have you done towards this?

Martin. Nothing at all.

Magistrate. Why, 'tis you or your Appearance.

Martin. I cannot help it.

Magistrate. Is it not *your* Master? How comes your Appearance to hurt these?

Martin. How do I know? He that appeared in the Shape of *Samuel*, a glorified Saint, may appear in any ones Shape.

It was then also noted in her, as in others like her, that if the Afflicted went to approach her, they were flung down to the Ground. And, when she was asked the reason of it, she said, *I cannot tell; it may be, the Devil bears me more Malice than another.*

III. The Court accounted themselves, alarum'd by these Things, to enquire further into the Conversation of the Prisoner; and see what there might occur, to render these Accusations further credible. Whereupon, *John Allen* of *Salisbury*, testify'd, That he refusing, because of the weakness of his Oxen, to Cart some Staves at the request of this *Martin*, she was displeased at it; and said, *It had been as good that he had; for his Oxen should never do him much more Service.* Whereupon, this Deponent said, *Dost thou threaten me, thou old Witch? I'l throw thee into the Brook:* Which to avoid, she flew over the Bridge, and escaped. But, as he was going home, one of his Oxen tired, so that he was forced to Unyoke him, that he might get him home. He then put his Oxen, with many more, upon *Salisbury* Beach, where Cattle did use to get *Flesh*. In a few days, all the Oxen upon the Beach were found by their Tracks, to have run unto the Mouth of *Merrimack-River*, and not returned; but the next day they were found come ashore upon *Plum-Island.* They that sought them, used all imaginable gentleness, but they would still run away with a violence, that seemed wholly Diabolical, till they came near the mouth of *Merrimack-River*; when they ran right into the Sea, swimming as far as they could be seen. One of them then swam back again, with a swiftness, amazing to the Beholders, who stood ready to receive him, and help up his tired Carcass: But the Beast ran furiously up into the Island, and from thence, thorough the Marshes, up into *Newbury* Town, and so up into the Woods; and there after a while found near *Amesbury.* So that, of fourteen good Oxen, there was only this saved: The rest were all cast up, some in one place, and some in another, Drowned.

IV. *John Atkinson* testifi'd, That he exchanged a Cow with a Son of *Susanna Martin's*, whereat she muttered, and was unwilling he should have it. Going to receive this Cow, tho he Hamstring'd her, and Halter'd her, she, of a Tame Creature, grew so mad, that they could scarce get her along. She broke all the Ropes that were fastned unto her, and though she were ty'd fast unto a Tree, yet she made her escape, and gave them such further trouble, as they could ascribe to no cause but Witchcraft.

V. *Bernard Peache* testifi'd, That being in Bed, on the Lord's-day Night, he heard a scrabbling at the Window, whereat he then saw *Susanna Martin* come in, and jump down upon the Floor. She took hold of this Deponent's Feet, and drawing his Body up into an Heap, she lay upon him near Two Hours; in all which time he could neither speak nor stir. At length, when he could begin to move, he laid hold on her Hand, and pulling it up to his Mouth, he bit three of her Fingers, as he judged, unto the Bone. Whereupon she went from the Chamber, down the Stairs, out at the Door. This Deponent thereupon called unto the People of the House, to advise them of what passed; and he himself did follow her. The People saw her not; but there being a Bucket at the Left-hand of the Door, there was a drop of Blood found upon it; and several more drops of Blood upon the Snow newly fallen abroad: There was likewise the print of her 2 Feet just without the Threshold; but no more sign of any Footing further off.

At another time this Deponent was desired by the Prisoner, to come unto an Husking of Corn, at her House; and she said, *If he did not come, it were better that he did!* He went not; but the Night following, *Susanna Martin,* as he judged, and another came towards him. One of them said, *Here he is!* but he having a Quarter-staff, made a Blow at them. The Roof of the Barn, broke his Blow; but following them to the Window, he made another Blow at them, and struck them down; yet they got up, and got out, and he saw no more of them.

About this time, there was a Rumour about the Town, that *Martin* had a Broken Head; but the Deponent could say nothing to that.

The said *Peache* also testifi'd the Bewitching the Cattle to Death, upon Martin's Discontents.

VI. *Robert Downer* testified, That this Prisoner being some Years ago prosecuted at Court for a Witch, he then said unto her, *He believed she was a Witch.* Whereat she being dissatisfied, said, *That some She-Devil would shortly fetch him away!* Which words were heard by others, as well as himself. The Night following, as he lay in his Bed, there came in at the Window, the likeness of a *Cat*, which flew upon him, took fast hold of his Throat, lay on him a considerable while, and almost killed him. At length he remembred what *Susanna Martin* had threatned the Day before; and with much striving he cried out, *Avoid, thou She-Devil! In the Name of God the Father, the Son, and the Holy Ghost, Avoid!* Whereupon it left him, leap'd on the Floor, and flew out at the Window.

And there also came in several Testimonies, that before ever *Downer* spoke a word of this Accident, *Susanna Martin* and her Family had related, *How this* Downer *had been handled!*

VII. *John Kembal* testified, that *Susanna Martin*, upon a Causeless Disgust, had threatned him, about a certain Cow of his, *That she should never do him any more Good:* and it came to pass accordingly. For soon after the Cow was found stark dead on the dry Ground, without any Distemper to be discerned upon her. Upon which he was followed with a strange Death upon more of his Cattle, whereof he lost in one Spring to the Value of Thirty Pounds. But the said *John Kembal* had a further Testimony to give in against the Prisoner which was truly admirable.

Being desirous to furnish himself with a Dog, he applied himself to buy one of this *Martin*, who had a Bitch with Whelps in her House. But she not letting him have his choice, he said, he would supply himself then at one *Blezdels*. Having mark'd a Puppy, which he lik'd at *Blezdels*, he met *George Martin*, the Husband of the Prisoner, going by, who asked him, *Whether he would not have one of his Wife's Puppies?* and he answered, *No*. The same Day, one *Edmond Eliot*, being at *Martin's* House, heard *George Martin* relate, where this *Kembal* had been, and what he had said. Whereupon *Susanna Martin* replied, *If I live, I'll give him Puppies enough!* Within a few days after, this *Kembal*, coming out of the Woods, there arose a little Black Cloud in the N. W. and *Kembal* immediately felt a force upon him, which made him not able to avoid running upon the stumps of Trees, that were before him, albeit he had a broad, plain Cart-way, before him; but tho' he had his Ax also on his Shoulder to endanger him in his Falls, he could not forbear going out of his way to tumble over them. When he came below the Meeting House, there appeared unto him, a little thing like a *Puppy*, of a Darkish Colour; and it shot backwards and forwards between his Legs. He had the Courage to use all possible Endeavours of Cutting it with his Ax; but he could not Hit it: the Puppy gave a jump from him, and went, as to him it seem'd into the Ground. Going a little further, there appeared unto him a Black Puppy, somewhat bigger than the first, but as Black as a Cole. Its Motions were quicker than those of his Ax; it flew at his Belly, and away; then at his Throat; so, over his Shoulder one way, and then over his Shoulder another way. His Heart now began to fail him, and he thought the Dog would have tore his Throat out. But he recovered himself, and called upon God in his Distress; and naming the Name of Jesus Christ, it vanished away at once. The Deponent spoke not one Word of these Accidents, for fear of affrighting his Wife. But the next Morning, *Edmond Eliot*, going into *Martin's* House, this Woman asked him where Kembal was? He replied, *At home, a Bed, for ought he knew.* She returned, *They say, he was frighted last Night.* Eliot asked, *With what?* She answered, *With Puppies.* Eliot asked, *Where she heard of it, for he had heard nothing of it?* She rejoined, *About the Town.* Altho' *Kembal* had mentioned the Matter to no Creature living.

VIII. *William Brown* testifi'd, That Heaven having blessed him with a most Pious and Prudent Wife, this Wife of his, one day met with *Susanna Martin*; but when she approach'd just unto her, *Martin* vanished out of sight, and left her extreamly affrighted. After which time, the said *Martin* often appear'd unto her, giving her no little trouble; and when she did come, she was visited with Birds, that sorely peck'd and prick'd her; and sometimes, a Bunch, like a Pullet's Egg, would rise in her Throat, ready to choak her, till she cry'd out, *Witch, you shan't choak me!* While this good Woman was in this extremity, the Church appointed a Day of Prayer, on her behalf; whereupon her Trouble ceas'd; she saw not *Martin* as formerly; and the Church, instead of their Fast, gave Thanks for her Deliverance. But a considerable while after, she being Summoned to give in some Evidence at the Court, against this *Martin*, quickly thereupon, this *Martin* came behind her, while she was milking her Cow, and said unto her, *For thy defaming her at Court, I'll make thee the miserablest Creature in the World.* Soon after which, she fell into a strange kind of distemper, and became horribly frantick, and uncapable of any reasonable Action; the Physicians declaring, that her Distemper was preternatural, and that some Devil had certainly bewitched her; and in that condition she now remained.

IX. *Sarah Atkinson* testify'd, That *Susanna Martin* came from *Amesbury* to their House at *Newbury*, in an extraordinary Season, when it was not fit for any to Travel. She came (as she said, unto *Atkinson*) all that long way on Foot. She brag'd and shew'd how dry she was; nor could it be perceived that so much as the Soles of her Shoes were wet. *Atkinson* was amazed at it; and professed, that she should her self have been wet up to the knees, if she had then came so far; but *Martin* reply'd, *She scorn'd to be Drabbled!* It was noted, that this Testimony upon her Trial, cast her in a very singular Confusion.

X. *John Pressy* testify'd, That being one Evening very unaccountably Bewildred, near a Field of *Martins*, and several times, as one under an Enchantment, returning to the place he had left, at length he saw a marvellous Light, about the bigness of an Half-bushel, near two Rod, out of the way. He went, and struck at it with a Stick, and laid it on with all his might. He gave it near forty blows; and felt it a palpable substance. But going from it, his Heels were struck up, and he was laid with his Back on the Ground, sliding, as he thought, into a Pit; from whence he recover'd by taking hold on the Bush; altho' afterwards he could find no such Pit in the place. Having, after his Recovery, gone five or six Rod, he saw *Susanna Martin* standing on his Left-hand, as the Light had done before; but they changed no words with one another. He could scarce find his House in his Return; but at length he got home extreamly affrighted. The next day, it was upon Enquiry understood, that *Martin* was in a miserable condition by pains and hurts that were upon her.

It was further testify'd by this Deponent, That after he had given in some Evidence against *Susanna Martin,* many years ago, she gave him foul words about it; and said, *He should never prosper more;* particularly, *That he should never have more than two Cows; that tho' he was never so likely to have more, yet he should never have them.* And that from that very day to this, namely for twenty years together, he could never exceed that number; but some strange thing or other still prevented his having any more.

XI. *Jervis Ring* testify'd, That about seven years ago, he was oftentimes and grievously oppressed in the Night, but saw not who troubled him; until at last he Lying perfectly Awake, plainly saw *Susanna Martin* approach him. She came to him, and forceably bit him by the Finger; so that the Print of the bite is now, so long after, to be seen upon him.

XII. But besides all of these Evidences, there was a most wonderful Account of one *Joseph Ring*, produced on this occasion.

This Man has been strangely carried about by *Dæmons*, from one *Witch-meeting* to another, for near two years together; and for one quarter of this time, they have made him, and keep him Dumb, tho' he is now again able to speak. There was one *T. H.* who having, as 'tis judged, a design of engaging this *Joseph Ring* in a snare of Devillism, contrived a while, to bring this *Ring* two Shillings in Debt unto him.

Afterwards, this poor Man would be visited with unknown shapes, and this *T. H.* sometimes among them; which would force him away with them, unto unknown Places, where he saw Meetings, Feastings, Dancings; and after his return, wherein they hurried him along through the Air, he gave Demonstrations to the Neighbours, that he had indeed been so transported. When he was brought unto these hellish Meetings, one of the first Things they still did unto him, was to give him a knock on the Back, whereupon he was ever as if bound with Chains, uncapable of stirring out of the place, till they should release him. He related, that there often came to him a Man, who presented him a *Book*, whereto he would have him set his Hand; promising to him, that he should then have even what he would; and presenting him with all the delectable Things, Persons, and Places, that he could imagin. But he refusing to subscribe, the business would end with dreadful Shapes, Noises and Screeches, which almost scared him out of his Wits. Once with the Book, there was a Pen offered him, and an Ink-horn with Liquor in it, that seemed like Blood: But he never toucht it.

This Man did now affirm, That he saw the Prisoner at several of those hellish Randezvouzes.

Note, this Woman was one of the most impudent, scurrilous, wicked Creatures in the World; and she did now throughout her whole Tryal, discover her self to be such an one. Yet when she was asked, what she had to say for her self? Her chief Plea was, *That she had lead a most virtuous and holy Life.*

IV.
THE TRYAL OF ELIZABETH HOW, AT THE
COURT OF OYER AND TERMINER, HELD BY ADJOURNMENT
AT SALEM, JUNE 30. 1692.

I.

E*lizabeth How* pleading *Not Guilty* to the Indictment of Witchcrafts, then charged upon her; the Court, according to the usual Proceedings of the Courts in *England*, in such Cases, began with hearing the Depositions of several afflicted People, who were grievously tortured by sensible and evident *Witchcrafts*, and all complained of the Prisoner, as the cause of their Trouble. It was also found that the Sufferers were not able to bear her *Look*, as likewise, that in their greatest Swoons, they distinguished her *Touch* from other Peoples, being thereby raised out of them.

And there was other Testimony of People to whom the shape of this *How*, gave trouble nine or ten years ago.

II. It has been a most usual thing for the bewitched Persons, at the same time that the *Spectres*, representing the *Witches*, troubled them, to be visited with Apparitions of *Ghosts*, pretending to have been Murdered by the *Witches* then represented. And sometimes the Confessions of the Witches afterwards acknowledged those very Murders, which these *Apparitions* charged upon them; altho' they had never heard what Informations had been given by the Sufferers.

There were such Apparitions of Ghosts testified by some of the present Sufferers; and the Ghosts affirmed, that this *How* had Murdered them: Which things were *fear'd* but not *prov'd*.

III. This *How* had made some Attempts of joyning to the Church at *Ipswich*, several years ago; but she was denyed an admission into that Holy Society, partly through a suspicion of Witchcraft, then urged against her. And there now came in Testimony, of preternatural Mischiefs, presently befalling some that had been Instrumental to debar her from the Communion whereupon she was intruding.

IV. There was a particular Deposition of *Joseph Stafford*, That his Wife had conceived an extream Aversion to this *How*, on the Reports of her Witchcrafts: But *How* one day, taking her by the Hand, and saying, *I believe you are not ignorant of the great Scandal that I lye under, by an evil Report raised upon me.* She immediately, unreasonably and unperswadeably, even like one Enchanted, began to take this Woman's part. *How* being soon after propounded, as desiring an Admission to the Table of the Lord, some of the pious Brethren were unsatisfy'd about her. The Elders appointed a Meeting to hear Matters objected against her; and no Arguments in the World could hinder this Goodwife *Stafford* from going to the Lecture. She did indeed promise, with much ado, that she would not go to the Church-meeting, yet she could not refrain going thither also. *How's* Affairs there were so canvased, that she came off rather *Guilty* than *Cleared*; nevertheless Goodwife *Stafford* could not forbear taking her by the Hand, and saying, *Tho' you are Condemned before Men, you are Justify'd before God.* She was quickly taken in a very strange manner, Ranting, Raving, Raging and crying out, *Goody* How *must come into the Church; she is a precious Saint; and tho' she be condemned before Men, she is Justify'd before God.* So she continued for the space of two or three Hours; and then fell into a Trance. But coming to her self, she cry'd out, *Ha! I was mistaken;* and afterwards again repeated, *Ha! I was mistaken!* Being asked by a stander by, *Wherein?* she replyed, *I thought Goody* How *had been a precious Saint of*

God, but now I see she is a Witch: She has bewitched me, and my Child, and we shall never be well, till there be a Testimony for her, that she may be taken into the Church. And *How* said afterwards, that she was very sorry to see *Stafford* at the Church-meeting mentioned. *Stafford*, after this, declared herself to be afflicted by the Shape of *How*; and from that Shape she endured many Miseries.

V. *John How*, Brother to the Husband of the Prisoner testified, that he refusing to accompany the Prisoner unto her Examination, as was by her desired, immediately some of his Cattle were Bewitched to Death, leaping three or four foot high, turning about, speaking, falling, and dying at once; and going to cut off an Ear, for an use, that might as well perhaps have been omitted, the Hand wherein he held his Knife was taken very numb, and so it remained, and full of Pain, for several Days, being not well at this very Time. And he suspected the Prisoner for the Author of it.

VI. *Nehemiah Abbot* testify'd, that unusual and mischievous Accidents would befal his Cattle, whenever he had any Difference with this Prisoner. Once, particularly, she wished his Ox choaked; and within a little while that Ox was choaked with a Turnep in his Throat. At another Time, refusing to lend his Horse, at the Request of her Daughter, the Horse was in a preternatural manner abused. And several other odd things of that kind were testified.

VII. There came in Testimony, that one Good-wife *Sherwin*, upon some Difference with *How*, was Bewitched; and that she dyed, charging this *How* with having an Hand in her Death. And that other People had their Barrels of Drink unaccountably mischieved, spoil'd and spilt, upon their displeasing of her.

The things in themselves were trivial, but there being such a Course of them, it made them the more considered. Among others, *Martha Wood*, gave her Testimony, That a little after her Father had been employed in gathering an account of *How's* Conversation, they once and again lost great Quantities of Drink out of their Vessels, in such a manner, as they could ascribe to nothing but Witchcraft. As also, That *How* giving her some Apples, when she had eaten of them, she was taken with a very strange kind of Amaze, insomuch that she knew not what she said or did.

VIII. There was likewise a Cluster of Depositions, That one *Isaac Cummings* refusing to lend his Mare unto the Husband of this *How*, the Mare was within a Day or two taken in a strange condition: The Beast seemed much abused, being bruised as if she had been running over the Rocks, and marked where the Bridle went, as if burnt with a red hot Bridle. Moreover, one using a Pipe of Tobacco for the Cure of the Beast, a blue Flame issued out of her, took hold of her Hair, and not only spread and burnt on her, but it also flew upwards towards the Roof of the Barn, and had like to have set the Barn on Fire: And the Mare dyed very suddenly.

IX. *Timothy Pearley* and his Wife, testifyd, Not only unaccountable Mischiefs befel their Cattle, upon their having of Differences with this Prisoner: but also that they had a Daughter destroyed by Witchcrafts; which Daughter still charged *How* as the Cause of her Affliction. And it was noted, that she would be struck down whenever *How* were spoken of. She was often endeavoured to be thrown into the Fire, and into the Water, in her strange Fits: Tho' her Father had corrected her for charging *How* with bewitching her, yet (as was testified by others also) she said, She was sure of it, and must dye standing to it. Accordingly she charged *How* to the very Death; and said, *Tho' How could afflict and torment her Body, yet she could not hurt her Soul:* And, *That the Truth of this matter would appear, when she should be dead and gone.*

X. *Francis Lane* testified, That being hired by the Husband of this *How* to get him a parcel of Posts and Rails, this *Lane* hired *John Pearly* to assist him. This Prisoner then told *Lane*, That she believed the Posts and Rails would not do, because *John Pearly* helped him; but that if he had got them alone, without *John Pearly's* help, they might have done well enough. When *James How* came to receive his Posts and Rails of *Lane*, *How* taking them up by the Ends, they, tho' good and sound, yet unaccountably broke off, so that *Lane* was forced to get thirty or forty more. And this Prisoner being informed of it, she said, She told him so before, because *Pearly* helped about them.

XI. Afterwards there came in the Confessions of several other (penitent) Witches, which affirmed this *How* to be one of those, who with them had been baptized by the Devil in the River, at *Newbury*-Falls: before which he made them there kneel down by the Brink of the River and worshiped him.

V.
THE TRIAL OF MARTHA CARRIER, AT THE
COURT OF OYER AND TERMINER, HELD BY ADJOURNMENT
AT SALEM, AUGUST 2. 1692.

I.

M*artha Carrier* was Indicted for the bewitching certain Persons, according to the Form usual in such Cases, pleading *Not Guilty,* to her Indictment; there were first brought in a considerable number of the bewitched Persons; who not only made the Court sensible of an horrid Witchcraft committed upon them, but also deposed, That it was *Martha Carrier,* or her Shape, that grievously tormented them, by Biting, Pricking, Pinching and Choaking of them. It was further deposed, That while this *Carrier* was on her Examination, before the Magistrates, the Poor People were so tortured that every one expected their Death upon the very spot, but that upon the binding of *Carrier* they were eased. Moreover the Look of *Carrier* then laid the Afflicted People for dead; and her Touch, if her Eye at the same time were off them, raised them again: Which Things were also now seen upon her Tryal. And it was testified, That upon the mention of some having their Necks twisted almost round, by the Shape of this *Carrier,* she replyed, *Its no matter though their Necks had been twisted quite off.*

II. Before the Trial of this Prisoner, several of her own Children had frankly and fully confessed, not only that they were Witches themselves, but that this their Mother had made them so. This Confession they made with great Shews of Repentance, and with much Demonstration of Truth. They related Place, Time, Occasion; they gave an account of Journeys, Meetings and Mischiefs by them performed, and were very credible in what they said.

Nevertheless, this Evidence was not produced against the Prisoner at the Bar, inasmuch as there was other Evidence enough to proceed upon.

III. *Benjamin Abbot* gave his Testimony, That last March was a twelvemonth, this *Carrier* was very angry with him, upon laying out some Land, near her Husband's: Her Expressions in this Anger, were, *That she would stick as close to* Abbot *as the Bark stuck to the Tree; and that he should repent of it afore seven Years came to an End, so as Doctor* Prescot *should never cure him.* These Words were heard by others besides *Abbot* himself; who also heard her say, *She would hold his Nose as close to the Grindstone as ever it was held since his Name was* Abbot. Presently after this, he was taken with a Swelling in his Foot, and then with a Pain in his Side, and exceedingly tormented. It bred into a Sore, which was launced by Doctor *Prescot*, and several Gallons of Corruption ran out of it. For six Weeks it continued very bad, and then another Sore bred in the Groin, which was also lanced by Doctor *Prescot.* Another Sore then bred in his Groin, which was likewise cut, and put him to very great Misery: He was brought unto Death's Door, and so remained until *Carrier* was taken, and carried away by the Constable, from which very Day he began to mend, and so grew better every Day, and is well ever since.

Sarah Abbot also, his Wife, testified, That her Husband was not only all this while Afflicted in his Body, but also that strange extraordinary and unaccountable Calamities befel his Cattel; their Death being such as they could guess at no Natural Reason for.

IV. *Allin Toothaker* testify'd, That *Richard*, the son of *Martha Carrier*, having some difference with him, pull'd him down by the Hair of the Head. When he Rose again, he was going to strike at *Richard Carrier*; but fell down flat on his Back to the ground, and had not power to stir hand or foot, until he told *Carrier* he yielded; and then he saw the shape of *Martha Carrier*, go off his breast.

This *Toothaker*, had Received a wound in the *Wars*; and he now testify'd, that *Martha Carrier* told him, *He should never be Cured*. Just afore the Apprehending of *Carrier*, he could thrust a knitting Needle into his wound, four inches deep; but presently after her being siezed, he was throughly healed.

He further testify'd, that when *Carrier* and he sometimes were at variance, she would clap her hands at him, and say, *He should get nothing by it*; whereupon he several times lost his Cattle, by strange Deaths, whereof no natural causes could be given.

V. *John Rogger* also testifyed, That upon the threatning words of this malicious *Carrier*, his Cattle would be strangely bewitched; as was more particularly then described.

VI. *Samuel Preston* testify'd, that about two years ago, having some difference with *Martha Carrier*, he lost a *Cow* in a strange Preternatural unusual manner; and about a month after this, the said *Carrier*, having again some difference with him, she told him; *He had lately lost a Cow, and it should not be long before he lost another*; which accordingly came to pass; for he had a thriving and well-kept *Cow*, which without any known cause quickly fell down and dy'd.

VII. *Phebe Chandler* testify'd, that about a Fortnight before the apprehension of *Martha Carrier*, on a Lords-day, while the Psalm was singing in the *Church*, this *Carrier* then took her by the shoulder and shaking her, asked her, *where she lived*: she made her no Answer, although as *Carrier*, who lived next door to her Fathers House, could not in reason but know who she was. Quickly after this, as she was at several times crossing the Fields, she heard a voice, that she took to be *Martha Carriers*, and it seem'd as if it was over her head. The voice told her, *she should within two or three days be poisoned*. Accordingly, within such a little time, one half of her right hand, became greatly swollen, and very painful; as also part of her Face; whereof she can give no account how it came. It continued very bad for some dayes; and several times since, she has had a great pain in her breast; and been so siezed on her leggs, that she has hardly been able to go. She added, that lately, going well to the House of God, *Richard*, the son of *Martha Carrier*, look'd very earnestly upon her, and immediately her hand, which had formerly been poisoned, as is abovesaid, began to pain her greatly, and she had a strange Burning at her stomach; but was then struck deaf, so that she could not hear any of the prayer, or singing, till the two or three last words of the Psalm.

VIII. One *Foster*, who confessed her own share in the Witchcraft for which the Prisoner stood indicted, affirm'd, that she had seen the prisoner at some of their *Witch-meetings*, and that it was this *Carrier*, who perswaded her to be a Witch. She confessed, that the Devil carry'd them on a pole, to a Witch-meeting; but the pole broke, and she hanging about *Carriers* neck, they both fell down, and she then received an hurt by the Fall, whereof she was not at this very time recovered.

IX. One *Lacy*, who likewise confessed her share in this Witchcraft, now testify'd, that she and the prisoner were once Bodily present at a *Witch-meeting* in *Salem Village*; and that she knew the prisoner to be a Witch, and to have been at a Diabolical sacrament, and that the prisoner was the undoing of her, and her Children, by enticing them into the snare of the Devil.

X. Another *Lacy*, who also confessed her share in this Witchcraft, now testify'd, that the prisoner was at the *Witch-meeting*, in *Salem Village*, where they had Bread and Wine Administred unto them.

XI. In the time of this prisoners Trial, one *Susanna Sheldon*, in open Court had her hands Unaccountably ty'd together with a Wheel-band, so fast that without cutting, it could not be loosed: It was done by a *Spectre*; and the Sufferer affirm'd, it was the *Prisoners*.

Memorandum. This Rampant Hag, *Martha Carrier*, was the person, of whom the Confessions of the Witches, and of her own Children among the rest, agreed, That the Devil had promised her, she should be *Queen of Heb*.

Having thus far done the Service imposed upon me; I will further pursue it, by relating a few of those Matchless Curiosities, with which the *Witchcraft* now upon us, has entertained us. And I shall Report nothing but with Good Authority, and what I would invite all my Readers to examine, while 'tis yet Fresh and New, that if there be found any mistake, it may be as willingly *Retracted*, as it was unwillingly *Committed*.

The First Curiositie.

I. 'Tis very Remarkable to see what an Impious and Impudent *imitation* of Divine Things, is Apishly affected by the Devil, in several of those matters, whereof the Confessions of our *Witches*, and the Afflictions of our *Sufferers* have informed us.

That Reverend and Excellent Person, Mr. *John Higginson*, in my Conversation with him, Once invited me to this Reflection; that the Indians which came from far to settle about *Mexico*, were in their Progress to that Settlement, under a Conduct of the *Devil*, very strangely Emulating what the Blessed God gave to *Israel* in the Wilderness.

Acosta, is our Author for it, that the Devil in their Idol *Vitzlipultzli*, governed that mighty Nation. 'He commanded them to leave their Country, promising to make them *Lords* over all the Provinces possessed by *Six* other Nations of Indians, and give them a Land abounding with all precious things. They went forth, carrying their Idol with them, in a Coffer of *Reeds*, supported by Four of their Principal *Priests*; with whom he still *Discoursed* in secret, Revealing to them the Successes, and Accidents of their way. He advised them, when to *March*, and where to *Stay*, and without his Commandment they moved not. The first thing they did, where-ever they came, was to Erect a *Tabernacle*, for their false god; which they set always in the midst of their Camp, and they placed the *Ark* upon an *Alter*. When they, Tired with pains, talked of, *proceeding no further* in their Journey, than a certain pleasant Stage, whereto they were arrived, this Devil in one Night, horribly kill'd them that had started this Talk, by pulling out their Hearts. And so they passed on till they came to *Mexico*.'

The Devil which *then* thus imitated what was in the Church of the *Old Testament*, now among *Us* would Imitate the Affairs of the Church in the *New*. The *Witches* do say, that they form themselves much after the manner of *Congregational Churches*; and that they have a *Baptism* and a *Supper*, and *Officers* among them, abominably Resembling those of our Lord.

But there are many more of these Bloody *Imitations*, if the Confessions of the *Witches* are to be Received; which I confess, ought to be but with very much Caution.

What is their stricking down with a fierce *Look*? What is their making of the Afflicted *Rise*, with a touch of their *Hand*? What is their Transportation thro' the *Air*? What is their Travelling *in Spirit*, while their Body is cast into a Trance? What is their causing of *Cattle* to run mad and perish? What is their Entring their Names in a *Book*? What is their coming together from all parts, at the Sound of a *Trumpet*? What is their Appearing sometimes Cloathed with *Light* or *Fire* upon them? What is their Covering of themselves and their Instruments with *Invisibility*? But a Blasphemous Imitation of certain Things recorded about our Saviour or His Prophets, or the Saints in the Kingdom of God.

A Second Curiositie.

II. In all the *Witchcraft* which now Grievously Vexes us, I know not whether anything be more Unaccountable, than the Trick which the Witches have to render themselves, and their Tools *Invisible*. *Witchcraft* seems to be the Skill of Applying the *Plastic Spirit* of the World, unto some unlawful purposes, by means of a Confederacy with *Evil Spirits*. Yet one would wonder how the *Evil Spirits* themselves can do some things; especially at *Invisibilizing* of the Grossest Bodies. I can tell the Name of an Ancient Author, who pretends to show the *way*, how a man may come to walk about *Invisible*, and I can tell the Name of another Ancient Author, who pretends to Explode that way. But I will not speak too plainly Lest I should unawares Poison some of my *Readers*, as the pious *Hemingius* did one of his *Pupils*, when he only by way of Diversion recited a *Spell*, which, they had said, would cure *Agues*. This much I will say; The notion of procuring *Invisibility*, by any *Natural Expedient*, yet known, is, I Believe, a meer Plinyism; How far it may be obtained by a *Magical Sacrament*, is best known to the Dangerous Knaves that have try'd it. But our *Witches* do seem to have got the knack: and this is one of the Things, that make me think, *Witchcraft* will not be fully understood, until the day when there shall not be one Witch in the World.

There are certain people very *Dogmatical* about these matters; but I'll give them only these three Bones to pick.

First, One of our bewitched people, was cruelly assaulted by a *Spectre*, that, she said, ran at her with a *spindle*: tho' no body else in the Room, could see either the *Spectre* or the *spindle*. At last, in her miseries, giving a snatch at the *Spectre*, she pull'd the *spindle* away, and it was no sooner got into her hand, but the other people then present, beheld, that it was indeed a Real, Proper, Iron *spindle*, belonging they knew to whom; which when they lock'd up very safe, it was nevertheless by *Demons* unaccountably stole away, to do further mischief.

Secondly, Another of our bewitched people, was haunted with a most abusive *Spectre*, which came to her, she said, with a *sheet* about her. After she had undergone a deal of Teaze, from the Annoyance of the *Spectre*, she gave a violent snatch at the sheet, that was upon it; wherefrom she tore a corner, which in her hand immediately became *Visible* to a Roomful of Spectators; a palpable Corner of a Sheet. Her Father, who was now holding her, catch'd that he might keep what his Daughter had so strangely siezed, but the unseen *Spectre* had like to have pull'd his hand off, by endeavouring to wrest it from him; however he still held it, and I suppose has it, still to show; it being but a few hours ago, namely about the beginning of this *October*, that this Accident happened; in the family of one *Pitman*, at *Manchester*.

Thirdly, A young man, delaying to procure Testimonials for his Parents, who being under confinement on suspicion of *Witchcraft*, required him to do that service for them, was quickly pursued with odd Inconveniences. But once above the Rest, an Officer going to put his *Brand* on the Horns of some *Cows,* belonging to these people, which tho' he had siez'd for some of their debts, yet he was willing to leave in their possession, for the subsistance of the poor Family; this young man help'd in holding the Cows to be thus branded. The three first *Cows* he held well enough; but when the hot Brand was clap'd upon the Fourth, he *winc'd* and *shrunk* at such a Rate, as that he could hold the Cow no longer. Being afterwards Examined about it, he confessed, that at that very instant when the *Brand* entered the *Cow's Horn,* exactly the like burning *Brand* was clap'd upon his own Thigh; where he has exposed the lasting marks of it, unto such as asked to see them.

Unriddle these Things,—*Et Eris mihi magnus Apollo.*

A Third Curiositie.

III. If a Drop of *Innocent Blood* should be shed, in the Prosecution of the *Witchcrafts* among us, how unhappy are we! For which cause, I cannot express my self in better terms, than those of a most Worthy Person, who lives near the present Center of these things. *The Mind of God in these matters, is to be carefully lookt into, with due Circumspection, that Satan deceive us not with his Devices, who transforms himself into an Angel of Light, and may pretend justice and yet intend mischief.* But on the other side, if the storm of Justice do now fall only on the Heads of those guilty *Witches* and *Wretches* which have defiled our Land, *How Happy!*

The Execution of some that have lately Dyed, has been immediately attended, with a strange Deliverance of some, that had lain for many years, in a most sad Condition, under, they knew not whose *evil hands.* As I am abundantly satisfy'd, That many of the Self-Murders committed here, have been the effects of a Cruel and Bloody *Witchcraft*, letting fly *Demons* upon the miserable *Seneca's*; thus, it has been admirable unto me to see, how a Devilish *Witchcraft*, sending Devils upon them, has driven many poor people to *Despair*, and persecuted their minds, with such Buzzes of *Atheism* and *Blasphemy*, as has made them even run *distracted with Terrors*: And some long *Bow'd down* under such a *spirit of Infirmity*, have been marvelously Recovered upon the death of the Witches.

One *Whetford* particularly ten years ago, challenging of *Bridget Bishop* (whose Trial you have had) with steeling of a Spoon, *Bishop* threatned her very direfully: presently after this, was *Whetford* in the Night, and in her Bed, visited by *Bishop*, with one *Parker*, who making the Room light at their coming in, there discoursed of several mischiefs they would inflict upon her. At last they pull'd her out, and carried her unto the Sea-side, there to *drown*, her; but she calling upon God, they left her, tho' not without Expressions of their Fury. From that very time, this poor *Whetford* was utterly spoilt, and grew a Tempted, Froward, Crazed sort of a Woman; a vexation to her self, and all about her; and many ways unreasonable. In this Distraction she lay, till those women were Apprehended, by the Authority; *then* she began to mend; and upon their Execution, was presently and perfectly Recovered, from the ten years madness that had been upon her.

A Fourth Curiositie.

IV. 'Tis a thousand pitties, that we should permit our Eyes, to be so *Blood-shot* with passions, as to loose the sight of many wonderful things, wherein the Wisdom and Justice of God, would be Glorify'd. Some of those things, are the frequent **Apparitions** of Ghosts, whereby many Old **Murders** among us, come to be considered. And, among many instances of this kind, I will single out one, which concerned a poor man, lately *Prest* unto Death, because of his Refusing to *Plead* for his Life. I shall make an Extract of a Letter, which was written to my Honourable Friend, *Samuel Sewal*, Esq.; by Mr. *Putman*, to this purpose;

'The Last Night my Daughter *Ann*, was grievously Tormented by Witches, Threatning that she should be *Pressed* to Death, before *Giles Cory*. But thro' the Goodness of a Gracious God, she had at last a little Respite. Whereupon there appeared unto her (she said) a man in a Winding Sheet, who told her that *Giles Cory* had Murdered him, by *Pressing* him to Death with his Feet; but that the Devil there appeared unto him, and Covenanted with him, and promised him, *He should not be Hanged*. The Apparition said, God Hardned his heart; that he should not hearken to the Advice of the Court, and so Dy an easy Death; because as it said, *It must be done to him as he has done to me*. The Apparition also said, That *Giles Cory*, was carry'd to the Court for this, and that the Jury had found the Murder, and that her Father knew the man, and the thing was done before she was born. Now Sir, This is not a little strange to us; that no body should Remember these things, all the while that *Giles Cory* was in Prison, and so often before the Court. For all people now Remember very well, (and the Records of the Court also mention it,) That about Seventeen Years ago, *Giles Cory* kept a man in his House, that was almost a Natural Fool: which Man Dy'd suddenly. A Jury was impannel'd upon him, among whom was Dr. *Zorobbabel Endicot*; who found the man bruised to Death, and having clodders of Blood about his Heart. The Jury, whereof several are yet alive brought in the man Murdered; but as if some Enchantment had hindred the Prosecution of the Matter, the Court Proceeded not against *Giles Cory*, tho' it cost him a great deal of Mony to get off.' Thus the Story.

The Reverend and Worthy Author, having at the Direction of His Excellency the Governour, so far Obliged the Publick, as to give some Account of the Sufferings brought upon the Countrey by Witchcraft; *and of the Tryals which have passed upon several Executed for the Same:*

Upon Perusal thereof, We find the Matters of Fact and Evidence, Truly reported. And a Prospect given, of the Methods of Conviction, *used in the Proceedings of the Court at* Salem

        Boston Octob. 11.   William Stoughton
            1692.   Samuel Sewall.

But is *New-England*, the only Christian Countrey, that hath undergone such Diabolical Molestations? No, there are other Good people, that have in this way been harassed; but none in circumstances more like to *Ours*, than the people of God, in *Sweedland*. The story is a very Famous one; and it comes to Speak English by the Acute Pen of the Excellent and Renowned Dr. *Horneck*. I shall only single out a few of the more Memorable passages therein Occurring; and where it agrees with what happened among ourselves, my Reader shall understand, by my inserting a Word of every such thing in **Black Letter**.

I. It was in the Year 1669. and 1670. That at *Mohra* in *Sweedland*, the **Devils** by the help of **Witches**, committed a most horrible outrage. Among other Instances of Hellish Tyranny there exercised. One was, that Hundreds of their Children, were usually in the Night fetcht from their Lodgings, to a Diabolical Rendezvouz, at a place they called, *Blockula*, where the Monsters that so Spirited them, **Tempted** them all manner of Ways to **Associate** with them. Yea, such was the perillous Growth of this

Witchcraft, that Persons of Quality began to send their Children into other Countries to avoid it.

II. The Inhabitants had earnestly sought God by **Prayer**; and **Yet** their Affliction **Continued**. Whereupon **Judges** had a Special **Commission** to find and root out the Hellish Crew; and the rather, because another County in the Kingdom, which had been so molested, was delivered upon the Execution of the *Witches*.

III. The **Examination**, was begun with a Day of **Humiliation**; appointed by Authority. Whereupon the Commissioners **Consulting**, how they might resist such a Dangerous Flood, the **Suffering Children**, were first Examined; and tho' they were Questioned **One** by **One** apart, yet their **Declarations All Agreed**. The **Witches** Accus'd in these Declarations, were then Examined; and tho' at first they obstinately **Denied**, yet at length many of them ingeniously **Confessed** the Truth of what the children had said; owning with Tears, that the **Devil**, whom they call'd *Locyta*, had **Stopt** their **Mouths**; but he being now **Gone** from them, they could **No Longer Conceal** the Business. The things by them **Acknowledged**, most wonderfully **Agreed** with what other Witches, in other places had confessed.

IV. They confessed, that they did use to **Call upon** the **Devil**, who thereupon would **Carry** them away, over the Tops of Houses, to a Green Meadow, where they gave themselves unto him. Only one of them said, That sometimes the *Devil* only took away her **Strength**, leaving her **Body** on the ground; but she went at other times in **Body** too.

V. Their manner was to come into the **Chambers** of people, and fetch away their children upon Beasts, of the

Devils providing: promising **Fine Cloaths** and other Fine Things unto them, to inveagle them. They said, they never had power to do thus, till of late; but now the Devil did **Plague** and **Beat** them, if they did not gratifie him, in this piece of Mischief. They said, they made use of all sorts of **Instruments** in their Journeys! Of **Men**, of **Beasts**, of **Posts**; the *Men* they commonly laid asleep at the place, whereto they rode them; and if the children mentioned the **Names** of them that stole them away, they were miserably **Scurged** for it, until some of them were killed. The **Judges** found the marks of the Lashes on some of them; but the Witches said, **They would Quickly vanish**. Moreover the Children would be in **strange Fits**, after they were brought Home from these Transportations.

VI. The **First Thing**, they said, they were to do at *Blockula*, was to give themselves unto the Devil, and **Vow** that they would serve him. Hereupon, they **cut their Fingers**, and with **Blood** writ their **Names** in his **Book**. And he also caused them to be **Baptised** by such **Priests**, as he had, in this Horrid company. In **some** of them, the **Mark** of the **cut Finger** was to be found; they said, that the Devil gave **Meat** and **Drink**, as to *Them*, so to the Children they brought with them: that afterwards their Custom was to *Dance* before him; and *swear* and *curse* most horribly; they said, that the Devil show'd them a great, Frightful, Cruel *Dragon*, telling them, **If they confessed any Thing**, he would let loose that Great Devil upon them; they added, that the Devil had a **Church**, and that when the **Judges** were coming, he told them, **he would kill them all**; and that some of them had **Attempted to Murder the Judges**, but **could not**.

VII. Some of the **Children**, talked much of a **White Angel**, which did use to **Forbid** them, what the Devil had bid them to do, and **Assure** them that these doings would

Not last long; but that what had been done was permitted for the wickedness of the People. This **White Angel**, would sometimes rescue the Children, from **Going in**, with the Witches.

VIII. The Witches confessed many mischiefs done by them, declaring with what kind of **Enchanted Tools**, they did their Mischiefs. They sought especially to **kill the Minister** of *Elfdale*, but could not. But some of them said, that such as they wounded, would Be recovered, upon or before their Execution.

IX. The **Judges** would fain have seen them show some of their **Tricks**; but they Unanimously declared, that, **Since they had confessed**, all, they found all their **Witchcraft** gone; and the Devil then Appeared very Terrible unto them, threatning with an **Iron Fork**, to thrust them into a Burning Pit, if they persisted in their Confession.

X. There were discovered no less than *threescore and ten* Witches in One Village, **three and twenty** of which **freely confessing** their Crimes, were condemned to dy. The rest, (**One** pretending she was with Child) were sent to *Fahluna*, where most of them were afterwards executed. Fifteen Children, which confessed themselves engaged in this Witchery, dyed as the rest. Six and Thirty of them between *nine* and *sixteen* years of Age, who had been less guilty, were forced to run the Gantlet, and be lashed on their hands once a Week, for a year together; twenty more who had less inclination to these Infernal enterprises, were lashed with Rods upon their Hands for three Sundays together, at the Church door; the number of the seduced Children, was about three hundred. This course, together with **Prayers**, in all the Churches thro' the Kingdom, issued in the deliverance of the Country.

XI. The most Accomplished Dr. *Horneck* inserts a most wise caution, in his preface to this Narrative, says he, *there is no Public Calamity, but some ill people, will serve themselves of the sad providence, and make use of it for their own ends; as* Thieves *when an house or town is on fire, will steal what they can.* And he mentions a Remarkable Story of a young Woman, at *Stockholm*, in the year 1676, Who accused her own Mother of being a Witch; and swore positively, that she had carried her away in the Night; the poor Woman was burnt upon it: professing her innocency to the last. But tho' she had been an Ill Woman, yet it afterwards prov'd that she was not *such* an one; for her Daughter came to the Judges, with hideous Lamentations, Confessing, That she had wronged her Mother, out of a wicked spite against her; whereupon the Judges gave order for her Execution too.

But, so much of these things; And, now, *Lord, make these Labours of thy Servant, Profitable to thy People.*

Matter Omitted in the Trials.

Nineteen Witches have been Executed at *New-England*, one of them was a Minister, and two Ministers more are Accus'd. There is a hundred Witches more in Prison, which broke Prison, and about two Hundred more are Accus'd, some Men of great Estates in *Boston*, have been accus'd for *Witchcraft*. Those Hundred now in Prison accus'd for Witches, were Committed by fifty of themselves being *Witches*, some of *Boston*, but most about *Salem*, and the Towns Adjacent. Mr. *Increase Mather* has Published a Book about *Witchcraft*, occasioned by the late Trials of Witches, which will be speedily printed in *London* by *John Dunton*.

THE DEVIL DISCOVERED.

2 Cor. II. 11. *We are not Ignorant of His* DEVICES.

Our Blessed Saviour has blessed us, with a counsil, as Wholsome and as Needful as any that can be given us, in *Math. 26.41. Watch and Pray, that yee Enter not into Temptation.* As there is a Tempting *Flesh*, and a Tempting *World*, which would seduce us from Our Obedience to the Laws of God, so there is a Busy *Devil*, who is by way of Eminency called, *The Tempter*; because by him, the Temptations of the *Flesh* and the *World* are managed.

It is not *One Devil* alone, that has Cunning or Power enough to apply the Multitudes of *Temptations*, whereby Mankind is daily diverted from the Service of God; No, the *High Places* of Our Air, are Swarming full of those *Wicked Spirits*, whose Temptations trouble us; they are so many, that it seems no less than a *Legion*, or more than twelve thousands may be spared, for the Vexation of one miserable man. But because those Apostate Angels, are all *United*, under one Infernal Monarch, in the Designs of Mischief, 'tis in the Singular Number, that they are spoken of. Now, the *Devil*, whose Malice and Envy, prompts him to do what he can, that we may be as unhappy as himself, do's ordinarily use more *Fraud*, than *Force*, in his assaulting of us; he that assail'd our First Parents, in a *Serpent*, will still *Act Like a Serpent*, rather than a *Lion*, in prosecuting of his wicked purposes upon us, and for us to guard against the *Wiles* of the *Wicked One*, is one of the greatest cares, with which our God ha's charged us.

We are all of us liable to various *Temptations* every day, whereby if we are carried aside from the strait *Paths of Righteousness*, we get all sorts of wounds unto our selves. Of *Temptations*, I may say, as the Wise Man said, of

Mortality; there is no discharge from that war. The *Devils* fell hard upon both *Adams,* nor may any among the Children of both, imagine to be excused. The *Son* of God Himself, had this *Dog* of Hell, barking at Him; and much more may the Children of *Men,* look to be thus Visited; indeed, there is hardly any *Temptation,* but what is, *Common to Man.* When I was considering, how to spend one Hour in Raising a most Effectual and Profitable *Breast-work,* against the inroads of this Enemy, I perceived it would be done, by a short answer to this.

Case.

What are those Usual Methods *of* Temptation, *with which the Powers of Darkness do assault the Children of Men?*

The *Corinthians,* having upon the Apostles Direction, Excommunicated one of their Society, who had married his Mother-in-law, & this, as it is thought, while his own Father was Living too; the Apostle encourages them to Re-admit that man, upon his very deep and sharp *Repentance.* He gives divers Reasons of his propounding this unto them; whereof one is, *Lest Satan should get advantage of them*; for, had the man miscarried, under any Rigour of the Sentence continued upon him, after his *Repentance,* 'tis well if the Church itself had not quickly fallen to pieces thereupon; besure, the Success of the Gospel had been more than a little Incommoded. The Apostle upon this Occasion, intimates, That *Satan* has his *Devices*; by which word are meant, Artifices or Contrivances used for the *Deceiving* of those that are Treated with them well, But what shall *we do* that we may come to this *Corinthian Attainment, We are not Ignorant of Satan's Devices?*

Truly, the Devil has *Mille Nocendi Artes*; and it will be impossible for us, to run over all the *Stratagems* and *Policies* of our Adversary. I shall only attempt a few Observations upon the *Temptations* of our Lord Jesus Christ: who was *Tempted in all things like unto us, except in our Sins*. When we read the *Temptations* of our Lord Jesus Christ, in the Fourth Chapter of *Matthew* There, Thence, you will understand, what was once counted so difficult; Even, *The way of a Serpent upon the Rock*. There are certain Ancient and Famous *Methods* which the Devil in his *Temptations*, does mostly accustome himself unto; which is not so much from any Barrenness, or Sluggishness in the Devil, but because he has had the Encouragement of a, *Probatum est*, upon those horrid Methods. How did the Devil assault the First *Adam*? It was with Temptations drawn from *Pleasure*, and *Profit*, and *Honour*, which, as the Apostle notes, in *1 Joh. 2.16.* are, *All that is in the World*. With the very same temptations it was, that he fell upon the Second *Adam* too. Now, in those *Temptations*, you will see the more *Usual Methods*, whereby the *Devil* would be Ensnaring of us; and I beseech you to attend unto the following Admonitions, as those *Warnings* of God, which the Lives of your souls depend upon your taking of.

There were especially Three *Remarkable* Assaults of *Temptations*, which the *Devil* it seems, visibly made upon our Lord; after he had been more invisibly for Forty dayes together *Tempting* of that Holy One; and we may make a few distinct *Remarks* upon them all.

§ The first of our Lords three Temptations is thus related, in *Mat. 4.3. He was an Hungry; and when the Tempter came to him, he said, If thou be the Son of God, Command that these Stones be made Bread.*

From whence, take these *Remarks*.

I. The Devil will ordinarily make our *Conditions*, to be the Advantages of his *Temptations*. When our Lord was *Hungry*, then *Bread! Bread!* shall be all the Cry of his Temptation; the Devil puts him upon a wrong step, for the getting of *Bread*. There is no Condition, but what has indeed some *Hunger* accompanying of it; and the Devil marks what it is, that we are *Hungry* for. One mans Condition makes him *Hunger* for Preferments, or Employments, another mans makes him *Hunger* for Cash or Land, or Trade; another mans makes him *Hunger* for Merriments, or Diversions: And the Condition of every Afflicted Man, makes him *Hunger* with Impatience for Deliverance. Now the Devil will be sure to suit his Perswasions with our *Conditions*. When he has our *Condition* to speak with him, & for him, then thinks he, *I am sure this man will now hearken to my Proposals!* Hence, if men are in *Prosperity*, the Devil will tempt them to Forgetfulness of God; if they are in *Adversity*, he will tempt them to Murmuring at God; in all the expressions of those impieties. Wise *Agur* was aware of this; in *Prov. 30.9.* says he, if a man be *Full*, he shall be tempted, *to deny God, and say, who is the Lord?* if a man be Poor, he shall be tempted, *to steal, and take the Name of God in vain.* The Devil will talk suitably; if you ponder your Conditions, you may expect you shall be tempted agreeably thereunto.

II. The Devil does often manage his *temptations*, by urging of our *Necessities*. Our Lord, was thus by the Devil bawl'd upon; *You want Bread, and you'll starve, if in my way you get it not.* The Devil will show some forbidden thing unto us, and plead concerning it, as of *Bread* we use to say, *it must be had. Necessity* has a wonderful compulsion in it. You may see what *Necessity* will do, if you read in *Deut. 28.56. the tender and the delicate Woman among you, her eye shall be evil towards the Children that she shall bear, for she shall eat them for want of all things.* The Devil will perswade us that there is a *Necessity* of our doing what he does propound unto us;

and then tho' the *Laws* of God about us were so many *Walls* of Stone, yet we shall break through them all. That little inconvenience, of our coming to beg our *Bread*, O what a fearful Representation does the Devil make of it! and when once the Devil scares us to think of a sinful thing, *it must be done*, we soon come to think, *it may be done*. When the Devil has frighted us into an Apprehension, that it is a *Needful* thing which we are prompted unto, he presently Engages all the Faculties of our Souls, to prove, that it may be a *Lawful* one; the Devil told *Esau, You'll dye if you don't sell your Birthright*; the Devil told *Aaron, You'll pull all the people about your ears, if you do not countenance their superstitions*; and then they comply'd immediately. Yea, sometimes if the Devil do but Feign a Necessity, he does thereby *Gain* the Hearts of Men; he did but feign a Need, when he told *Saul, the Cattel must be spared, and the sacrifice must be precipitated*, & he does but feign a Need, when he tells many a man, *if you do no servile work on the* Sabbath-day, *and if you don't Rob God of his evening, you'll never subsist in the world*. All the denials of God, in the world, use to be from this Fallacy impos'd upon us. It never can be necessary for us to violate any Negative Commandment in the Law of our God; where God says, *thou shalt not*, we cannot upon any pretence reply, I *must*. But the Devil will put a most formidable and astonishing face of necessity upon many of those *Abominable things, which are hateful to the soul of God*. He'll say nothing to us about, the one thing needful; but the petite and the sorry *Need-nots* of this world, he'll set off with most bloody Colours of *Necessity*. He will not say, *'tis necessary for you to maintain the Favour of your God, and secure the* welfare of your Soul; but he'll say, *'tis necessary for you to keep in with your Neighbours; and that you and yours may have a good Living among them*.

III. The Devil does insinuate his most Horrible *Temptations*, with pretence, of much *Friendship* and

Kindness for us. He seemed very unwilling that our Lord should want any thing that might be comfortable for him; but, he was a *Devil* still! The *Devil* flatters our Mother *Eve*, as if he was desirous to make her more Happy than her Maker did; but there was the *Devil* in that flattery. *Sub Amici fallere Nomen,*——to Salute men with profers to do all manner of Service for them; and at the same time to Stab them as *Joab* did *Abner* of old; this is just like the *Devil*, and the *Devil* truly has many Children that Imitate him in it. Some very Affectionate Things were spoken once unto our Lord; *Lord, be it far from thee, that thou shouldest suffer any Trouble!* But our Lords Answer was, in *Mat. 16.23 Get thee behind me Satan.* The Devil will say to a man, *I would have thee to Consult thy own Interest, and I would have Trouble to be far from thee.* He speaks these *Fair Things*, by the Mouths of our professed Friends unto us, as he did by the Tongue of a Speckled Snake unto our Deluded Parents at the first. But all this while, 'tis a Direction that has been wisely given us; *When he speaks fair, Believe him not, for there are seven Abominations in his Heart.*

IV. Things in themselves *Allowable* and *Convenient*, are oftentimes turned into sore *Temptations* by the Devil. He press'd our Lord unto the making of *Bread*; Why, that very thing was afterwards done by our Lord, in the Miracles of the *Loaves*; and yet it is now a motion of the *Devil, Pray, make thy self a Little Bread*. The Devil will frequently put men by, from the doing of a *seasonable Duty*; but how? Truly by putting us upon another *Duty*, which may be at that juncture a most *Unseasonable* Thing. It is said in *Eccl. 8.5. A Wise Mans heart discerns both Time and Judgment.* The *Ill-Timing* of good Things, is One of the chief Intregues, which the Devil has to Prosecute. The Devil himself, will Egg us on to many a *Duty*; and why so? But because at that very Time a more proper and Useful Duty, will have a *Supersedeas* given thereunto. And, thus there are many

Things, whereof we can say, though no more than this, yet so much as this, *They are Lawful ones,* by which Lawful Things——*Perimus Omnes.* Where shall we find that the Devil has laid our most fatal Snares? Truly, our Snares are on the *Bed,* where it is *Lawful* for us to Sleep; at the *Board,* where it is *Lawful* for us to Sit; in the *Cup,* where 'tis *Lawful* to Drink; and in the *Shops,* where we have *Lawful* Business to do. The *Devil* will decoy us, unto the utmost Edge of the *Liberty* that is *Lawful* for us; and then one Little push, hurries us into a Transgression against the Lord. And the *Devil* by Inviting us to a *Lawful* thing, at a wrong time for it, Layes us under further Entanglement of Guilt before God. 'Tis *Lawful* for People to use Recreations; but in the Evening of the Lords Day, or the Morning of any Day, how Ensnaring are they! The *Devil* then too commonly bears part in the Sport. If *Promiscuous Dancing* were Lawful; though almost all the Christian Churches in the World, have made a Scandal of it; yet for Persons to go presently from a *Sermon* to a *Dance,* is to do a thing, which Doubtless the *Devil* makes good Earnings of.

V. To *distrust* Gods Providence and Protection, is one of the worst things, into which the Devil by his *Temptations* would be hurrying of us. He would fain have driven our Lord unto a Suspicion of Gods care about Him, said the Devil, *You may dy for lack of Bread, if you do not look better after your self, than God is like to do for you.* It is an usual thing for Persons to dispair of Gods *Fatherly Care* Concerning them; they torture themselves with distracting and amazing Fears, that they shall come to want before they dy; Yea, they even say with *Jonas,* in *Chap. 2.4. I am cast out of the sight of God;* He wont look after me! But it is the Devil that is the Author of all such Melancholly Suggestions in the minds of men. It is a thought that often raises a Feaver in the Hearts of *Married* Persons, when Charges grow upon them; *God will never be able in the way of my Calling, to feed and cloath all my Little Folks.* It is a Thought with which *Aged* persons are often tormented, *Tho' God has all my dayes hitherto supplied me, yet I shall be pinched with Straits before I come to my Journeys end.* 'Tis a malicious Devil that raises these *Evil surmisings* in the hearts of Men. And sometimes a distemper of Body affords a Lodging for the Devil, from whence he shoots the cruel Bombs of such *Fiery Thoughts* into the minds of many other persons. With such thoughts does the Devil choose to persecute us; because thereby we come to *Forfeit* what we *Question*. We *Question* the Care of God, and so we *Forfeit* it, until perhaps the Devil do utterly *drown us in Perdition*. Our God says, *Trust in the Lord, and do good, and verily thou shall be fed*. But the Devil says, *don't you trust in God; be afraid that you shall not be fed;* and thus he hinders men from the *doing of Good*.

VI. There is nothing more Frequent in the *Temptations* of the Devil, then for our *Adoption* to be doubted, because of our *Affliction*. When our Lord was in his Penury, then says the Devil, *If thou be the Son of God;* he now makes an *If,* of it; *What? the Son of God, and not be able to Command a Bit of Bread!* Thus, when we are in very Afflictive Circumstances, this will be the Devils Inference, *Thou art not a Child of God*. The Bible says in *Heb. 12.7. If you are Chastened, it is a shrow'd sign that you can't be Children*. Since he can't Rob us of our *Grace*, he would Rob us of our *Joy;* and therefore having Accused us unto God, he then Accuses God unto us. When *Israel* was weak and faint in the Wilderness, then did *Amalek* set upon them; just so does the Devil set upon the people of God, when their Losses, their Crosses, their Exercises have Enfeebled their Souls within them; and what says the Devil? E'en the same that was mutter'd in the Ear of the Afflicted *Job, Is not this the Uprightness of thy Ways? Remember, I pray thee, who ever perished, being Innocent? If thou wert a Child of God, He would never follow thee, with such Testimonies of his Indignation.*

This is the *Logic* of the Devil; and he thus interrupts that patience, and that Chearfulness wherewith we should *suffer the will of God.*

VII. To dispute the Divine Original and Authority of *Gods Word*, is not the least of those *Temptations* with which the Devil troubles us. God from Heaven, had newly said unto our Lord, *this is my Beloved Son*; but now the Devil would have him to make a dispute of it, *If thou be the son of God.* The Devil durst not be so Impudent, and Brasen fac'd, as to bid men use *Pharaohs* Language, *Who is the Lord, that I should obey his voice?* But he will whisper into our Ears, what he did unto our Mother *Eve* of old, *It is not the Lord that hath spoken what you call his Word.* The Devil would have men say unto the *Scripture*, what they said unto the *Prophet*, in *Jer. 43.2. Thou speakest falsely; the Lord our God hath not sent thee to speak what thou sayst unto us*; & he would fain have secret & cursed Misgivings in our hearts, *that things are not altogether so as the Scripture has represented them.* The Devil would with all his heart make one huge Bonefire of all the Bibles in the world; & he has got Millions of persecutors to *assist him in the suppression of that miraculous book. It was the* devil *once in the tongue of a Papist*, that cry'd out, *A plague on this bible; this 'tis that does all our mischief.* But because he can't *Suppress* this Book, he sets himself, to *Disgrace* it all that he can. Altho' the Scripture carries its *own Evidence* with it, and be all over, so pure, so great, so true, and so powerful, that it is impossible it should proceed from any but God alone; yet the Devil would gladly bring some Discredit upon it, as if it were but some *Humane Contrivance*; Of nothing, is the Devil more desirous, than this; That we should not count, *Christ* so precious, *Heaven* so Glorious, *Hell* so Dreadful, and *Sin* so odious, as the Scripture has declared it.

§ The Second of our Lords Three Temptations, is related after this manner, in *Mat. 4.5, 6. Then the Devil taketh him up, into the Holy City, and setteth him upon a Pinacle of the Temple; and saith unto him, if thou be the Son of God, cast thy self down; for it is written, He shall give his Angels charge concerning thee, and in their Hands, they shall bear thee up, lest at any time thou dash thy Foot against a Stone.*

From whence take these *Remarks*.

I. The places of the greatest *Holiness* will not secure us from Annoyance by the *Temptations* of the Devil, to the greatest wickedness. When our Lord was in the Holy City, the Devil fell upon him there. Indeed, there is now no proper *Holiness* of *Places* in our Days; the Signs and Means of Gods more special Presence are not under the Gospel, ty'd unto any certain *places*: Nevertheless there are *places*, where we use to enjoy much of God; and where, altho' God visit not the *Persons* for the sake of the *Places*, yet he visits the *Places* for the sake of the *Persons*. But, I am to tell you that the Devil will visit those *Places* and best *Persons* there. No *Place*, that I know of, has got such a *Spell* upon it, as will always keep the Devil out. The *Meeting-House* wherein we Assemble for the Worship of God, is fill'd with many Holy People, and many Holy Concerns continually; but if our Eyes were so refined as the Servant of the Prophet had his of old, I suppose we should now see a Throng of *Devils* in this very place. The Apostle has intimated, that Angels come in among us; there are Angels it seems that hark, how I *Preach*, and how you *Hear*, at this Hour. And our own sad Experience is enough to intimate, That the *Devils* are likewise Rendevouzing here. It is Reported, in *Job 1.5. When the Sons of God came to present themselves before the Lord, Satan came also among them.* When we are in our Church-Assemblies, O how many *Devils*, do you imagine, croud in among us! There is a *Devil* that rocks one to Sleep, there is a *Devil* that makes another to be thinking of, he scarce knows what himself; and there is a *Devil*, that makes another, to be pleasing himself with wanton and wicked Speculations. It is also possible, that we have our *Closets*, or our *Studies*, gloriously perfumed with Devotions every day; but alas, can we shut the Devil out of them? No, Let us go where we will, we shall still find a Devil nigh unto us. Only, when we come to Heaven, we shall be out of his reach for ever; *O thou foul Devil; we are going where thou canst not come!* He was hissed out of *Paradise*, and shall never enter it any more. Yea, more than so, when the *New Jerusalem* comes down into the *High Places* of our Air, from whence the Devil shall then be banished, there shall be no Devil within the Walls of that Holy City. *Amen, Even so Lord Jesus, Come quickly.*

II. Any other acknowledgments of the Lord Jesus Christ, will be permitted by the Temptations of the Devil, provided those Acknowledgments of him, which are *True* and *Full*, may be thereby prevented. What was it, that the Devil hurried our Lord Jesus Christ unto the Top of the *Temple* for? Surely it could not meerly be to find *Precipices*; any part of the Wilderness would have afforded *Them*. No, it was rather to have *Spectators*. And why so, Why, the carnal Jews had an Expectation among them; that *Elias* was to fly from Heaven to the Temple; and the Devil seems willing, that our Lord should be cry'd up for *Elias*, among the giddy multitude; or any thing in the World, tho never so considerable otherwise, rather than to be received as the Christ of God. The Devil will allow his Followers to think very highly of the Lord Jesus Christ; O but he is very lothe to have them think, *All.* We read in *Col. 1.19. It has pleased the Father, that in Him there should all Fullness dwell.* But it is pleasing to the Devil that we deny something of the Immense *Fullness*, which is in our Lord. The Devil would confess to our Lord, *Thou art the Holy One of God!* but then he claps in, *Thou art Jesus of Nazareth;* which was to conceal our Lords being *Jesus of Bethlehem,* and so his being, *The True Messiah.* All the *Heresies*, and all the Persecutions, that ever plagued the Church of God, have still been, to strike at some *Glory* of our Lord Jesus Christ. A Christ Entirely Acknowledged, will save the Souls of them that so Acknowledge Him; but, says the Devil, *Whatever tides I must not give way to that.* As they say, the Devil makes Witches unable to utter all the *Lords Prayer*, or some such System of Religion, without some Deprevations of it; thus the Devil will consent that we may make a very large Confession of the Lord Jesus Christ; only he will have us to deprave it, at least in some one Important Article. Some one Honour, some one Office, and some one *Ordinance* of the Lord Jesus Christ, must be always left unacknowledged, by those that will do as the Devil would have them.

III. *High Stations* in the Church of God, lay men open to violent and peculiar *Temptations* of the Devil. When our Lord was upon the *Pinacle*, that is not the *Fane*, or *Spire*, but the *Battlements* of the *Temple*, there did the Devil pester him, with singular Molestations, and he therein seems to intend an Entanglement for the Jews, as well as for our Lord. Believe me they that stand High, cannot stand safe. The Devil is a *Nimrod*, a mighty Hunter; and common or little Game, will not serve his Turn: he is a *Leviathan*, of whom we may say, as in *Job. 41.34. He beholds all high things.* Men of high Attainments, and Men of high Employments, in the Church of God, must look, like *Peter* to be more *Sifted*, and like *Paul*, to be more *Buffeted* than other Men. *Ferunt Summos Fulmina Montes.*——The Devil can raise a Storm, when God permitteth it, but as for those Men that stand near Heaven, the Devil will attack them with his most cruel storms of Thunder and Lightening. It was said, *let him that standeth take heed;* but we may say, *They that stand most high, have cause to take most heed.* The Devil is a *Goliah*; and when he finds a *Champion*, he'l be sure most fiercely to Combate such a Man. He is for, *Killing many Birds with one stone;* and he knows that he shall hinder a world of *Good*, and produce a world of *Ill*, if once he can bring a Man Eminently Stationed into his Toyls. Hence 'tis that the *Ministers* of God, are more dogg'd by the Devil, than other persons are. Especially such *Ministers*, as more in the highest Orb of Serviceableness; and most of all such *Ministers* as have spent many years in Laudable Endeavours to be serviceable; Those Ministers are the *Stars* of Heaven, at which the *Tayl* of the *Dragon*, will give the most sweeping and most stinging strokes; the Devil will find that for them, that shall make them *Walk softly* all their Days. These are the Men, that have creepled, and vexed the Devil more than other Men; for which the Devil has an old Quarrel with them. O Neighbours, little do you think, what black Days of Mourning, and Fasting, and Praying before the Lord, a Raging Devil does fill the lives of such *Men of God* withall.

IV. The Devil will make a deceitful and unfaithful use of the *Scriptures* to make his *Temptations* forceable. When the Devil Solicited our Lord, unto an evil thing, he quoted the *Ninty First* Psalm unto him, tho' indeed he fallaciously clip'd it, and maim'd it, of one clause very material in it. O never does the Devil make such dangerous Passes at us, as when he does wrest our *own Sword* out of our Hands, and push *That* upon us. We have to defend us, that Weapon in *Eph. 6.16. The Sword of the Spirit, which, is the word of God*; but when the Devil has that very Weapon to fight us with, he makes terrible work of it. When the Devil would poyson men with false *Doctrines*, he'l quote Scriptures for them; a *Quaker* himself, will have the First Chapter of *John* always in his mouth. When the Devil would perswade men to vile *Actions*, he'l quote Scriptures for them; he'l encourage men to go on in Sin, by showing them, where 'tis said, *The Lord is ready to Pardon.* I say this, The one story of *Davids* Fall, in the Scripture, has been made by the Devil an Engine for the Damnation of many Millions. The Devil will fright men from doing those things, that are, *the*

Things of their Peace; but How? He'l turn a *Scripture* into a *Scare-crow* for them. The Devil will fright them from all constant Prayer to God, by quoting that Scripture, *The Sacrifice of the Wicked, is an Abomination to the Lord*; the Devil will fright them from the Holy Supper of God, by quoting that Scripture, *He that Eats and Drinks unworthily, Eats and Drinks damnation to himself.* And thus the Devil will by some abused Scripture, Terrifie the Children of God; the Scripture is written as we are told, *For our Comfort*; but it is quoted by the Devil, *for our terror.* How many Godly Souls have been cast into sinful Doubts and Fears, by the Devils foolish glosses upon that Scripture, *He that doubts is Damned*; and that, *the fearful shall have their portion in the burning Lake*; The Devil sometimes has play'd the *Preacher*, but I say, *Beware all silly Souls when such a fool is Preaching.*

V. Grievous and Pulling Hurries to *Self-Murder* are none of the smallest outrages, which the Devil in his *Temptations* commits upon us. Why, did the Devil say to our Lord, *Cast thy self down*, but in hopes that our Lord would have broke his Bones, in the fall? The Devil is an *Old Murtherer*; and he loves to *Murder* men; but no *Murder* gives him so much satisfaction, as that which at his instigation, men perpetrate upon themselves. We see that such as are *Bewitched* and *Possessed* by the Devil, do quickly lay violent hands upon themselves, if they be not watched continually, and we see that when persons have begun that *Unnatural* business of *killing themselves*, there is a *Preternatural* Stupendious Prodigious Assistance, by the Devil given thereunto. When people are going to Harm themselves, we call upon them, like those to the Jailor, in *Acts 16.28. Do thy self no harm!* And we have this Argument for it, *It is the Devil that is dragging of you to this mischief; but will you believe, will you obey such an one as the Devil is?* What was it that made *Judas* to strangle himself? We read it was when the *Devil was in him.* I suppose there are few *self-*

murderers, but what are first very strangely fallen into the Devils hands; and possibly, 'tis by some Extraordinary *Discontent,* against God, or *back-sliding* from him, that the Devil first entred into those disturbed Souls. Indeed, some very great Saints of God, have sometimes had hideous Royls raised by the Devil in their minds; untill they have e'en cry'd out with *Job, I choose strangling rather than Life;* and sometimes the ill Humours or Vapours in the Bodies of such Good Men, do so harbour the Devil that they have this woful motion every day thence made unto them; *You must Kill your self! you must! you must!* But it is rarely any other than a *Saul,* an *Abimelek,* an *Achitophel,* or a *Judas;* rarely any other, than a very Reprobate, whom the Devil can drive, while the man is *Compos Mentis,* to Consummate such a Villany. Yea, no Child of God, in his Right Senses can go so far in this impiety, as to be left without all Time and Room for true *Repentance* of the Crime; 'tis *thus* done, by none but those that go to the Devil. A *self-murder,* acted by one that is upon other accounts a Reasonable man, is but such an attempt of Revenge upon the God that made him, as none but one full of the Devil can be guilty of. If any of you are Dragoon'd by the Devil, unto the murdering of your selves, my Advice to you is, *Disclose it, Reveal it, make it known immediately.* One that Cut his own Throat among us, Expired crying out, *O that I had told! O that I had told.* You may spoil the Devil, if you'l *Tell* what he is a doing of.

VI. Presumptuous and Unwarrantable *Trials* of the Blessed God, are some of those things whereinto the Devil would fain hook us with his *Temptations.* This was that which the Devil would have brought our Lord unto, even, *A tempting of the Lord our God.* It is the charge of our God upon us, in *Deut. 6.16. Thou shalt not Tempt the Lord thy God.* But that which the Devil *Tries,* is, to put us upon *Trying* in a sinful way, whether God be such a God as indeed he is. 'Tis true as to the ways of Obedience, our

God says unto us, *Prove me, in those ways; Try, whether I won't be as good as my Word.* But then there are ways of *Presumption,* wherein the Devil would have us to trie, what a God it is, *With whom we have to do.* The Devil would have us to trie the Purpose of God, about our selves or others; but how? By going to the *Devil* himself; by Consulting *Astrologers,* or *Fortune Tellers;* or perhaps by letting the Bible fall open, to see what is the first Sentence we light upon. The Devil would have us trie the Mercy of God, but how? By running into *Dangers,* which we have no call unto. He would have us trie the Power of God; but how? By looking for good things, without the use of Means for the getting of them. He would have us trie the Justice of God; but how? By venturing upon Sin in a *Corner,* with an Imagination that God will never bring us out. He would have us trie the Promise of God; but how? By *Limiting* the Lord, unto such or such a way of manifesting Himself, or else believing of nothing at all. He would have us trie the Threatning of God; but how? By going on impenitently in those things, for which the *Wrath of God comes upon the Children of Disobedience.* Thus would the Devil have us to affront the Majesty of Heaven every day.

VII. The *Temptations* of the Devil, aim at puffing and bloating of us up, with *Pride;* as much perhaps as any one iniquity. The Devil would have had Our Lord make a *Vain glorious* Discovery of himself unto the World, by *Flying in the air,* so as no mortal can. *Hoc Ithacus velit*—the Devil would have us to soar aloft, and not only to be above other men, but also to *know* that we are so, *Pride* is the Devils own sin; and he affects especially to be, *The King over the Children of Pride,* it is a caution in *1 Tim. 3.6.* A Pastor must not be *A Novice; Lest being lifted up with Pride, He fall into the condemnation of the Devil. (Summo ac Pio cum Tremore Hunc Textum Legamus nos Ministri Juvenes!)* Accordingly, the Devil would have us to be inordinately taken and moved with what *Excellencies* our God has bestowed upon us. If our *Estates* rise, he would have us rise in our Spirits too. If we have been blessed with Beauty, with Breeding, with Honour, with Success, with Attire, with Spiritual Priviledges, or with Praise-worthy Performances; Now says the Devil, *Think thy self better than other Men.* Yea, the Devil would have us arrogate unto our selves, those *Excellencies* which really we never were owners of; and *Boast of a false Gift*. He would have us moreover to Thirst after Applause among others that may see Our *Excellencies*! and be impatient if we are not accounted *some-body*. He would have us furthermore, to aspire after such a *Figure*, as God has never yet seen fitting for us; and croud into some *High Chair* that becomes us not. Thus would the Devil Elevate us into the *Air*, above our Neighbours; and why so? 'Tis that we may be punished with such *Falls*, as may make us cry out with *David, O my Bones are broken with my Falls!* The Devil can't endure to see men lying in the *Dust*; because there is no falling thence. He is a *Fallen Spirit* himself, and it pleases him to see the *Falls* of men.

§ The Third of Our Lords Three Temptations, is related in such Terms as these. *Matth. 4.8, 9. Again the Devil taketh him up, into an exceeding High Mountain, and sheweth him all the Kingdoms of the world, and the glory of them: and saith unto him, all these things will I give thee, if thou wilt fall down and Worship me.* From whence take these Remarks.

I. The Devil in his *Temptations* will set the Delight of this world before us; but he'll set a fair, and a false *Varnish* upon those Delights. They were some unknown *Perspectives*, which the Devil had, both for the Refracting of the *Medium*, and for the Magnifying of the Object, whereby he gave our Lord at once a prospect of the whole Roman Empire; but what was it? It was the *World*, and the *Glory* of it; he says not a word of the *World*, and the *Trouble* of it. No sure; not a word of that; the Devil will not have his Hook so barely expos'd unto us. The Devil sets off the Delights of Sin, which he offers unto us, with a stretched and raised Rhetorick; but he will not own, *That in the midst of our Laughter, our Heart shall be sorrowful;* and *That the end of our Mirth shall be Heaviness.* There is but one Glass in the Spectacles, with which the Devil would have us to read, those passages in *Eccles. 11.9. Rejoyce, O young Man in thy youth, and let thy Heart chear thee in the Dayes of thy youth, and walk in the ways of thy Heart, and in the sight of thine Eyes.* Thus far the Devil would have us to Read; and he'll make many a fine Comment upon it; he'll tell us, That if we'll follow the Courses of the World, we shall swim in all the Delights of the World. But he is not willing you should Read out the next words; *But know thou, that for all these things God shall bring thee into Judgment.* O he's loth we should be aware of the dreadful Issues, and Reckonings that our Worldly Delights will be attended with. He sets before us, *The Pleasures of Sin;* but he will not say, *These are but for a Season.* He sets before us, *The sweet Waters of Stealth;* but he will not say, *There is Death in the Pot.* He is a *Mountebank,* that will bestow nothing but Romantic Praises upon all that he makes us the Offers of.

II. There are most Hellish *Blasphemies* often buzz'd by the *Temptations* of the Devil, into the minds of the best Men alive. What a most Execrable Thing was here laid before our Lord Himself: Even, To own the *Devil as God!* a thing that can't be uttered, without unutterable Horror of Soul. The best man on earth, may have such *Fiery Darts* from Hell shot into his mind. One that was acted by the *Devil,* had the impudence to propound this unto such a good man as *Job, Curse God.* And the Devil pleases himself, by chusing the Hearts of good men, with his base Injections, *That there is no God,* or, *That God is not a Righteous God;* and a thousand more such things, too Devilish to be mentioned. A good man is extreamly grieved at it, when he hears a *Blasphemy* from the mouth of another man; said the Psalmist, in *Psal. 44.15, 16. My Confusion is continually before me, for the voice of him that Blasphemeth.* But much more when a good man finds a *Blasphemy* in his own Heart; O it throws him into most Fevourish Agonies of Soul. For this cause, a mischievous Devil, will *Flie blow* the Heart of such a man, with such Blasphemous Thoughts, as make him crie out, *Lord I am e'n weary of my life.* Yea, the Devil serves the man just as the Mistress of *Joseph* dealt with him; he importunes the man to think wickedly from Day to Day; and if the man refuse, he cries out at last, *Behold, what wicked thoughts this man has lodging in him.* Sayst thou so? *Satan!* No, they are Baits of thy own; and at thy Door alone shall they be laid for ever.

III. There is a sort of Witchcrafts in those things, whereto the Temptations of the Devil would inveigle us. To worship the Devil is Witchcraft, and under that notion was our Lord urged unto sin. We are told in *1 Sam. 15.23. Rebellion is as the sin of Witchcraft:* When the Devil would have us to sin, he would have us to do the things which the forlorn Witches use to do. Perhaps there are few persons, ever allured by the Devil unto an Explicit Covenant with himself. If any among ourselves be so, my councel is, that you hunt the Devil from you, with such words as the Psalmist had, *Be gone, Depart from me, ye evil Doers, for I will keep the Commandments of my God.* But alas, the most of men, are by the Devil put upon doing the things that are Analogous to the worst usages of Witches. The Devil says to the sinner, *Despise thy Baptism, and all the Bond of it, and all the Good of it.* The Devil says to the sinner, *Come, cast off the Authority of God, and refuse the Salvation of Christ for ever.* Yea, the Devil who is called, *The God of this World,* would have us to take Him for Our God, and rather Hear Him, Trust Him, Serve Him, than the God that formed us.

IV. The *Temptations* of the Devil do Tug and Pull for nothing more, than that the Rulers of the World may yield

Homage unto him. Our Lord has had this by his Father Engag'd unto him, *That he shall one day be Governour of the Nations.* The Devil doe's extreamly dread the approach of that Illustrious time, when *The Kingdom of God shall come and his Will be done, as in Heaven, and on Earth.* For this cause it was that he was desirous, Our Lord should rather have accepted of him, that Kingdom, which *Antichrist* afterwards accepted of him, for the Establishment of *Devil-worship*, in the World. I may tell you, The Devil is mighty unwilling, that there should be one *Godly Magistrate* upon the face of the Earth. Such is the influence of *Government*, that the Devil will every where stickle mightily, to have that siding with him. What *Rulers* would the Devil have, to command all mankind, if he might have his will? Even, such as are called in *Psal. 94.20. The throne of iniquity, which frames mischief by a Law*; such as will promote Vice, by both Connivance, and Example; and such as will oppress all that shall be *Holy, and Just, and Good.* All men have cause therefore to be jealous, what Use the Devil may make of them, with reference to the Affairs of Government; but Rulers may most of all think, that the Lord Jesus from Heaven calls upon them, *Satan has desired that he might Sift you, and have you; O Look to it, what side you take.*

Thus have you in the Temptations of our Lord, seen the principal of those Devices, which the Devil has to Entrap our Souls. But what shall we now do, that we may be fortified against those Devices? O that we might be well furnished with the *Whole Armour of God!* But me thinks, there were some things attending the Temptations of our Lord, which would especially Recommend those few Hints unto us for our Guard.

First, If you are not fond of Temptation, be not fond of Needless, or Too much Retirement. Where was it, that the Devil fell upon our Lord? it was when he was Alone in the Wilderness. We should all have our Times to be Alone every Day; and if the Devil go to scare us out of our Chambers, with such a Bugbear, as that he'll appear to us, yet stay in spite of his teeth, stay to finish your Devotions; he Lyes, he dare not shew his head. But on the other-side by being too solitary, we may lay our selves too much open to the Devil; You know who says, *Wo to him that is alone.*

Secondly, Let an *Oracle* of God be your defence against a *Temptation* of *Hell.* How did our Lord silence the *Devil?* It was with an, *It is written!* And *all* his Three Citations were from that one Book of *Deuteronomy.* What a *full* Armoury then have we, in *all* the sacred Pages that lie before us? Whatever the Words of the *Devil* are, drown them with the words of the *Great God.* Say, *It is Written* The *Belshazzar* of *Hell* will Tremble and Withdraw, if you show these *Hand-Writings* of the Lord.

Lastly, Since the Lord Jesus Christ has conquered all the *Temptations* of the Devil, Flie to that Lord, Crie to that Lord, that He would give you a share in his Happy Victory. It was for Us that our Lord overcome the Devil: and when he did but say, *Satan, Get hence,* away presently the Tygre flew: Does the Devil molest Us? Then let us Repair to our Lord, who says, *I know how to succour the Tempted.* Said the *Psalmist, Psal. 61.2. Lead me to the Rock that is higher than I.* A Woman in this Land being under the Possession of Devils, the Devils within her, audibly spoke of diverse Harms they would inflict upon her; but still they made this answer, *Ah! She Runs to the Rock! She Runs to the Rock!* and that hindered all. O this *Running to the Rock*; 'tis the best Preservation in the World; the *Vultures* of *Hell* cannot prey upon the *Doves* in the *Clefts* of that *Rock.* May our God now lead us thereunto.

A FURTHER ACCOUNT OF THE TRYALS OF THE New-England Witches.

WITH THE OBSERVATIONS
Of a Person who was upon the Place several Days when the suspected Witches were first taken into Examination.

To which is added,

Cases of Conscience
Concerning Witchcrafts and Evil Spirits Personating Men.

Written at the Request of the Ministers of *New-England*.

By *Increase Mather*, President of *Harvard* Colledge.

Licensed and Entred according to Order.

London: Printed for **J. Dunton**, at the *Raven* in the *Poultrey*. 1693. Of whom may be had the *Third Edition* of Mr. *Cotton Mather's First Account* of the Tryals of the *New-England* Witches, Printed on the same size with this *Last Account*, that they may bind up together.

A True Narrative of some Remarkable Passages relating to sundry Persons afflicted by *Witchcraft* at *Salem* Village in *New-England*, which happened from the *19th.* of *March* to the *5th.* of *April,* 1692.

Collected by Deodat Lawson.

On the Nineteenth day of *March* last I went to *Salem* Village, and lodged at *Nathaniel Ingersol's* near to the Minister Mr. *P.'s* House, and presently after I came into my Lodging, Capt. *Walcut's* Daughter *Mary* came to Lieut. *Ingersol's* and spake to me; but suddenly after, as she stood by the Door, was bitten, so that she cried out of her Wrist, and looking on it with a Candle, we saw apparently the marks of Teeth, both upper and lower set, on each side of her Wrist.

In the beginning of the Evening I went to give Mr. *P.* a Visit. When I was there, his Kinswoman, *Abigail Williams*, (about 12 Years of Age) had a grievous fit; she was at first hurried with violence to and fro in the Room (though Mrs. *Ingersol* endeavoured to hold her) sometimes making as if she would fly, stretching up her Arms as high as she could, and crying, *Whish, Whish, Whish,* several times; presently after she said, there was Goodw. *N.* and said, *Do you not see her? Why there she stands!* And she said, Goodw. *N.* offered her the Book, but she was resolved she would not take it, saying often, *I wont, I wont, I wont take it, I do not know what Book it is: I am sure it is none of God's Book, it is the Devil's Book for ought I know.* After that, she ran to the Fire, and begun to throw Fire-brands about the House, and run against the Back, as if she would run up Chimney, and, as they said, she had attempted to go into the Fire in other Fits.

On Lords Day, the Twentieth of *March*, there were sundry of the afflicted Persons at Meeting, as Mrs. *Pope*, and Goodwife *Bibber*, *Abigail Williams*, *Mary Walcut*, *Mary Lewes*, and Doctor *Grigg's* Maid. There was also at Meeting, Goodwife *C.* (who was afterward Examined on suspicion of being a *Witch*:) They had several sore Fits in the time of Publick Worship, which did something interrupt me in my first Prayer, being so unusual. After *Psalm* was sung *Abigail Williams* said to me, *Now stand up, and name your Text!* And after it was read, she said, *It is a long Text.* In the beginning of Sermon, Mrs. *Pope*, a Woman afflicted, said to me, *Now there is enough of that.* And in the Afternoon, *Abigail Williams*, upon my referring to my *Doctrine*, said to me, *I know no Doctrine you had, If you did name one, I have forgot it.*

In Sermon time, when Goodwife *C.* was present in the Meeting-House, *Ab. W.* called out, *Look where Goodwife C. sits on the Beam suckling her Yellow Bird betwixt her fingers! Ann Putman*, another Girle afflicted, said, *There was a Yellow Bird sat on my Hat as it hung on the Pin in the Pulpit*; but those that were by, restrained her from speaking loud about it.

On *Monday* the *21st.* of *March*, the Magistrates of *Salem* appointed to come to Examination of Goodwife *C.* And about Twelve of the Clock they went into the Meeting-House, which was thronged with Spectators. Mr. *Noyes* began with a very pertinent and pathetical *Prayer*; and

Goodwife *C.* being called to answer to what was alledged against her, she desired to go to *Prayer*, which was much wondred at, in the presence of so many hundred People: The Magistrates told her, they would not admit it; they came not there to hear her Pray, but to Examine her, in what was Alledged against her. The Worshipful Mr. *Hathorne* asked her, *Why she afflicted those Children?* She said, she did not Afflict them. He asked her, who did then? She said, *I do not know; How should I know?* The Number of the Afflicted Persons were about that time Ten, *viz.* Four Married Women, Mrs. *Pope,* Mrs. *Putman,* Goodwife *Bibber,* and an Ancient Woman, named *Goodall;* three Maids, *Mary Walcut, Mercy Lewes,* at *Thomas Putman's,* and a Maid at *Dr. Griggs's;* there were three Girls from 9 to 12 Years of Age, each of them, or thereabouts, *viz. Elizabeth Parris, Abigail Williams,* and *Ann Putman;* these were most of them at Goodwife *C.'s* Examination, and did vehemently Accuse her in the Assembly of Afflicting them, by *Biting, Pinching, Strangling, &c.* And that they in their Fits see her Likeness coming to them, and bringing a *Book* to them; she said, she had no *Book;* they affirmed, she had a *Yellow Bird,* that used to suck betwixt her Fingers, and being asked about it, if she had any *Familiar Spirit,* that attended her? she said, *She had no Familiarity with any such thing.* She was a *Gospel Woman:* Which Title she called her self by; and the Afflicted Persons told her, Ah! she was *A Gospel Witch. Ann Putman* did there affirm, that one day when Lieutenant *Fuller* was at Prayer at her Father's House, she saw the shape of Goodwife *C.* and she thought Goodwife *N.* Praying at the same time to the Devil; she was not sure it was Goodwife *N.* she thought it was; but very sure she saw the shape of Goodwife *C.* The said *C.* said, they were poor distracted Children, and no heed to be given to what they said. Mr. *Hathorne* and Mr. *Noyes* replyed, It was the Judgment of all that were present, they were *Bewitched,* and only she the Accused Person said, they were *Distracted.* It was observed several times, that if she did but bite her under lip in time of Examination, the Persons afflicted were bitten on their Arms and Wrists, and produced the *Marks* before the Magistrates, Ministers, and others. And being watched for that, if she did but *Pinch* her Fingers, or *Grasp* one Hand hard in another, they were Pinched, and produced the *Marks* before the Magistrates, and Spectators. After that, it was observed, that if she did but lean her *Breast* against the Seat in the Meeting-House, (being the *Bar* at which she stood), they were afflicted. Particularly Mrs. *Pope* complained of grievous Torment in her *Bowels*, as if they were torn out. She vehemently accused the said *C.* as the Instrument, and first threw her Muff at her; but that flying not home, she got off her *shoe*, and hit Goodwife *C.* on the Head with it. After these Postures were watched, if the said *C.* did but stir her Feet, they were afflicted in their *Feet*, and stamped fearfully. The afflicted Persons asked her, why she did not go to the Company of Witches which were before the Meeting-House Mustering? Did she not hear the *Drum* beat? They accused her of having Familiarity with the *Devil*, in the time of Examination, in the shape of a Black *Man* whispering in her Ear; they affirmed, that her *Yellow Bird* sucked betwixt her Fingers in the Assembly; and Order being given to see if there were any sign, the Girl that saw it, said, it was too late now; she had removed a *Pin*, and put it on her *Head*; which was found *there* sticking upright.

They told her, she had Covenanted with the *Devil* for ten Years, six of them were gone, and four more to come. She was required by the Magistrates to answer that Question in the Catechism, *How many persons be there in the Godhead?* She answered it but oddly, yet was there no great thing to be gathered from it; she denied all that was charged upon her, and said, *They could not prove a Witch*; she was that Afternoon Committed to *Salem* Prison; and after she was in Custody, she did not so appear to them, and afflict them as before.

On Wednesday the *23d.* of *March*, I went to *Thomas Putman's*, on purpose to see his Wife: I found her lying on the Bed, having had a sore Fit a little before; she spake to me, and said, she was glad to see me; her Husband and she both desired me to Pray with her while she was sensible; which I did, though the Apparition said, *I should not go to Prayer*. At the first beginning she attended; but after a little time, was taken with a Fit; yet continued silent, and seemed to be *Asleep*: When Prayer was done, her Husband going to her, found her in a *Fit*; he took her off the Bed, to set her on his Knees, but at first she was so stiff, she could not be bended; but she afterwards sat down, but quickly began to strive violently with her *Arms* and *Leggs*; she then began to Complain of, and as it were to Converse Personally with, Goodwife *N*. saying, *Goodwife N. Be gone! Be gone! Be gone! are you not ashamed, a Woman of your Profession, to afflict a poor Creature so? What hurt did I ever do you in my life? You have but two Years to live, and then the Devil will torment your Soul; for this your Name is blotted out of God's Book, and it shall never be put in God's Book again; be gone for shame, are you not afraid of that which is coming upon you? I know, I know what will make you afraid; the wrath of an Angry God, I am sure that will make you afraid; be gone, do not torment me, I know what you would have* (we judged she meant, *her Soul*) *but it is out of your reach; it is cloathed with the white Robes of Christ's Righteousness.* After this, she seemed to dispute with the Apparition about a particular *Text* of Scripture. The Apparition seemed to deny it; (the Womans Eyes being fast closed all this time) she said, *She was sure there was such a Text*, and she would tell it; and then the Shape would be gone, for, said she, *I am sure you cannot stand before that Text!* Then she was sorely Afflicted, her Mouth drawn on one side, and her Body strained for about a Minute, and then said, *I will tell, I will tell; it is, it is, it is*, three or four times, and then was afflicted to hinder her from telling, at last she broke forth, and said, *It is the third Chapter of the Revelations.* I did something scruple the reading it, and did let my scruple appear, lest Satan should make any Superstitiously to improve the Word of the Eternal God. However, tho' not versed in these things, I judged I might do it this once for an Experiment. I began to *read*, and before I had near read through the first Verse, she opened her Eyes, and was well; this Fit continued near half an hour. Her Husband and the Spectators told me, she had often been so relieved by reading Texts that she named, something pertinent to her Case; as *Isa. 40.1. Isa. 49.1. Isa. 50.1.* and several others.

On Thursday the Twenty-Fourth of *March*, (being in course the Lecture-Day at the Village,) Goodwife. *N.* was brought before the Magistrates Mr. *Hathorne* and Mr. *Corwin*, about Ten of the Clock in the Forenoon, to be Examined in the Meeting-House, the Reverend Mr. *Hale* begun with Prayer, and the Warrant being read, she was required to give Answer, *Why she afflicted those persons?* She pleaded her own Innocency with earnestness. *Thomas Putman's* Wife, *Abigail Williams*, and *Thomas Putman's* Daughter accused her that she appeared to them, and afflicted them in their Fits; but some of the others said, that they had seen her, but knew not that ever she had hurt them; amongst which was *Mary Walcut*, who was presently after she had so declared bitten, and cryed out of her in the Meeting-House, producing the *Marks* of *Teeth* on her wrist. It was so disposed, that I had not leisure to attend the whole time of Examination, but both Magistrates and Ministers told me, that the things alledged by the afflicted, and defences made by her, were much after the same manner as the former was. And her motions did produce like effects, as to *Biting, Pinching, Brusing, Tormenting*, at their *Breasts*, by her *Leaning*, and when bended back, were as if their Backs were broken. The afflicted Persons said, the *Black Man* whispered to her in the Assembly, and therefore she could not hear what the Magistrates said unto her. They said also, that she did then ride by the Meeting-House, behind the *Black Man*. *Thomas Putman's* Wife had a grievous Fit in the time of Examination, to the very great impairing of her strength, and wasting of her spirits, insomuch as she could hardly move hand or foot when she was carried out. Others also were there grievously afflicted, so that there was once such a hideous scrietch and noise (which I heard as I walked at a little distance from the Meeting-House) as did amaze me, and some that were within, told me the whole Assembly was struck with Consternation, and they were afraid, that those that sate next to them were under the Influence of *Witchcraft*. This Woman also was that day committed to *Salem* Prison. The Magistrates and Ministers also did inform me, that they apprehended a Child of *Sarah G.* and examined it, being between 4 and 5 years of Age. And as to matter of Fact, they did unanimously affirm, that when this *Child* did but cast its Eye upon the afflicted Persons, they were tormented; and they held her *Head*, and yet so many as her *Eye* could fix upon were afflicted. Which they did several times make careful Observation of: The afflicted complained, they had often been *Bitten* by this Child, and produced the marks of *a small set of teeth* accordingly; this was also committed to *Salem* Prison, the Child looked *hail, and well* as other Children. I saw it at Lieut. *Ingersol's*. After the Commitment of Goodw. *N. Tho. Putman's* Wife was much better, and had no violent Fits at all from that *24th.* of March, to the *5th.* of *April.* Some others also said they had not seen her so frequently appear to them, to hurt them.

On the *25th.* of *March* (as Capt. *Stephen Sewal* of *Salem* did afterwards inform me) *Eliz. Paris* had sore Fits at his House, which much troubled *himself, and his Wife,* so as he told me they were almost discouraged. She related, that the great *Black Man* came to her, and told her, if she would be ruled by him, she should have whatsoever she desired, and go to a *Golden City.* She relating this to Mrs. *Sewal,* she told the Child, it was the *Devil*, and he was a *Lyar from the Beginning*, and bid her tell him so, if he came again: which she did accordingly, at the next coming to her, in her Fits.

On the *26th.* of *March*, Mr. *Hathorne*, Mr. *Corwin*, and Mr. *Higison*, were at the Prison-Keeper's House to Examine the Child, and it told them there, it had a little *Snake* that used to suck on the lowest Joynt of its Fore-Finger; and when they enquired where, pointing to other places, it told them, not there, but *there*, pointing on the lowest Joint of the Fore-Finger, where they observed a deep Red Spot, about the bigness of a *Flea-bite*; they asked who gave it that *Snake*? whether the great Black Man? It said no, its Mother gave it.

The 31 of *March* there was a *Publick Fast* kept at *Salem* on account of these Afflicted Persons. And *Abigail Williams* said, that the Witches had a *Sacrament* that day at an house in the Village, and that they had *Red Bread* and *Red Drink*. The first of *April*, *Mercy Lewis*, *Thomas Putman's* Maid, in her Fit, said, they did eat *Red Bread*, like *Man's Flesh*, and would have had her eat some, but she would not; but turned away her head, and spit at them, and said, *I will not Eat, I will not Drink, it is Blood, &c.*, she said, *That is not the Bread of Life; that is not the Water of Life; Christ gives the Bread of Life; I will have none of it!* The first of *April* also *Mercy Lewis* aforesaid saw in her Fit a *White Man*, and was with him in a glorious Place, which had no *Candles* nor *Sun*, yet was full of Light and *Brightness*; where was a great Multitude in White glittering Robes, and they Sung the Song in the fifth of *Revelation*, the 9th verse, and the 110 *Psalm*, and the 149 *Psalm*; and said with her self, *How long shall I stay here! let me be along with you:* She was loth to leave this place, and grieved that she could tarry no longer. This *white Man* hath appeared several times to some of them, and given them notice how long it should be before they had another Fit, which was sometimes a day, or day and half, or more or less, it hath fallen out accordingly.

The 3d of *April*, the Lord's-day, being Sacrament-day, at the Village, *Goodw. C.* upon Mr. *Parris's* naming his Text, *John 6.70. One of them is a Devil*, the said *Goodw. C.* went immediately out of the Meeting-House, and flung the Door after her violently, to the amazement of the Congregation. She was afterwards seen by some in their Fits, who said, *O* Goodw. C. *I did not think to see you here!* (and being at their *Red bread and drink*) said to her, *Is this a time to receive the Sacrament, you ran away on the Lord's-Day, and scorned to receive it in the Meeting-House, and, Is this a time to receive it? I wonder at you!* This is the sum of what I either saw my self, or did receive Information from persons of undoubted Reputation and Credit.

Remarks of things more than ordinary about the Afflicted Persons.

1. They are in their Fits tempted to be *Witches*, are shewed the List of the Names of others, and are tortured, because they will not yeild to Subscribe, or meddle with, or touch the Book, and are promised to have present Belief if they would do it.

2. They did in the Assembly mutually *Cure* each other, even with a *Touch* of their Hand, when Strangled, and otherwise Tortured; and would endeavour to get to their Afflicted, to relieve them.

3. They did also foretel when anothers Fit was a-coming, and would say, *Look to her!* she will have a Fit presently, which fell out accordingly, as many can bear witness, that heard and saw it.

4. That at the same time, when the *Accused* Person was present, the *Afflicted Persons* saw her Likeness in other places of the Meeting-House, suckling her *Familiar,* sometimes in one place and posture, and sometimes in another.

5. That their Motions in their Fits are *Preternatural,* both as to the manner, which is so strange as a well person could not Screw their Body into; and as to the violence also it is preternatural being much beyond the Ordinary force of the same person when they are in their right mind.

6. The *eyes* of some of them in their fits are exceeding fast closed, and if you ask a question they can give no answer, and I do believe they cannot hear at that time, yet do they plainly converse with the Appearances, as if they did discourse with real persons.

7. They are utterly pressed against any persons *Praying* with them, and told by the appearances, they shall not go to *Prayer,* so *Tho. Putman's* wife was told, *I should not Pray;* but she said, *I should:* and after I had done, reasoned with the *Appearance, Did not I say he should go to Prayer.*

8. The forementioned *Mary W.* being a little better at ease, the Afflicted persons said, *she had signed the Book;* and that was the reason she was better. Told me by *Edward Putman.*

Remarks concerning the Accused.

1. For introduction to the discovery of those that afflicted them, It is reported Mr. *Parris's* Indian Man, and Woman, made a Cake of *Rye Meal,* and the Childrens water, baked it in the Ashes, and gave it to a Dog, since which they have discovered, and seen particular persons hurting of them.

2. In Time of Examination, they seemed little affected, though all the Spectators were much grieved to see it.

3. *Natural* Actions in them produced *Preternatural* actions in the Afflicted, so that they are their own *Image* without any *Poppits* of Wax or otherwise.

4. That they are accused to have a Company about 23 or 24 and they did *Muster in Armes*, as it seemed to the Afflicted Persons.

5. Since they were confined, the Persons have not been so much Afflicted with their appearing to them, *Biteing* or *Pinching* of them &c.

6. They are reported by the Afflicted Persons to keep dayes of *Fast* and dayes of *Thanksgiving*, and *Sacraments*; Satan endeavours to Transforme himself to an *Angel of Light*, and to make his Kingdom and Administrations to resemble those of our Lord Jesus Christ.

7. Satan Rages Principally amongst the Visible Subjects of Christ's Kingdom and makes use (at least in appearance) of some of them to Afflict others; that *Christ's Kingdom, may be divided against it self*, and so be weakened.

8. Several things used in *England* at Tryal of Witches, to the Number of 14 or 15 which are wont to pass instead of, or in Concurrence with *Witnesses*, at least 6 or 7 of them are found in these accused: see *Keebles Statutes*.

9. Some of the most solid Afflicted Persons do affirme the same things concerning *seeing* the accused *out* of their Fitts as well as *in* them.

10. The Witches had a *Fast*, and told one of the Afflicted Girles, she must not *Eat*, because it was *Fast Day*, she said,

she *would*: they told her they would *Choake* her then; which when she did eat, was endeavoured.

A FURTHER ACCOUNT OF THE TRYALS OF
THE NEW-ENGLAND WITCHES, SENT IN A LETTER FROM
THENCE, TO A GENTLEMAN IN LONDON.

Here were in *Salem, June 10, 1692*, about 40 persons that were afflicted with horrible torments by *Evil Spirits*, and the afflicted have accused 60 or 70 as Witches, for that they have *Spectral appearances* of them, tho the Persons are absent when they are tormented. When these Witches were Tryed, several of them confessed a contract with the Devil, by signing his Book, and did express much sorrow for the same, declaring also thir *Confederate Witches*, and said the Tempters of them desired 'em to sign the *Devils Book*, who tormented them till they did it. There were at the time of *Examination*, before many hundreds of Witnesses, strange Pranks play'd; such as the taking Pins out of the Clothes of the afflicted, and thrusting them into their flesh, many of which were taken out again by the *Judges* own hands. Thorns also in like kind were thrust into their flesh; the accusers were sometimes *struck dumb, deaf, blind*, and sometimes lay as if they were dead for a while, and all foreseen and declared by the afflicted just before it 'twas done. Of the afflicted there were two Girls, about *12 or 13 years of age*, who saw all that was done, and were therefore called the *Visionary Girls*; they would say, *Now he, or she, or they, are going to bite or pinch the Indian*; and all there present in Court saw the visible marks on the *Indians* arms; they would also cry out, *Now look, look, they are going to bind such an ones Legs*, and all present saw the same person spoken of, fall with her Legs twisted in an extraordinary manner; Now say they, we shall all fall, and immediately 7 or 8 of the afflicted fell down, with *terrible shrieks and Out-crys*; at the time when one of the Witches was *sentenc'd, and pinnion'd* with a Cord, at the same time was the afflicted *Indian* Servant going home, (being about 2 or 3 miles out of town,) and had both his Wrists at the same instant bound about with a like Cord, in the same manner as she was when she was sentenc'd, but with that violence, that the Cord entred into his flesh, not to be untied, nor hardly cut——Many *Murders* are suppos'd to be in this way committed; for these Girls, and others of the afflicted, say, *they see Coffins, and bodies in Shrowds,* rising up, and looking on the accused, crying, *Vengeance, Vengeance on the Murderers*——Many other strange things were transacted before the Court in the time of their Examination; and especially one thing which I had like to have forgot, which is this, One of the accus'd, whilst the rest were under Examination, was drawn up by a Rope to the Roof of the house where he was, and would have been choak'd in all probability, had not the Rope been presently cut; the Rope hung at the Roof by some *invisible tye,* for there was no hole where it went up; but after it was cut the *remainder* of it was found in the Chamber just above, lying by the very place where it hung down.

In *December 1692,* the Court sate again at *Salem* in *New-England,* and cleared about 40 persons suspected for Witches, and Condemned three. The Evidence against these three was the same as formerly, so the Warrant for their Execution was sent, and the *Graves digged* for the said three, and for about five more that had been Condemned at *Salem* formerly, but were Repreived by the Governour.

In the beginning of *February 1693,* the Court sate at *Charles-Town* where the Judge exprest himself to this effect.

That who it was that obstructed the Execution of Justice, or hindred those good proceedings they had made, he knew not, but thereby the Kingdom of Satan was advanc'd, &c. *and the Lord have mercy on this Country:* and so declined coming any more into Court. In his absence *Mr. D——* sate as Chief Judge 3 several days, in which time 5 or 6 were clear'd by Proclamation, and almost as many by Trial; so that all are acquitted.

The most remarkable was an Old Woman named *Dayton,* of whom it was said, *If any in the World were a Witch, she was one, and had been so accounted 30 years.* I had the Curiosity to see her tried; she was a decrepid Woman of about 80 years of age, and did not use many words in her own defence. She was accused by about 30 Witnesses; but the matter alledged against her was such as needed little apology, on her part not one passionate word, or immoral action, or evil, was then objected against her for 20 years past, only strange accidents falling out, after some Christian admonition given by her, as saying, *God would not prosper them, if they wrong'd the Widow.* Upon the whole, there was not proved against her any thing worthy of Reproof, or just admonition, much less so heinous a Charge.

So that by the *Goodness* of God we are once more out of present danger of this *Hobgoblin Monster,* the standing Evidence used at *Salem* were called, but did not appear.

There were others also at *Charles-town* brought upon their *Tryals,* who had formerly confess'd themselves to be Witches; but upon their tryals deny'd it, and were all clear'd; So that at present there is no *further prosecution of any.*

CASES of Conscience Concerning
Evil Spirits
Personating MEN;
WITCHCRAFTS,
Infallible Proofs of Guilt in such as are Accused with that CRIME.

All Considered according to the Scriptures, History, Experience, and the Judgment of many Learned MEN.

By *Increase Mather*, President of *Harvard* Colledge at *Cambridge*, and Teacher of a Church at *Boston* in *New England*.

PROV. xxii. xxi.
——*That thou mightest Answer the Words of Truth, to them that send unto thee.*

Efficiunt Dæmones, ut quæ non sunt, sic tamen, quasi sint, conspicienda hominibus exhibeant. Lactantius Lib. 2. Instit. Cap. 15. *Diabolus Consulitur, cum iis mediis utimur aliquid Cognoscendi, quæ a Diabolo sunt introducta. Ames Cas. Cons.* L. 4. Cap. 23.

Printed at *Boston,* and Re-printed at *London,* for **John Dunton**, at the *Raven* in the *Poultrey.* 1693.

CHRISTIAN READER.

So *Odious and Abominable is the Name of a Witch, to the Civilized, much more the Religious part of Mankind, that it is apt to grow up into a Scandal for any, so much as to enter some sober cautions against the over hasty suspecting, or too precipitant Judging of Persons on this account. But certainly, the more execrable the Crime is, the more critical care is to be used in the exposing of the Names, Liberties, and Lives of Men (especially of a Godly Conversation) to the imputation of it. The awful hand of God now upon us, in letting loose of evil Angels among us to perpetrate such horrid Mischiefs, and suffering of Hell's Instruments to do such fearful things as have been scarce heard of; hath put serious persons into deep Musings, and upon curious Enquiries what is to be done for the detecting and defeating of this tremendous design of the grand Adversary: And, tho' all that fear God are agreed,* That no evil is to be done, that good may come of it; *yet hath the Devil obtained not a little of his design, in the divisions of Reuben, about the application of this Rule.*

That there are Devils and Witches, the Scripture asserts, and experience confirms, That they are common enemies of Mankind, and set upon mischief, is not to be doubted: That the Devil can (by Divine Permission) and often doth vex men in Body and Estate, without the Instrumentality of Witches, is undeniable: That he often hath, and delights to have the concurrence of Witches, and their consent in harming men, is consonant to his native Malice to Man, and too lamentably exemplified: That Witches, when detected and convinced, ought to be exterminated and cut off, we have God's warrant for, Exod. 22.18. Only the same God who hath said, thou shalt not suffer a Witch to live; *hath also said,* at the Mouth of two Witnesses, or three Witnesses shall he that is worthy of Death, be put to Death: But at the Mouth of one Witness, he shall not be put to Death, *Deut. 17.6. Much debate is made about what is sufficient Conviction, and some have (in their Zeal) supposed that a less clear evidence ought to pass in this than in other Cases, supposing that else it will be hard (if possible) to bring such to condign Punishment, by reason of the close conveyances that there are between the Devil and Witches; but this is a very dangerous and unjustifiable tenet. Men serve God in doing their Duty, he never intended that all persons guilty of Capital Crimes should be discovered and punished by men in this Life, though they be never so curious in searching after Iniquity. It is therefore exceeding necessary that in such a day as this, men be informed what is Evidence and what is not. It concerns men in point of Charity; for tho' the most shining Professor may be secretly a most abominable Sinner, yet till he be detected, our Charity is bound to Judge.according to what appears: and notwithstanding that a clear evidence must determine a case; yet presumptions must be weighed against presumptions, and Charity is not to be forgone as long as it has the most preponderating on its side. And it is of no less necessity in point of Justice; there are not only Testimonies required by God, which are to be credited according to the Rules given in his Word referring to witnesses: But there is also an Evidence supposed to be in the Testimony, which is throughly to be weighed, and if it do not infallibly prove the Crime against the person accused, it ought not to determine him guilty of it; for so a righteous Man may be Condemned unjustly. In the case of Witchcrafts we know that the Devil is the immediate Agent in the Mischief done, the consent or compact of the Witch is the thing to be Demonstrated.*

Among many Arguments to evince this, that which is most under present debate, is that which refers to something vulgarly called Spectre Evidence, *and a certain sort of Ordeal or trial by the sight and touch. The principal Plea to justifie the convictive*

Evidence in these, is fetcht from the Consideration of the Wisdom and Righteousness of God in Governing the World, which they suppose would fail, if such things were permitted to befal an innocent person; but it is certain, that too resolute conclusions drawn from hence, are bold usurpations upon spotless Sovereignty: *and tho' some things if suffered to be common, would subvert this Government, and disband, yea ruine Humane Society; yet God doth sometimes suffer such things to evene, that we may thereby know how much we are beholden to him, for that restraint which he lays upon the Infernal Spirits, who would else reduce a World into a Chaos. That the Resolutions of such Cases as these is proper for the Servants of Christ in the Ministry cannot be denied; the seasonableness of doing it now, will be justified by the Consideration of the necessity there is at this time of a right Information of men's Judgments about these things, and the danger of their being misinformed.*

The Reverend, Learned, and Judicious Author of the ensuing Cases, is too well known to need our Commendation: All that we are concerned in, is to assert our hearty Consent to, and Concurrence with the substance of what is contained in the following Discourse: *And, with our hearty Request to God, that he would discover the depths of this Hellish Design; direct in the whole management of this Affair; prevent the taking any wrong steps in this dark way; and that he would in particular Bless these faithful Endeavours of his Servant to that end, we Commend it and you to his Divine Benediction.*

William Hubbard.	John Baily.
Samuel Phillips.	Jabez Fox.
Charles Morton.	Joseph Gerrish.
James Allen.	Samuel Angier.

Michael Wigglesworth.

Samuel Whiting, *Sen.*

Samuel Willard.

John Wise.

Joseph Capen.

Nehemiah Walter.

CASES OF CONSCIENCE CONCERNING WITCHCRAFTS.

The First Case that I am desired to express my Judgment in, is this, *Whether it is not Possible for the Devil to impose on the imaginations of Persons Bewitched, and to cause them to Believe that an Innocent, yea that a Pious person does torment them, when the Devil himself doth it; or whether Satan may not appear in the Shape of an Innocent and Pious, as well as of a Nocent and Wicked Person, to Afflict such as suffer by Diabolical Molestations?*

The Answer to the Question must be Affirmative; Let the following Arguments be duely weighed in the Ballance of the Sanctuary.

Argu. 1. There are several Scriptures from which we may infer the Possibility of what is Affirmed.

1. We find that the *Devil by the Instigation of the Witch at Endor appeared in the Likeness of the Prophet Samuel.* I am

not ignorant that some have asserted that, which, if it were proved, would evert this Argument, *viz.* that it was the true and not a delusive *Samuel* which the Witch brought to converse with *Saul.* Of this Opinion are some of the Jewish Rabbies and some Christian Doctors and many late Popish Authors amongst whom *Cornel. a Lapide* is most elaborate. But that it was a *Dæmon* representing *Samuel* has been evinced by learned and Orthodox Writers: especially *Peter Martyr, Balduinus Lavater,* and our incomparable *John Rainolde.* I shall not here insist on the clearing of that, especially considering, that elsewhere I have done it: only let me add, that the Witch said to *Saul, I see Elohim,* i. e. *A God;* (for the whole Context shows, that a single Person is intended) *Ascending out of the Earth. 1 Sam. 28.13.* The Devil would be Worshipped as a God, and *Saul* now, that he was become a *Necromancer,* must bow himself to him. Moreover, had it been the true *Samuel* from Heaven reprehending *Saul,* there is great Reason to believe, that he would not only have reproved him for his sin, in not executing Judgment on the *Amalekites;* as in Ver. 18. But for his Wickedness in consulting with Familiar Spirits: For which Sin it was in special that he died. *2 Chron. 10.13.* But in as much as there is not one word to testify against that Abomination, we may conclude that it was not real *Samuel* that appeared to *Saul:* and if it were the Devil in his likeness, the Argument seems very strong, that if the Devil may appear in the form of a Saint in Glory, much more is it possible for him to put on the likeness of the most Pious and Innocent Saint on Earth. There are, who acknowledge that a *Dæmon* may appear in the shape of a Godly Person, *But not as doing Evil.* Whereas the Devil in *Samuel's* likeness told a pernicious Lye, when he said, *Thou hath disquieted me.* It was not in the Power of *Saul,* nor of all the Devils in Hell, to disquiet a Soul in Heaven, where *Samuel* had been for Two years before this Apparition. Nor did the *Spectre* speak true, when he said, *Thou and thy Sons shall be with me:* Tho' *Saul* himself at his Death went to be with the Devil, his Son *Jonathan* did not so. Besides, (which suits with the matter in hand) the Devil in *Samuels* shape confirmed *Necromancy* and *Cursed Witchery*. He that can in the likeness of Saints encourage Witches to Familiarity with Hell, may possibly in the likeness of a Saint afflict a Bewitched Person. But this we see from Scripture, Satan may be permitted to do.

And whereas it is objected, that the Devil may appear indeed in the form of Dead Persons, but that he cannot represent such as are living; The contrary is manifest. No Question had *Saul* said to the Witch, bring me *David* who was then living, she could as easily have shown living *David* as dead *Samuel*, as easily as that great Conjurer of whom *Wierus* speaks, brought the appearance of *Hector* and *Achilles*, and after that of *David* before the Emperour *Maximilian*.

And that evil Angels have sometimes appeared in the likeness of living absent persons, is a thing abundantly confirmed by History.

Austin tells us of one that went for resolution in some intricate Questions to a Philosopher, of whom he could get no Answer; but in the Night the Philosopher comes to him, and resolves all his Doubts. Not long after, he demanded the reason why he could not answer him in the Day as well as in the Night; The Philosopher professed he was not with him in the Night, only acknowledged that he dreamed of his having such conversation of his Friend, but he was all the time at home, and asleep. *Paulus* and *Palladius* did both of them profess to *Austin*, that one in his shape, had divers times, and in divers places appeared to them: *Thyreus* mentions several Apparitions of absent living persons, which happened in his time, and which he had the certain knowledge of. A Man that is in one place cannot (*Autoprosopos*) at the same time be in another. It remains then that such *Spectres* are Prodigious and Supernatural, and not without Diabolical Operation. It has been Controverted among Learned Men, whether innocent Persons may not by the malice and deluding Power of the Devil be represented as present amongst Witches at their dark Assemblies. The mentioned *Thyreus* says, that the Devil may, and often does represent the forms of Innocent Persons out of those Conventions, and that there is no Question to be made of it, but as to his natural Power and Art he is able to make their shapes appear amongst his own Servants, but he supposeth the Providence of God will not suffer such an Injury to be done to an Innocent Person. With him *Delrio*, and *Spineus* concur. But *Cumanus* in his *Lucerna Inquisitorum* (a Book which I have not yet seen) defends the Affirmative in this Question. *Bins Fieldius* in his Treatise, concerning the Confession of Witches, inclines to the Negative, only he acknowledges *Dei extraordinaria Permissione posse Innocentes sic representari*. And he that shall assert, that Great and Holy God never did nor ever will permit the Devil thus far to abuse an Innocent Person, affirms more than he is able to prove. The story of *Germanus* his discovering a Diabolical illusion of this nature, concerning a great number of Persons that seemed to be at a Feast when they were really at home and asleep, is mentioned by many Authors. But the particulars insisted on, do sufficiently evince the Truth of what we assert, *viz*. That the Devil may by Divine Permission appear in the shape of Innocent and Pious Persons. Nevertheless, It is evident from another Scripture, *viz*. that in *2 Cor. 11.14. For Satan himself is transformed into an Angel of Light.* He seems to be what he is not, and makes others seem to be what they are not. He represents evil men as good, and good men as evil. The Angels of Heaven, (who are the Angels of Light) love Truth and Righteousness, the Devil will seem to do so too; and does therefore sometimes lay before men excellent good Principles and exhort them (as he did *Theodore*

Maillit) to practise many things, which by the Law of Righteousness they are obliged unto, and hereby he does more effectually deceive. Is it not strange, that he has sometimes intimated to his most devoted servants, that if they would have familiar Conversation with him, they must be careful to keep themselves from enormous Sins, and pray constantly for Divine Protection? But so has he transformed himself into an Angel of Light, as *Boissardus* sheweth. He has frequently appeared to Men pretending to be a good Angel, so to *Anatolius* of old; and the late instances of Dr. *Dee* and *Kellet* are famously known. How many deluded *Enthusiasts* both in former and latter times have been imposed on by Satans appearing visibly to them, pretending to be a good Angel. And moreover, he may be said to transform himself into an *Angel of Light*, because of his appearing in the Form of *Holy Men*, who are the *Children of Light*, yea in the shape and habit of Eminent Ministers of God. So did he appear to Mr. *Earl* of *Colchester* in the likeness of Mr. *Liddal* an Holy Man of God, and to the *Turkish Chaous* Baptized at *London, Anno 1658.* pretending to be Mr. *Dury* an Excellent Minister of Christ. And how often has he pretended to be the Apostle *Paul* or *Peter* or some other celebrated Saint? Ecclesiastical Histories abound with Instances of this nature. Yea, sometimes he has transfigured himself into the Form of Christ. It is reported that he appeared to St. *Martin* Gloriously arrayed, as if he had been Christ. So likewise to *Secundellus*, and to another Saint, who suspecting it was Satan, transforming himself into an *Angel of Light* had this expression, *If I may see Christ in Heaven it is enough, I desire not to see him in this World*; whereupon the *Spectre* vanished. It has been related of *Luther*, that after he had been Fasting and Praying in his Study, the Devil come pretending to be Christ, but *Luther* saying, *away thou confounded Devil, I acknowledge no Christ but what is in my Bible*, nothing more was seen. Thus then the Devil is able (by Divine Permission) to Change himself into what form or figure he pleaseth,

Omnia transformat sese in miracula rerum.

A Third Scripture to our purpose is that, in *Rev. 12.10.* where the Devil is called the *Accuser of the Brethren.* Such is the malice and impudence of the Devil, as that he does accuse good Men, and that before God, and that not only of such Faults as they really are guilty of, he accused *Joshua* with his filthy Garments, when through his Indulgence some of his Family had transgressed by unlawful Marriages, *Zach. 3.23.* with *Ezra. 10.18.* but also with such Crimes, as they are altogether free from. He represented the Primitive Christians as the vilest of men, and as if at their Meetings they did commit the most nefandous Villanies that ever were known; and that not only Innocent, but Eminently Pious Persons should thro' the malice of the Devil be accused with the Crime of Witchcraft, is no new thing. Such an Affliction did the Lord see meet to exercise the great *Athanasius* with only the Divine Providence did wonderfully vindicate him from that as well as from some other foul Aspersions. The *Waldenses* (altho' the Scriptures call them *Saints, Rev. 13.7.*) have been traduced by Satan and by the World as horrible Witches; so have others in other places, only because they have done extraordinary things by their Prayers: It is by many Authors related, that a City in *France* was molested with a Diabolical *Spectre*, which the People were wont to call *Hugon*; near that place a number of Protestants were wont to meet to serve God, whence the Professors of the true reformed Religion were nic-named *Hugonots*, by the Papists, who designed to render them before the World, as the Servants and Worshippers of that *Dæmon*, that went under the name of *Hugon*. And how often have I read in Books written by Jesuits, that *Luther* was a Wizard, and that he did himself confess that he had familiarity with

Satan! Most impudent Untruths! nor are these things to be wondered at, since the Holy Son of God himself was reputed a *Magician,* and one that had Familiarity with the greatest of Devils. The Blaspheming Pharisees said, *he casts out the Devils thro' the Prince of Devils, Matth. 9.34.* There is then not the best Saint on Earth (Man or Woman) that can assure themselves that the Devil shall not cast such an Imputation upon them. *It is enough for the Disciple that he be as his Master, and the Servant as his Lord: If they have called the Master of the House Beelzebub, how much more them of his Household, Matth. 10.25.* It is not for men to determine how far the Holy God may permit the wicked one to proceed in his Accusations. The sacred story of *Job* giveth us to understand, that the Lord whose ways are past finding out, does for wise and holy Ends suffer Satan by immediate Operation, (and consequently by Witchcraft) greatly to afflict innocent Persons, as in their Bodies and Estates, so in their Reputations. I shall mention but one Scripture more to confirm the Truth in hand: It is that in *Eccles. 9.2, 3.* where it is said, *All things come alike to all, there is one event to the Righteous and to the Wicked, as is the Good, so is the Sinner, this is an evil amongst all things under the Sun, that there is one Event happeneth to all.* And in *Eccles. 7.15.* 'tis said, *There is a just man that perisheth in his Righteousness.*

From hence we infer, that there is no outward Affliction whatsoever but may befal a good Man; now to be represented by Satan as a Tormentor of Bewitched or Possessed Persons, is a sore Affliction to a good man. To be tormented by Satan is a sore Affliction, yet nothing but what befel *Job,* and a Daughter of *Abraham,* whom we read of in the Gospel: To be represented by Satan as tormenting others, is an Affliction like the former; the Lord may bring such extraordinary Temptations on his own Children, to afflict and humble them, for some Sin they have been guilty of before him. A most wicked Person in St. *Ives*, got a Knife, and went with it to a Ministers House, designing to stab him, but was disappointed; afterwards Conscience being awakened, the Devil appears to this Person in the Shape of that Minister, with a Knife in his hand exhorting to Self-murder: Was not here a Punishment suitable to the Sin which that Person had been guilty of? Perhaps some of those whom Satan has represented as committing Witchcrafts, have been tampering with some foolish and wicked Sorceries, tho' not to that degree, which is Criminal and Capital by the Laws both of God and Men; for this Satan may be permitted so to scourge them; or it may be, they have misrepresented and abused others, for which cause the Holy God may justly give Satan leave falsely to represent them.

Have we not known some that have bitterly censured all that have been complained of by bewitched Persons, saying it was impossible they should not be guilty; soon upon which themselves or some near Relations of theirs, have been to the lasting Infamy of their Families, accused after the same manner, and Personated by the Devil! Such tremendous Rebukes on a few, should make all men to be careful how they joyn with Satan in Condemning the Innocent.

Arg. 2. *Because it is possible for the Devil in the Shape of an innocent Person to do other mischiefs.* As for those who acknowledge that Satan may personate a pious Person, but not to do mischief, their Opinion has been confuted by more than a few unhappy Instances. Mr. *Clark* speaks of a Man that had been an Atheist, or a Sadduce, not believing that there are any Devils or any (to us) invisible World; this Man was converted, but as a Punishment of his Infidelity, evil Angels did often appear to him in the Shape of his most intimate Friends, and would sometimes seduce him into great Inconveniences. It has been elsewhere, and but now noted, that a *Dæmon* in the shape of excellent Mr. *Dury* appeared to the *Turkish Chaos, Anno. 1658.* to disswade him from prosecuting his desires of Baptism into the Name of Christ: Also to Mr. *Earle* in the likeness of his Friends, to discourage him from doing things lawful and good. A multitude of *Jews* were once deluded by a Person pretending to be *Moses* from Heaven, and that if they would follow him they should pass safe through the Sea (as did their Fathers of old through the Red Sea) whereby great numbers of them were deceived and perished in the Waters. Learned and judicious Men have concluded that this *Moses Creensis* was a *Dæmon*, transforming himself into *Moses*: And that the Devil has frequently appeared in the shape of famous Persons to the end that he might seduce Men into Idolatry, (a Sin equal to that of Witchcraft) no Man that has made it his Concern to enquire into things of this nature can be ignorant. Many Examples of this kind are collected by Mr. *Bromhall* in his *Treatise of Spectres, and the cunning Devil, to strengthen Men in their worshipping of Saints departed:* And by Mr. *Bovet* in his *Pandemonium.* It is credibly reported that the Devil in the likeness of a faithful Minister (as St. *Ives* before mentioned, near *Boston* in *Lincolnshire*) came to one that was in trouble of Mind, telling her the longer she lived, the worse it would be for her; and therefore advising her to Self-murder: An eminent Person still living had the account of this Matter from Mr. *Cotton* (the famous Teacher of both *Bostons.*) He was well acquainted with that Minister, who related to him the whole Story, with all the Circumstances of it: For Mr. *Cotten* was so affected with the Report, as to take a Journey on purpose to the Town where this happened, that so he might obtain a satisfactory account about it, which he did. Some Authors say, that a *Dæmon* appeared in the form of *Sylvanus* (*Hierom's* Friend) attempting a dishonest thing, the Devil thereby designing to blast the Reputation of a famous Bishop. I have in another Book mentioned that celebrated Instance concerning an honest Citizen in *Zurick* (the Metropolis of *Helvetia*) in whose shape the Devil appeared, committing an abominable Fact (not fit to be named) very early in the Morning, seen by the Prefect of the City, and his Servant; they were amazed to behold a Man of good Esteem for his Conversation, perpetrating a thing so vile and abominable; but going from the *Spectre* in the Field, to the Citizen's House in the Town, they found him at home, and in his Bed, nor had he been abroad that Morning, which convinced them, that what they saw was an Illusion of the Devil: This Passage is mentioned as a thing known and certain by *Lavater* in his Treatise of *Spectres*, who was a most learned and judicious Preacher in that City. Our *Juel* saith of him, that he must ingeniously confess, that he never understood *Solomon's Proverbs* until *Lavater* expounded them to him: That Book of his *De Spectris* hath been published in *Latin*, High and Low *Dutch*, *French*, *Italian*. The learned *Zanchy* speaks highly of it, professing that he had read it both with Pleasure and Profit. *Voetius* takes notice of that passage which we have quoted out of *Lavater* as a thing memorable.

Some Popish Authors argue, That the Devil cannot personate an innocent Man as doing an act of Witchcraft, because then he might as well represent them as committing Theft, Murder, *&c*. And if so, there would be no living in the World: But I turn the Argument against them, he may (as the mentioned Instances prove) personate honest Men as doing other Evils; and no solid Reason can be given why he may not as well personate them under the Notion of Witches, as under the Notion of Thieves, Murderers, and Idolaters: As for the Objection, that then there would be no living in the World, we shall consider it under the next Argument.

Arg. 3. *If Satan may not represent one that is not a Covenant Servant of his, as afflicting those that are bewitched or possessed, then it is either because he wants Will, or Power to do this, or because God will never permit him thus to do.* No man but a Sadduce doubts of the ill will of Devils; nothing is more pleasing to the Malice of those wicked Spirits than to see Innocency wronged: And the Power of the Enemy is such, as that having once obtained a Divine Concession to use his Art, he can do this and much more than this amounts unto: We know by Scripture-Revelation, that the Sorcerers of *Egypt* caused many untrue and delusive Representations before *Pharaoh* and his Servants. *Exod. 7.11, 22.* and *8.7.* And we read of the working of Satan in all Power and Signs, and lying Wonders. *2 Thess. 2.9.* His Heart is beyond what the wisest of Men may pretend unto: He has perfect skill in Opticks, and can therefore cause that to be visible to one, which is not so to another, and things also to appear far otherwise then they are: He has likewise the Art of Limning in the Perfection of it, and knows what may be done by Colours. It is an odd passage which I find in the *Acta Eruditorum,* printed by *Lipsick,* that about Thirty-two Years ago an indigent Merchant in *France* was instructed by a *Dæmon,* that with Water of *Borax* he might colour Taffities, so as to cause them to glister and look very gay: He searcheth into the Nature, Causes, and Reasons of things, whereby he is able to produce wonderful effects. So that if he does not form the Shape of an innocent Person as afflicting others, it is not from want of either will or power. They that affirm, that God never did, nor ever will permit him thus to do, alledge that it is inconsistent with the Righteousness and Providence of God, in governing Humane Affairs thus to suffer Men to be imposed on: It must be acknowledged that the Divine Providence has taken care, that the greatest part of Mankind shall not be left to unavoidable Deception, so as to be always abused by the mischievous Agents of Hell, in the Objects of plain Sence: But yet it is not for sinful and silly Mortals to prescribe Rules to the most High in his Government of the World, or to direct him how far he may permit Satan to use his power: I am apt to think that there are some amongst us, who if they had lived in *Job's* days, and seen the Devil tormenting of him, and heard him complaining of being scared with Dreams, and terrified with Night-visions, they would have joined with his uncharitable Friends in censuring him as a most guilty Person: But we should consider, that the most high God doth sometimes deal with Men in a way of absolute Sovereignty, performing the thing which is appointed for them, and many such things are with him: If he does destroy the *perfect with the wicked, and laugh at the tryal of the innocent,* (*Job 9.22, 23.*) Who shall enter into his Councils! who has given him a Charge over the Earth! or who has disposed the whole World! Men are not able to give an account of his ordinary Works, much less of his secret Counsels, and the dark Dispensations of his Providence: They do but darken Counsel by Words without Knowledge when they undertake it: If we are not able to see how this or that can stand with the Righteousness of him that governs the World, shall we say that the Almighty will pervert Judgment? or that he that governs the Earth hateth Right? Shall we condemn him that is most just? But whereas 'tis objected; where is Providence? And how shall Men live on the Earth, if the Devil may be permitted to use such Power? I demand, where was Providence, when Satan had Power to cause Sons of *Belial* to lye and swear away the Life of innocent *Naboth,* laying such Crimes to his charge as he was never guilty of? And what an Hour of Darkness was it? How far was the Power of Hell permitted to prevail, when Christ the Son of God was accused, condemned, and hanged for a Crime that he never was guilty of? That was the strangest Providence that has happened since the World began, and yet in the Issue the most glorious: We must therefore distinguish between what does ordinarily come to pass by the Providence of God, and things which are extraordinary: It is not an usual thing for a *Naboth* to have his Life taken from him by false Accusations, or for an

Athanasius or a *Susanna* to be charged, and perhaps brought before Courts of Judicature for Crimes of which they were altogether innocent.

But if we therefore conclude, that such a thing as this can never happen in the World, we shall offend against the Generation of the Just: It is not ordinary for Devils to be permitted to reveal the secret Sins of Men; yet this has been done more than once or twice: Nor is it ordinary for *Dæmons* to steal Money out of Mens Pockets, and Purses, or Wine and Cyder out of their Cellars. Yet some such Instances have there been amongst our selves. It is not usual for Providence to permit the Devil to come from Hell and to throw Fire on the tops of Houses, and to cause a whole Town to be burnt to Ashes thereby; there would (it must be confessed) be no living in the World, if evil Angels should be permitted to do thus when they had a mind to it; nevertheless, Authors worthy of Credit, tell us, that this has sometimes happened. Both *Erasmus* and *Cardanus* write that the Town of *Schiltach* in *Germany*, was in the Month of *April*, 1533. set on fire by a Devil, and burnt to the ground in an Hour's space: 'Tis also reported by *Sigibert, Aventinus* and others, that some Cottages and Barns in a Town called *Bingus* were fired by a wicked *Genius*; that spiteful *Dæmon* said it was for the Impieties of such a Man whom he named, that he was sent to molest them: The poor Man to satisfie his Neighbours, who were ready to Stone him, carried an hot Iron in his Hand, but receiving no hurt thereby, he was judged to be innocent. It is not ordinary for a Devil upon the dying Curse of a Servant, to have a Commission from Heaven to tear and torment a bloody cruel Master; yet such a thing may possibly come to pass. There is a fearful Story to this purpose, in the account of the *Bucuneers* of *America*, wherein my Author relates that a Servant, who was *Spirited* or *Kidnapt* (as they call it) into *America*, falling into the Hands of a Tyrannical Master, he ran away from him, but being taken and brought back, the hard-hearted Tyrant lashed him on his naked Back, until his Body ran in an entire stream of Blood; to make the Torment of this miserable Creature intolerable, he anointed his Wounds with Juice of Lemon mingled with Salt and Pepper, being ground small together, with which torture the miserable Wretch gave up the Ghost, with these dying Words, *I beseech the Almighty God, Creator of Heaven and Earth, that he permit a wicked Spirit, to make thee feel as many Torments before thy Death, as thou hast caused me to feel before mine:* Scarce four days were past after this horrible Fact, when the Almighty Judge gave Permission to the Father of Wickedness to possess the Body of that cruel Master, and to make him lacerate his own Flesh until he died, belike surrendring his Ghost into the Hands of the infernal Spirit, who had tormented his Body: But of this Tragical Story enough.

To proceed, Is it not usual for Persons after their Death to appear unto the Living: But it does not therefore follow, that the great God will not suffer this to be: For both in former and latter Ages, Examples thereof have not been wanting: No longer since than the last Winter, there was much discourse in *London* concerning a Gentlewoman, unto whom her dead Son (and another whom she knew not) had appeared: Being then in *London,* I was willing to satisfie my self, by enquiring into the Truth of what was reported; and on *Febr. 23. 1691.* my Brother (who is now a Pastor to a Congregation in that City) and I discoursed the Gentlewoman spoken of; she told us, that a Son of hers, who had been a very civil young Man, but more airy in his Temper than was pleasing to his serious Mother, being dead, she was much concerned in her Thoughts about his Condition in the other World; but a Fortnight after his Death he appeared to her, saying, *Mother you are solicitous about my Spiritual Welfare; trouble your self no more, for I am happy,* and so vanished; should there be a continual

Intercourse between the Visible and Invisible World, it would breed Confusion. But from thence to infer, that the great Ruler of the Universe will never permit any thing of this nature to be, is an inconsequent Conclusion; it is not usual for Devils to be permitted to come and violently carry away persons through the Air, several miles from their Habitations: Nevertheless, this was done in *Sweedland* about twenty Years ago, by means of a cursed Knot of Witches there. And a learned Physician now living, giveth an account of several Children, who by Diabolical Frauds were stollen from their Parents, and others left in their room: And of two, that in the night-time a Line was by invisible Hands put about their Necks, with which they had been strangled, but that some near them happily prevented it. *V. Germ. Ephem. Anno 1689.* pag. 51. 516.

Let me further add here; It has very seldom been known, that Satan has Personated innocent Men doing an ill thing, but Providence has found out some way for their Vindication; either they have been able to prove that they were in another place when that Fact was done, or the like. So that perhaps there never was an Instance of any innocent Person Condemned in any Court of Judicature on Earth, only through Satans deluding and imposing on the Imaginations of Men, when nevertheless, the Witnesses, Juries, and Judges, were all to be excused from blame.

Arg. 4. *It is certain both from Scripture and History, that Magicians by their Inchantments and Hellish Conjurations, may cause a false Representation of Persons and Things.* An inchanted eye shall see such things as others cannot discern; it is a thing too well known to be denied, that some by rubbing their eyes with a bewitched Water, have immediately thereupon seen that which others could not discern; and there are Persons in the World, who have a strange *Spectral sight.* Mr. *Glanvil* speaks of a Dutchman that could see Ghosts which others could perceive nothing of. There are in *Spain* a sort of men whom they call *Zahurs*, these can see into the Bowels of the Earth; they are able to discover Minerals and hidden Treasures; nevertheless, they have their extraordinary sight only on *Tuesdays* and *Fridays*, and not on the other days of the Week. *Delrio* saith, that when he was at *Madrid, Anno Dom. 1575.* he saw some of these strange sighted Creatures. Mr. *George Sinclare*, in his Book Entituled, *Satans Invisible World discovered*, has these Words, 'I am undoubtedly informed, that men and women in the High-lands can discern Fatality approaching others, by seeing them in the Waters or with Winding Sheets about them. And that others can lecture in a Sheeps shoulder-bone a Death within the Parish seven or eight Days before it come. It is not improbable but that such Preternatural Knowledge comes first by a Compact with the Devil, and is derived downward by Succession to their Posterity: Many such I suppose are Innocent, and have this sight against their Will and Inclination.' Thus Mr. *Sinclare*, I concur with his supposal, that such Knowledge is originally from Satan, and perhaps the Effect of some old Inchantment. There are some at this day in the World, that if they come into a House where one of the Family will die within a Fortnight, the smell of a dead Corpse offends them to such a degree, as that they cannot stay in that House. It is reported that near unto the Abby of St. *Maurice* in *Burgundy* there is a Fishpond in which are Fishes put according to the number of the Monks of that place; if any one of them happened to be sick, there is a Fish seen to Float and Swim above Water half dead, and if the Monk shall die, the Fish a few days before dieth. In some parts in *Wales* Death-lights or Corps Candles (as they call them) are seen in the night time going from the House where some body will shortly die, and passing in to the Church-yard. Of this, my Honoured and never to be forgotten Friend Mr. *Richard Baxter*, has given an Account in his

Book about Witchcrafts lately Published: what to make of such things, except they be the effects of some old Inchantment, I know not; nor what Natural Reason to assign for that which I find amongst the Observations of the *Imperial Academy* for the Year 1687, *viz.* That in an Orchard where are choice *Damascen* Plumbs, the Master of the Family being sick of a *Quartan Ague*, whilst he continued very ill, four of his Plumb-trees instead of Damascens brought forth a vile sort of yellow Plumbs: but recovering Health, the next Year the Tree did (as formerly) bear Damascens again; but when after that he fell into a fatal Dropsie, on those Trees were seen not Damascens, but another sort of Fruit. The same Author gives Instances of which he had the certain knowledge, concerning Apple-trees and Pear-trees, that the Fruit of them would on a sudden wither as if they had been baked in an Oven, when the owners of them were mortally sick. It is no less strange that in the Illustrious Electoral House of *Brandenburg* before the Death of some one of the Family Feminine Spectres appeared: and often in the Houses of Great men, Voices and Visions from the Invisible World have been the Harbingers of Death. When any Heir in the Worshipful Family of the *Breertons* in *Cheshire* is near his Death, there are seen in a Pool adjoyning, Bodies of Trees swimming for certain days together, on which Learned *Cambden* has this note, *These and such like things are done either by the Holy Tutelar Angels of Men, or else by the Devils, who by Gods Permission mightily shew their Power in this Inferiour World.* As for Mr. *Sinclare's* Notion that some Persons may have a *second Sight*, (as 'tis termed) and yet be themselves Innocent, I am satisfied that he judgeth right; for this is common amongst the *Laplanders*, who are horribly addicted to Magical Incantations: They bequeath their *Dæmons* to their Children as a Legacy, by whom they are often assisted (like Bewitched Persons as they are) to see and do things beyond the Power of Nature. An Historian who deserves Credit, relates, that a certain

Laplander gave him a true and particular Account of what had happened to him in his Journey to *Lapland*; and further complained to him with Tears, that things at great distance were represented to him, and how much he desired to be Delivered from that Diabolical Sight, but could not; this doubtless was caused by some Inchantment. But to proceed to what I intend; the Eyes of Persons by reason of Inchanting Charms, may not only see what others do not, but be under such power of Fascination, as that things which are not, shall appear to them as real: The Apostle speaks of *Bewitched Eyes, Gal. 3.1.* and we know from Scripture, that the Imaginations of men have by Inchantments been imposed upon; and Histories abound with very strange Instances of this Nature: The old Witch *Circe* by an Inchanted Cup caused *Ulysses* his Companions to imagine themselves to be turned into Swine; and how many Witches have been themselves so bewitched by the Devil, as really to believe that they were transformed into Wolves, or Dogs, or Cats. It is reported of *Simon Magus*, that by his Sorceries he would so impose on the Imaginations of People, as that they thought he had really changed himself into another sort of Creature. *Opollonius* of *Tyana* could out do *Simon* with his Magick: The great *Bohemian* Conjurer *Zyto* by his Inchantments, caused certain Persons whom he had a mind to try his Art upon, to imagine that their Hands were turned into the Feet of an Ox, or into the Hoofs of a Horse, so that they could not reach to the Dishes before them to take any thing thence; he sold Wisps of Straw to a Butcher who bought them for Swine; that many such prestigious Pranks were played, by the unhappy *Faustus*, is attested by *Camerarius, Wyerus, Voetius, Lavater,* and Lonicer.

There is newly Published a Book (mentioned in the *Acta Eruditorum*) wherein the Author (*Wiechard Valvassor*) relates, that a *Venetian* Jew instructed him (only he would not attend his Instructions) how to make a Magical Glass which should represent any Person or thing according as he should desire. If a Magician by an Inchanted Glass can do this, he may as well by the help of a Dæmon cause false *Idæas* of Persons and Things to be impressed on the Imaginations of bewitched Persons; the Blood and Spirits of a Man, that is bitten with a Mad-Dog, are so envenomed, as that strange Impressions are thereby made on his Imagination: let him be brought into a Room where there is a Looking-Glass, and he will (if put upon it) not only say but swear that he sees a Dog, tho' in truth there is no Dog it may be within 20 Miles of him; and is it not then possible for the Dogs of Hell to poyson the Imaginations of miserable Creatures, so as that they shall believe and swear that such Persons hurt them as never did so? I have heard of an Inchanted Pin, that has caused the Condemnation and Death of many scores of innocent Persons. There was a notorious *Witchfinder* in *Scotland*, that undertook by a Pin, to make an infallible Discovery of suspected Persons, whether they were Witches or not, if when the Pin was run an Inch or two into the Body of the accused Party no Blood appeared, nor any sense of Pain, then he declared them to be Witches; by means hereof my Author tells me no less then 300 persons were Condemned for Witches in that Kingdom. This Bloody Jugler after he had done enough in *Scotland*, came to the Town of *Berwick* upon *Tweed*; an honest Man now living in *New-England* assureth me, that he saw the Man thrust a great Brass Pin two Inches into the Body of one, that some would in that way try whether there was Witchcraft in the Case or no: the accused Party was not in the least sensible of what was done, and therefore in danger of receiving the Punishment justly due for Witchcraft; only it so happened, that Collonel *Fenwick* (that worthy Gentleman, who many years since lived in *New-England*) was then the Military Governour in that Town; he sent for the Mayor and Magistrates advising them to be careful and cautious in their proceedings; for he told them, it might be an

Inchanted Pin, which the Witchfinder made use of: Whereupon the Magistrates of the place ordered that he should make his Experiment with some other Pin as they should appoint: But that he would by no means be induced unto, which was a sufficient Discovery of the Knavery and Witchery of the Witchfinder. There is a strange Diabolical Energy goeth along with *Incantations*. If *Balak* had not known that he would not have sent for *Balaam*, to see whether he could inchant the Children of *Israel*. The Scripture intimates that Inchantments will keep a Serpent from biting, *Eccles. 10.11*. A Witch in *Sweedland* confessed, that the Devil gave her a wooden Knife; and that if she did but touch any living thing with that Knife, it would die immediately: And that there is a wonderful Power of the Devil attending things inchanted, we have confirmed by a prodigious Instance in Major *Weir*, a *Scotch* Man: That wretched Man was a perfect Prodigy; a Man of great Parts; esteemed a Saint, yet lived in secret Uncleanness with his own Sister for thirty four Years together: After his wickedness was discovered, he did not seem to be troubled at any of his Crimes, excepting that he had caused a poor Woman to be publickly whipped, because she reported that she had seen him committing Bestiality; which thing was true, only the Woman could not prove it. This horrid Creature, if he had his *Inchanted Staff* in his Hand could pray to admiration, and do extraordinary things, as is more amply related in the Postscript to Mr. *Sinclares* his Book before mentioned: But if he had not his Inchanted Rod to lean upon, he could not transform himself into an Angel of Light: But by all these things we may conclude, that it is not impossible, but that a guilty Conjurer, that so he may render himself the less suspected, may by his Magical Art and Inchantment, cause innocent Persons to be represented as afflicting those whom the Devil and himself are the Tormentors of.

Arg. 5. *The Truth we affirm is so evident, as that many Learned and Judicious Men have freely subscribed unto it.*

The memorable Relation of the Devils assuming the shape of an innocent Citizen in *Zurick*, is in the Judgment of that great Divine *Lud Lavater*, of weighty Consideration: And he declares, that he does therefore mention it, that so Judges might be cautelous in their Proceedings in Cases of this nature, inasmuch as the Devil does often in that way intangle innocent Persons, and bring them into great Troubles. His Words are, *Hanc Historiam ideo recito, ut Judices, in hujusmodi, Casibus cauti sint: Diabolus enim hac via sæpe innocentibus insidiatur.* He confirms what he saith by reciting a Passage out of *Alertus Granzius*, who writes that the Devil was seen in the shape of a Nobleman to come out of the Empress's Chamber: But to clear her Innocency, she (according to the superstitious *Ordeals* then in fashion) walked blindfold over a great many of glowing hot Irons without touching any of them. *Voetius* in his Disputation of *Spectres* proposeth that Question, whether the Devil may not untruly personate a Godly Man, and answers in the Affirmative: And withal adds, that it is a sufficient Argument (*ad hominem*) to answer the Papists with their own Histories, which give Instances of Satan's appearing in the Figure of Saints, nay of Christ himself. And in his Discourse concerning the *Operations of Dæmons* he has the like *Problem*, whether the Devil may not possibly put on the shape of a true Believer, a real Saint, not only of such as are dead, but still living, and answers, *Quidni?* Why not? It is true Popish *Casuists* do generally incline to the Negative in this Question: Nevertheless, the Instance of *Germanus*, who saw a Company of honest People represented by the Devil, as if they had been feasting together, when they were really asleep in their Beds, does a little puzzle them, so as that they are necessitated to take up with this Conclusion, *That by an extraordinary Permission of God, innocent Persons may be represented by*

Satan in the Nocturnal Conventicles of Witches: And if so, much more as afflicting bewitched Persons. *Delrio* giveth an account of an innocent Monk, whose Reputation was indangered by a *Dæmon's* appearing in his shape. He writes more like a Divine than Jesuits use to do, when he saith that, *It is not absolutely to be denied, but that the Devils may exhibite the Forms of innocent Persons, if God permit it, who when he does permit it, usually by some Providence discovers the Fraud of the Devils, that so the Innocent may be vindicated, or if not, it is to bring them to repentance for some Sin, or to try their Patience.* It is rare to see such Words dropping from the Pen of a Jesuit: As for Protestant Writers, I cannot call to mind one of any Note, that does deny the Possibility of the Affirmative, in the Question before us. Dr. *Henkelius* has lately published a learned and elaborate Discourse concerning the right Method of curing such as are obsessed with *Cacodæmons,* in which he asserts, that *Satan may possibly assume the Form of innocent and pious Persons, that so he might thereby destroy their Reputations, and expose them to undue Punishments.* As for our *English* Divines, there are not many greater *Casuists* than Mr. *Perkins*; nor do I know any one that has written on the Case of Witchcraft with more Judgment and Clearness of Understanding: He has these Words, "If a Man being dangerously sick and like to die upon suspicion, will take it on his death, that such an one has bewitched him, it is an allegation which may move the Judge to examine the Party, but it is of no moment for Conviction." The like is asserted by Mr. *Cooper,* Mr. *Bernard,* (once a famous Minister at *Batcomb* in *Somerset*) his Book called *A Guide to Grand Jury-men in Cases of Witchcraft,* is a solid and wise Treatise. What his Judgment was in the Case now under debate, we may see, *pag.* 209, 210. where his Words are these; "An Apparation of the Party suspected, whom the Afflicted in their Fits seem to see, is a great suspicion; yet this is but a presumption, tho' a strong one, because these Apparitions are wrought by the Devil, who can represent to the

Phansie such as the Parties use to fear, in which his representation he may well lye as in his other Witness: For if the Devil can represent to the Witch a seeming *Samuel*, saying, I see Gods ascending out of the Earth, to beguile *Saul*, may we not think he can represent a common ordinary Person, Man or Woman unregenerate, tho' no Witch to the Phansie of vain Persons, to deceive them and others that will give Credit to the Devil." Thus Mr. *Bernard*.

As for the Judgment of the Elders in *New-England*, so far as I can learn, they do generally concur with Mr. *Perkins*, and Mr. *Bernard*. This I know, that at a Meeting of Ministers at *Cambridge, August 1. 1692.* where were present seven elders besides the President of the *Colledge*, the Question then discoursed on, was, *Whether the Devil may not sometimes have a Permission to represent an innocent Person as tormenting such as are under Diabolical Molestations?* The Answer which they all concurred in, was in these words, *viz. That the Devil may sometimes have a Permission to represent an innocent Person as tormenting such as are under Diabolical Molestations; but that such things are rare and extraordinary, especially when such Matters come before Civil Judicatures:* And that some of the most eminent Ministers in the Land, who were not at that Meeting are of the same Judgment, I am assured: And I am also sure, that in Cases of this nature the *Priest's Lips should keep Knowledge, and they should seek the Law at his Mouth, Mal. 2.7.*

Arg. 6. *Our own Experience has confirmed the Truth of what we affirm.*

I have in another Book given an account concerning *Elizabeth Knap* of *Groton*, who complained that a Woman as eminent for Piety as any in that Town, did appear to her, and afflict her: But afterwards she was satisfied that

that Person never did her any harm, but that the Devil abused them both. About two Years ago, a bewitched Person in *Chelmsford* in her Fits, complained that a worthy good Man, a near Relation of hers did afflict her: So did she likewise complain of another Person in that town of known integrity and Piety.

I have my self known several of whom I ought to think that they are now in Heaven, considering that they were of good Conversation, and reputed Pious by those that had the greatest Intimacy with them, of whom nevertheless, some complained that their Shapes appeared to them, and threatned them: Nor is this answered by saying, we do not know but those Persons might be Witches: We are bound by the Rule of Charity to think otherwise: And they that censure any, meerly because such a sad Affliction as their being falsly represented by Satan has befallen them, do not do as they would be done by. I bless the Lord, it was never the portion allotted to me, nor to any Relation of mine to be thus abused: But no Man knoweth what may happen to him, since *there be just Men unto whom it happeneth according to the Work of the Wicked, Eccles. 8.14.* But what needs more to be said, since there is one amongst our selves whom no Man that knows him, can think him to be a Wizzard, whom yet some bewitched Persons complained of, that they are in his Shape tormented: And the Devils have of late accused some eminent Persons.

It is an awful thing which the Lord has done to convince some amongst us of their Error: This then I declare and testifie, that to take away the Life of any one, meerly because a *Spectre* or Devil, in a bewitched or possessed Person does accuse them, will bring the Guilt of innocent Blood on the Land, where such a thing shall be done: Mercy forbid that it should, (and I trust that as it has not it never will be so) in *New-England.* What does such an Evidence amount unto more than this: Either such an one did afflict such an one, or the Devil in his likeness, or his Eyes were bewitched.

The things which have been mentioned make way for, and bring us unto the second Case, which is to come under our Consideration, *viz.*

If one bewitched is struck down at the Look or cast of the Eye of another, and after that recovered again by a Touch from the same Person, Is not this an infallible Proof, that the Person suspected and complained of is in League with the Devil?

Answer; It must be owned that by such things as these Witchcrafts and Witches have been discovered more than once or twice: And that an ill Fame, or other Circumstances attending the suspected Party, this may be a Ground for Examination; but this alone does not afford sufficient Matter for Conviction: As *Spectres* or *Devils* appearing in the Shapes of Men that have been murdered, declaring that they were murdered by such Persons and in such a place, may give just occasion to the Magistrate for Enquiry into the Matter: One great Witch-Advocate confesseth, that by this means Murders have been brought to light; yet that alone, if other Circumstances did not concur, would not by the Law of God take away the Life of any Man. If my Reader pleaseth, he shall hear what old Mr. *Bernard* of *Batcomb* saith to a Case not unlike to this, and the former: His Words are these, 'The naming of the suspected in their Fits, and also where they have been, and what they have done here or there, as Mr. *Throgmorton's* Children could do, and that often and ever found true; this is a great Presumption: yet is this but a Presumption, because this is only the Devils Testimony, who can lie, and that more often than speak Truth. Christ would not allow his Witness of him in a point most true; nor St. *Paul* in the due Praises of him and *Sylas*; his Witness then may not be received as sufficient in case of ones Life: He may accuse an Innocent, as I shewed before in Mr. *Edmund's* giving over his Practice to find Stollen Goods; and Satan we read would accuse *Job* to God himself to be an Hypocrite, and to be ready to be a Blasphemer, and he is called the Accuser of the Brethren. Albeit, I cannot deny but this has very often proved true, yet seeing the Devil is such an one as you heard, Christian Men should not take his Witness, to give in Verdict upon Oath, and so swear that the Devil has therein spoken the Truth; be it far from good men to confirm any Word of the Devil by Oath, if it be not an evident Truth without the Devil's Testimony, who in speaking the Truth, has a lying Intent, and speaks some Truths of things done, which may be found to be so, that he may wrap with them some pernicious Lye, which cannot be tried to be true, but must rest upon his own testimony to ensnare the Blood of the Innocent.' Thus Mr. *Bernard* resolved the Case above sixty Years ago; and truly in my Opinion like a Wise and Orthodox Divine, what he says, reacheth both this and the former Case. Dr. *Cotta* (a Learned Physician) in his Book, about *The Tryal of Witchcraft, shewing the true and right Method of the Discovery, with a Confutation of Erroneous ways* (which Book he dedicates to the Right Honourable Sir *Edward Cook*, Lord Chief Justice of *England*,) He discourses concerning *Exploration of Witches by the touch of the Witch curing the touched bewitched*, and sheweth the Fallibility and Vanity of that way of Tryal, tho' he had often seen Persons bewitched in that way immediately delivered from the present Fit or Agony which was upon them: But he taketh it to be a Diabolical Miracle. He argueth thus, 'No Man can doubt but that the Vertue wherewith this touch was indued, is supernatural: If it be so, How can man to whom nothing is simply possible that is not natural be justly reputed an Agent therein? If he cannot be esteemed in himself any possible or true Agent, then it remaineth that he can only be interested therein as an Accessary in Consent, or as a Servant unto a Superior Power: If that

Superior Power be the Devil, the least reasonable doubt, whether the Devil alone, or with the Consent or Contract of the suspected Person has produced that wonderful effect; with what Religion or Reason can any Man incline rather to credit the Devil's mouth in the Bewitched, than to pity the Accused, and believe them against the subtility of a deceitful Devil: If the Devil by Divine Permission may cause supernatural Concomitances and Consequences to attend the natural Actions of Men without their allowance, as is manifest in possessed Persons, how is it reasonable and just that the Impositions of the Devil should be imputed unto any Man: And (saith he) God forbid that the Devil's Signs and Wonders, nay his Truths should become any legal Allegations or Evidences in Law. We may therefore conclude it unjust, that the forenamed miraculous Effect by the Devil wrought and imputed by the Bewitched, should be esteemed an infallible mark against any Man, as therefore convinced for that the Devil and the Bewitched have so decyphered him!' Thus that Learned Man. But to the Case in hand, I have several things to offer.

1. *It is possible that the Persons in Question may be possessed with Cacodæmons:* That bewitched Persons are many times really possessed with evil Spirits, is most certain. And as Mr. *Perkins* observes, no Man can prove but that Witchcraft might be the Cause of many of those Possessions, which we read of in the Gospel: And that Devils have been immitted into the Bodies of miserable Creatures by Magicians and Witches, Histories and Experience do abundantly testifie. *Hierom* relates concerning a certain Virgin, that a young Man, whose Amours she despised, prevailed with a Magician to send an evil Spirit into her, by means whereof she was strangely besotted. 'Tis reported of *Simon Magus*, that after he had used an Hellish Sacrifice, to be revenged of some that had called him a great Witch, he caused infernal Spirits to

enter into them. Many confessing Witches have acknowledged, that they were the Cause of such and such Persons being possessed of evil Angels, as *Thyræus* and others have observed: Now no Credit ought to be given to what *Dæmons* in such as are by them obsessed shall say. Our Saviour by his own unerring Example has taught us not to receive the Devil's Testimony in any thing. The Papists are justly condemned for bringing Diabolical Testimony to confirm the Principles of their Religion. *Peter Cotton* the Jesuite enquired of the Devil in a possessed Person, what was the clearest Scripture to prove Purgatory. At the time when *Luther* died, all the possessed People in the *Netherlands* were quiet: The Devils in them, said the Reason was, because *Luther* had been a great Friend of theirs, and they owed him that respect as to go as far as *Germany* to attend his Funeral. Another time when there was a talk of some Ministers of the Reformed Religion, the Devils in the Obsessed laughed and said, they were not at all afraid of them, for the *Calvinists* and they were very good Friends. The Jesuits insult with these Testimonies as if they were Divine Oracles: But the Father of Lyes is never to be believed: He will utter twenty great truths to make way for one lye: He will accuse twenty Witches, if he can but thereby bring one innocent Person into trouble: He mixeth Truths with Lyes, that so those truths giving credit unto lyes, Men may believe both, and so be deceived: And whereas some say, that the Persons in question are only bewitched and not possessed, let it be considered that possessed Persons are called *Energumens* from ΕΡΓΟΜΑΙ *Agitor*. They whose Bodies are preternaturally agitated, so as to be in danger of being thrown into the Fire, or into the Water, though they may be bewitched, are undoubtedly possessed with *Dæmons*, *Mark 9.22, 25*. Learned Men give it as a most certain sign of Possession, when the afflicted Party can see and hear that which no one else can discern any thing of, and when they can discover secret things, *Acts 6.16.* past, or future, as a possessed Person in *Germany* foretold the War which broke out in the Year, 1546. And when the Limbs of miserable Creatures, are bent and disjointed so as could not possible be without a Luxation of Joints, were it not done by a preternatural Hand, and yet no hurt raised thereby that argueth Possession. Also, when Persons are by the Devil cast into Fits, in the which they speak of things, that afterwards they have no remembrance of, or, if they are by cruel Devils tortured, so as to cause horrendous Clamours in the distressed Sufferers, that's another sign of Obsession by evil Spirits: If all these things concur in the Persons concerning where the Question is, we may conclude them to be *Dæmoniacks*: And if so, no *Juror* can with a safe Conscience look on the Testimony of such, as sufficient to take away the Life of any Man.

2. *Falling down by the cast of an Eye proceeds not from a natural, but an arbitrary Cause*; not from any Poyson in the Eye of the Witch, but from the Agency of some *Dæmon*: The opinion of Fascination by the Eye is an old Fable, and (saith Mr. *Perkins*) as fond as old. *Pliny* speaks of a People that killed folks by looking on them; and he adds, that they had two Apples in each Eye: and *Tully* writes of women who had two Apples in one Eye that always did mischief with their meer looks; so *Ovid, Pupula duplex fulminat*. And *Plutarch* writes that some persons have such a Poyson in their Eyes, as that their Friends and Familiars are Fascinated thereby; nay he speaks of one that Bewitched himself sick by looking on his own Face in a Glass: Others write of Fascination by a meer Prolation of Words; and for ought I know, there may be as much Witchery in the Tongue as there is in the Eye. *Sennertus* has discovered the Superstition of these Fancies; Sight does not proceed from an Emission of Rays from the Eye, but by a reception of the visible Species; and if it be (as Philosophers conclude) an innocent Action and not an Emission of optick Spirits,

so that sight as such, does receive something from the Object, and not act upon it, the Notion of Fascination by the Eye is unphilosophical: It is true, that sore Eyes will affect those that look upon them, *Dum spectant Oculi Læsos, Leduntur & ipsi,* for which a natural Reason is easily to be assigned; but if the Witches Eyes are thus infected with a natural Contagion, Whence is it, that only Bewitched Persons are hurt thereby? If the vulgar Error concerning the *Basilisks* killing with the Look of his Poysonful Eye were a Truth, whatever person that Serpent cast his Eye upon would be poysoned. So if Witches had a physical Venom in their Eyes, others as well as Fascinated Persons would be sensible thereof; there is as much Truth in this fancy of Physical Venom in the Eye of a Witch, as there is in what *Pliny* and others relate concerning the *Thibians, viz.* that they have two Apples in one Eye, and the Effigies of an Horse in the other Eye; and that they are a people that cannot be drowned.

3. As for that which concerns the Bewitched Persons being recovered out of their Agonies by the Touch of the suspected Party, it is various and fallible.

For sometimes the afflicted Person is made sick, (instead of being made whole) by the Touch of the Accused; sometimes the Power of Imagination is such, as that the Touch of a Person innocent and not accused shall have the same effect. It is related in the Account of the Tryals of Witches at *Bury* in *Suffolk* 1664, during the time of the Tryal, there were some Experiments made with the Persons afflicted, by bringing the accused to touch them, and it was observed that by the least Touch of one of the supposed Witches, they that were in their Fits, to all mens Apprehension wholly deprived of all Sense and Understandings, would suddenly shriek out and open their Hands.

Mr. Serjeant *Keeling* did not think that sufficient to Convict the Prisoners, for admitting that the Children were in truth Bewitched, yet (saith he) it cannot be applyed to the Prisoners upon the Imagination only of the Parties afflicted; for if that might be allowed, no Person whatsoever can be in safety, for perhaps they might fancy another Person who might altogether be innocent in such matters: To avoid this Scruple it was privately desired by the Judge, that some Gentlemen there in Court would attend one of the distempered Persons in the farther part of the Hall, whilst she was in her Fits, and then to send for one of the Witches to try what would happen, which they did accordingly. One of them was conveyed from the Bar, and brought to the Afflicted Maid. They put an Apron before her Eyes, and then another person (not the Witch) touched her, which produced the same effect, as the Touch of the Witch did in the Court. Whereupon the Gentlemen returned much unsatisfied. *Bodin* relates, that a Witch who was Tryed at *Nants*, was commanded by the Judges to touch a Bewitched person, a thing often practised by the Judges of *Germany* in the *Imperial Chamber*. The Witch was extreamly unwilling, but being Compelled by the Judges, she cryed out, *I am undone*; and as soon as ever she touched the Afflicted person, the Witch fell down dead, and the other recovered. That horrid Witch of *Salisbury*, *Ann Bodenham* who had been Servant to the Notorious Conjurer Dr. *Lamb*, could not bear the sight of one that was Bewitched by her. As soon as ever she saw the Afflicted Person, she ran about shrieking, and crying, and roaring after an hideous manner, that the Devil would tear her in pieces, if that person came near her. And whilst the Witch was in such Torment, the Bewitched was at ease. By these things we see, that the Laws and Customs of the Kingdom of darkness, are not always and in all places the same.

And it is good for men to concern themselves with them as little as may be.

I think there is weight in Dr. *Cotta's* Argument, *viz.*

That the Gift of healing the Sick and Possessed, was a special Grace and Favour of God, for the Confirmation of the Truth of the Gospel, but that such a Gift should be annexed to the Touch of Wicked Witches, as an infallible sign of their guilt, is not easie to be believed. It is a thing well known, that if a person possessed by an Evil Spirit, is (as oft it so happens) never so outragious whilst a good man is Praying with and for the Afflicted, let him lay his hand on them, and the Evil Spirit is quiet. I hope this is no evidence of any Covenant, or voluntary Communion between the Good Man that is Praying and the Evil Spirit; no more does the Case before us evince any such thing.

4. *There are that Question the Lawfulness of the Experiment.* For if this healing power in the Witch is not a Divine but a Diabolical Gift, it may be dangerous to meddle too much with it. If the Witch may be ordered to touch afflicted Persons in order to their healing or recovery out of a sick Fit, why may not the Diseased Person be as well ordered to touch the Witch for the same cause? And if to touch him, why not to scratch him and fetch Blood out of him, which is but an harder kind of touch? But as for this Mr. *Perkins* doubts not to call it a *Practice of Witchcraft*. It is not safe to meddle with any of the Devils Sacraments or Institutions; *For my own part, I should be loath to say to a Man, that I knew or thought was a Witch, do you look on such a Person, and see if you can Witch them into a Fit, and there is such an afflicted Person do you take them by the Hand, and see if you can Witch them well again. If it is by vertue of some Contract with the Devil that witches have Power to do such things, it is hard to conceive how they can be bid to do them, without being too much concerned in that Hellish Covenant.* I

take it to be (as elsewhere I have expressed) a solid Principle, which the Learned *Sennertus* insists on, *viz. That they who force another to do that which he cannot possibly do, but by vertue of a Compact with the Devil, have themselves implicitely Communion with the Diabolical Covenant.* The Devil is pleased and honoured when any of his Institutions are made use of; this way of discovering Witches, is no better than that of putting the Urine of the afflicted Person into a Bottle, that so the Witch may be tormented and discovered: The Vanity and Superstition of which practice I have formerly shewed, and testified against. *There was a Conjurer his name was* Edward Drake *who taught a Man to use that Experiment for the Relief of his afflicted Daughter, who found benefit thereby;* But we ought not to practice Witchcraft to discover Witches, nor may we make use of a *White healing Witch* (as they call them) to find out a *Black and Bloody one.* And how did men first come to know that Witches would be discovered in such ways as these, which have been mentioned? If Satan himself were the first Discoverer (as there is reason to believe) the experiment must needs have deceit in it. See Dr. Willet on *Exod. 7. Quest. 9.* And such Experiments better become Pagans or Papists than Professors in *New-England*; whereas 'tis pleaded, that such things are practised by the Judges of the Imperial Chamber, I reply, that those Judges (as *Bodin* relates, *Lib. 3. Dæmon. Cap. 6.*) have required suspected Witches to pronounce over the afflicted persons, these words, *I bless thee in the Name of the Father, &c.* upon which they have immediately recovered; but is the dark day come upon us, that such Superstitions as these shall be practised in *New-England*: The Lord Jesus forbid it. See *Baldwin's* Testimony against the Practice of the *Camera Imperialis,* Cas. Consc. L. 3. c. 3. p. 634.

5. *If the Testimony of a bewitched or possessed Person, is of validity as to what they see done to themselves, then it is so as to*

others, whom they see afflicted no less than themselves: But what they affirm concerning others, is not to be taken for Evidence. Whence had they this Supernatural Sight? It must needs be either from Heaven or from Hell: If from Heaven, (as *Elisha's* Servant, and *Balaam's* Ass could discern Angels) let their Testimony be received: But if they had this Knowledge from Hell, tho' there may possibly be truth in what they affirm, they are not legal Witnesses: For the Law of God allows of no Revelation from any other Spirit but himself, *Isa. 8.19.* It is a Sin against God to make use of the Devil's help to know that which cannot be otherwise known: And I testify against it, as a great Transgression, which may justly provoke the Holy One of *Israel*, to let loose Devils on the whole Land, *Luke 4.35.* See Mr. *Bernard's* Guide to Juries in Cases of Witchcraft, p. 136, 137, 138. And *Brockmand*, *Theol. de Angelis*, p. 227. Altho' the Devil's Accusations may be so far regarded as to cause an enquiry into the truth of things, *Job 1.11, 12. & 2.5, 6.* yet not so as to be an Evidence or Ground of Conviction: The Persons, concerning whom the Question is, see things through Diabolical Mediums; on which account their Evidence is not meer humane Testimony; and if it be in any part Diabolical, it is not to be owned as Authentick; for the Devil's Testimony ought not to be received neither in whole nor in part.

6. I am told by credible Persons, who say it is certainly true, that a bewitched Person has complained that she was cast into Fits by the Look of a Dog; and that she was no more able to bear the sight of that Dog, than of the Person whom she accused as bewitching her: And that thereupon the Dog was shot to death: This Dog was no Devil; for then they could not have killed him. I suppose no one will say that Dogs are Witches: It remains then that the casting down with the Look is no infallible sign of a Witch.

7. It has always been said, that it is a difficult thing to find out Witches: But if the Representation of such a Person as afflicting, or the Look or Touch be an infallible proof of the guilt of Witchcraft in the Persons complained of, 'tis the easiest thing in the World to discover them; for it is done to our hand, and there needs no enquiry into the Matter.

8. *Let them say this is an infallible Proof, produce any Word out of the Law of God which does in the least countenance that Assertion:* The Word of God instructs Jurors and Judges to proceed upon clear humane Testimony, *Deut. 35.30.* But the Word no where giveth us the least Intimation, that every one is a Witch, at whose look the bewitched Person shall fall into Fits; nor yet that any other means should be used for the discovery of Witches, than what may be used for the finding out of Murderers, Adulterers, and other Criminals.

9. Sometimes Antipathies in Nature have strange and unaccountable Effects. I have read of a Man that at the sight of his own Son, who was no Wizzard would fall into Fits. There are that find in their Natures an averseness to some Persons whom they never saw before, of which they can give no better an account than he in *Martial*, concerning *Sabidius*.

Non Amo te Sabidi, nec possum dicere quare.

That some Persons at the Sight of Bruit-Creatures, Cats, Spiders, *&c.* nay, at the sight of Cheeses, Milk, Apples, will fall into Fits, is too well known to be denied. *Pensingius* in his Learned Discourse *De Pulvere Sympathetico*, p. 128. saith, there was one in the City of *Groning* that could not bear the sight of a Swine's Head: And that he knew another who was not able to look on the Picture thereof. *Amatus Lusitanus* speaks of one that at the sight of a Rose would swoon away: This proveth that the falling into a Fit at the sight of another is not always a sign of Witchcraft. It may proceed from Nature, and the Power of Imagination.

To conclude; Judicious *Casuists* have determined, that to make use of those *Media* to come to the Knowledge of any Matter, which have no such power in them by Nature, nor by Divine Institution is an Implicit going to the Devil to make a discovery: Now there is no natural Power in the Look or Touch of a Person to bewitch another; nor is this by Divine Institution the means whereby Witchcraft is discovered: Therefore it is an unwarrantable Practice.

We proceed now to the third Case proposed to Consideration; If the things which have been mentioned are not infallible Proofs of Guilt in the accused Party, it is then Queried, *Whether there are any Discoveries of this Crime, which Jurors and Judges may with a safe Conscience proceed upon to the Conviction and Condemnation of the Persons under Suspicion?*

Let me here premise Two things,

1. The Evidence in this Crime ought to be as clear as in any other Crimes of a Capital nature. The Word of God does no where intimate, that a less clear Evidence, or that fewer or other Witnesses may be taken as sufficient to convict a Man of Sorcery, which would not be enough to convict him were he charged with another evil worthy of Death, *Numb. 35.30.* if we may not take the Oath of a distracted Person, or of a possessed Person in a Case of Murder, Theft, Felony of any sort, then neither may we do it in the Case of Witchcraft.

2. Let me premise this also, that there have been ways of trying Witches long used in many Nations, especially in

the dark times of Paganism and Popery, which the righteous God never approved of. But which (as judicious Mr. *Perkins* expresseth it in plain *English*) were invented by the Devil, that so innocent Persons might be condemned, and some notorious Witches escape: Yea, many Superstitious and Magical experiments have been used to try Witches by: Of this sort is that of scratching the Witch, or seething the Urine of the Bewitched Person, or making a Witch-cake with that Urine: And that tryal of putting their Hands into scalding Water, to see if it will not hurt them: And that of sticking an Awl under the Seat of the suspected Party, yea, and that way of discovering Witches by tying their Hands and Feet, and casting them on the Water, to try whether they will sink or swim: I did publickly bear my Testimony against this Superstition in a Book printed at *Boston* eight Years past.

I hear that of late some in a Neighbour Colony have been playing with this Diabolical invention: It is to be lamented, that in such a *Land of Uprightness* as *New-England* once was, a Practice which Protestant Writers generally condemn as sinful, and which the more sober and learned Men amongst Papists themselves have not only judged unlawful, but (to express it in their own terms) to be no less than a *Mortal Sin*, should ever be heard of. Were it not that the coming of Christ to judge the Earth draweth near, I should think that such Practices are an unhappy Omen that the Devil and Pagans will get these dark Territories into their Possession again: But that I may not be thought to have no reason for my calling the impleaded Experiment into Question, I have these things further to alledge against it.

1. It has been rejected long agone, by Christian Nations as a thing Superstitious and Diabolical: In *Italy* and *Spain* it is wholly disused; and in the *Low-Countries*, and in *France*, where the Judges are Men of Learning. In some parts of

Germany old *Paganism* Customs are observed more than in other Countries, nevertheless all the *Academies* throughout *Germany* have disapproved of this way of Purgation.

2. The Devil is in it, all Superstition is from him; and when Secret things, or latent Crimes, are discovered by superstitious Practices, some Compact and Communion with the Devil is the Cause of it, as *Austin* has truly intimated; and so it is here; for if a Witch cannot be drowned, this must proceed either from some natural Cause, which it doth not, for it is against Nature for Humane Bodies, when Hands and Feet are tied, not to sink under the Water: Besides, they that plead for this Superstition, say that if Witches happen to be condemned for some other Crime and not for Witchcraft, they will not swim like a Cork above Water, which Cause sheweth that the Cause of this Natation is not *Physical*: And if not, then either it must proceed from a Divine Miracle to save a Witch from drowning; or lastly, it must be a diabolical Wonder: This superstitious Experiment is commonly known by the Name of, *The Vulgar Probation*, because it was never appointed by any lawful Authority, but from the Suggestion of the Devil taken up by the rude Rabble: And some learned Men are of Opinion, that the first *Explorator* (*being a white Witch*) did explicitly covenant with the Devil, that he should discover latent Crimes in this way: And that it is by Virtue of that first Contract that the Devil goeth to work to keep his Servants from sinking, when this Ceremony of his ordaining is used. Moreover, we know that *Diabolus est Dei Simia*, the Devil seeks to imitate Divine Miracles. We read in Ecclesiastical Story, that some of the Martyrs when they were by Persecutors ordered to be drowned, prov'd to be immersible: This Miracle would the Devil imitate in causing Witches, who are his Martyrs, not to sink when they are cast into the Waters.

3. This way of Purgation is of the same nature with the old *Ordeals* of the Pagans. If Men were accused with any Crime, to clear their innocency, they were to take an hot Iron into their Hands, or to suffer scalding Water to be poured down their Throats, and if they received no hurt thereby they were acquitted. This was the Devil's Invention, and many times (as the Devil would have it) they that submitted to these Tryals suffered no inconvenience. Nevertheless, it is astonishing to think what innocent Blood has been shed in the World by means of this *Satanical* device. Witches have often (as *Sprenger* observes) desired that they might stand or fall by this Tryal by hot Iron, and sometimes come off well: Indeed, this *Ordeal* was used in other Cases, and not in Cases of Witchcraft only: And so was the *Vulgar Probation* by casting into the Water practiced upon Persons accused with other Crimes as well as that of Witchcraft: How it came to be restrained to that of Witchcraft I cannot tell; it is as supernatural for a Body whose Hands and Feet are tied to swim above the Water, as it is for their Hands not to feel a red hot Iron. If the one of these *Ordeals* is lawful to be used, then so is the other too: But as for the fiery *Ordeal* it is rejected and exploded out of the World; for the same reason then the tryal by Water should be so.

4. It is a tempting of God when Men put the Innocency of their Fellow-Creatures upon such tryals; to desire the Almighty to shew a Miracle to clear the Innocent, or to convict the Guilty is a most presumptuous tempting of him. Was it not a Miracle when *Peter* was kept from sinking under the Water by the Omnipotency of Christ? As for Satan, we know that his Ambition is to make his Servants believe that his Power is equal to God's, and that therefore he can preserve whom he pleaseth. I have read of certain Magicians, who were seen walking on the Water: If then guilty Persons shall float on the Waters, either it is the Devil that causes them to do so, (as no doubt it is) and

what have Men to do to set the Devil on work; or else it is a Divine Miracle, like that of *Peter's* not sinking, or that of the Iron that swam at the Word of *Elisha*. And shall Men try whether God will work a Miracle to make a discovery? If a Crime cannot be found out but by Miracle, it is not for any Judge on Earth to usurp that Judgment which is reserved for the Divine Throne.

5. This pretended Gift of Immersibility attending Witches, is a most fallible deceitful thing; for many a Witch has sunk under the Water. *Godelmannus* giveth an account of six notorious and clearly convicted Witches, that when they were brought to their *vulgar Probation*, sunk down under the Water like other Persons; *Althusius* affirms the like concerning others; in the *Bohemian* History it is related, that *Uratslaus* the King of *Bohemia*, extirpated Witches out of his Kingdom, some of which he delivered to the Ax, others of them to the Fire, and others of them he caused to be drowned: If Witches are immersible, how came they to die by drowning in *Bohemia*? Besides, it has sometimes been known that Persons who have floated on the Water when the Hangman has made the Experiment on them, have sunk down like a Stone, when others have made the tryal.

6. The Reasons commonly alledged for this Superstition are of no moment: It is said they hate the Water; whereas they have many times desired that they might be cast on the Water in order to their purgation: It is alledged, that Water is used in *Baptism*, therefore Witches swim: A weak Phansie; all the Water in the World is not consecrated Water. Cannot Witches eat Bread or drink Wine, notwithstanding those Elements are made use of in the Blessed Sacrament: But (say some) the Devils by sucking of them make them so light that the Water bears them;

whereas some Witches are twice as heavy as many an innocent Person: Well, but then they are possessed with the Devil: Suppose so; Is the Devil afraid if they should sink, that he should be drowned with them? But why then were the *Gadarens* Hogs drowned when the Devil was in them.

These things being premised, I answer the Question affirmatively; *There are Proofs for the Conviction of Witches which Jurors may with a safe Conscience proceed upon, so as to bring them in guilty.* The Scripture which saith, *Thou shalt not suffer a Witch to live,* clearly implies, that some in the World may be known and proved to be Witches: For until they be so, they may and must be suffered to live. Moreover we find in Scripture, that some have been convicted and executed for Witches: For *Saul cut off those that had familiar Spirits, and the Wizzards out of the Land, 1 Sam. 28.9.*

It may be wondered that *Saul* who did like him that said, *Flectere si nequeo Superos Acheronta Movebo,* should cause the Wizzards in the Land to be put to death. The *Jewish Rabbies* say, the reason was, because those Wizzards foretold that *David* should be King. It is (as Mr. *Gaul* observes) the Opinion of some learned Protestants, that *Saul* in his Zeal did over do: And that under the Pretext of Witches he slew the *Gibeonites,* for which that Judgment followed, *2 Sam. 21.1. Neither* (saith Mr. *Gaule*) *want we the storied Examples of God's Judgments upon those that defamed, prosecuted and executed them for Witches, that indeed were none.* But we have in the Scripture the Example of a better Man than *Saul* to encourage us to make enquiry after Wizzards and Witches in order to their Conviction and Execution. This did the rarest King that ever lived caused to be done, *viz. Josiah, 2 Kings 23.24. The Workers with familiar Spirits and the Wizzards, that were spied in the Land of* Judah, *did* Josiah *put away, that he might perform the*

Words of the Law. It seems there were some that sought to hide those Workers of Iniquity, but that incomparable King spied them out, and rid the Land and the World of them.

Q. But then the Enquiry is, *What is sufficient Proof?*

A. This Case has been with great Judgment answered by several Divines of our own, particularly by Mr. *Perkins*, and Mr. *Bernard*; also Mr. *John Gaul* a worthy Minister at *Staughton*, in the County of *Huntington*, has published a very Judicious Discourse, called, *Select Cases of Conscience touching Witches and Witchcrafts*, Printed at *London* A.D. 1646. wherein he does with great Prudence and Evidence of Scripture light handle this and other Cases: Such Jurors as can obtain those Books, I would advise them to read, and seriously as in the fear of God to consider them, and so far as they keep to the Law and to the Testimony, and speak according to that Word, receive the Light which is in them. But the Books being now rare to be had, let me express my Concurrence with them in these two particulars.

1. *That a free and voluntary Confession of the Crime made by the Person suspected and accused after Examination, is a sufficient Ground of Conviction.*

Indeed, If Persons are Distracted, or under the Power of *Phrenetick Melancholy*, that alters the Case; but the Jurors that examine them, and their Neighbours that know them, may easily determine that Case; or if Confession be extorted, the Evidence is not so clear and convictive; but if any Persons out of Remorse of Conscience, or from a Touch of God in their Spirits, confess and shew their Deeds, as the Converted Magicians in *Ephesus* did, *Acts 19.18, 19.* nothing can be more clear. Suppose a Man to be suspected for Murder, or for committing a Rape, or the like nefandous Wickedness, if he does freely confess the Accusation, that's ground enough to Condemn him. The Scripture approveth of Judging the wicked Servant out of his own Mouth, *Luke 19.22.* It is by some objected, that Persons in Discontent may falsly accuse themselves. I say, if they do so, and it cannot be proved that they are false Accusers of themselves, they ought to dye for their Wickedness, and their Blood will be upon their own Heads; the Jury, the Judges, and the Land is Clear: I have read a very sad and amazing, and yet a true Story to this purpose.

There was in the Year 1649, in a Town called *Lauder* in *Scotland*, a certain woman accused and imprisoned on suspicion of Witchcraft, when others in the same Prison with her were Convicted, and their Execution ordered to be on the Monday following, she desired to speak with a Minister, to whom she declared freely that she was guilty of Witchcraft, acknowledging also many other Crimes committed by her, desiring that she might die with the rest: She said particularly that she had Covenanted with the Devil, and was become his Servant about twenty years before, and that he kissed her and gave her a Name, but that since he had never owned her. Several Ministers who were jealous that she accused herself untruly, charged it on her Conscience, telling her that they doubted she was under a Temptation of the Devil to destroy her own Body and Soul, and adjuring her in the Name of God to declare the Truth: Notwithstanding all this, she stifly adhered to what she had said, and was on Monday morning Condemned, and ordered to be Executed that day. When she came to the place of Execution, she was silent until the Prayers were ended, then going to the Stake where she was to be Burnt, she thus expressed herself, *All you that see me this day! Know ye that I am to die as a Witch, by my own Confession! and I free all Men, especially the Ministers and Magistrates, from the guilt of my Blood, I take it wholly on my self, and as I must make answer to the God of Heaven, I declare I am as free from Witchcraft as any Child, but being accused by a Malicious Woman, and Imprisoned under the Name of a Witch, my Husband and Friends disowned me, and seeing no hope of ever being in Credit again, through the Temptation of the Devil, I made that Confession to destroy my own Life, being weary of it, and chusing rather to Die than to Live.* This her lamentable Speech did astonish all the Spectators, few of whom could restrain from Tears. The Truth of this Relation (saith my Author) is certainly attested by a worthy Divine now living, who was an Eye and an Ear-Witness of the whole matter; but thus did that miserable Creature suffer Death, and this was a just Execution. When the *Amalekite* confessed that he killed *Saul*, whom he had no legal Authority to meddle with, although 'tis probable that he belyed himself, *David* gave order for his Execution, and said to him, *Thy Blood be upon thy Head, for thy Mouth hath Testified against thee, 2 Sam. 1.16*. But as for the Testimony of Confessing Witches against others, the case is not so clear as against themselves, they are not such credible Witnesses, as in a Case of Life and Death is to be desired: It is beyond dispute, that the Devil makes his Witches to dream strange things of themselves and others which are not so. There was (as Authors beyond Exception relate) in appearance a sumptuous Feast prepared, the Wine and Meat set forth in Vessels of Gold; a certain Person whom an amorous young Man had fallen in Love with, was represented and supposed to be really there; but *Apollonius Tyanæus* discovered the Witchery of the Business, and in an instant all vanished, and nothing but dirty Coals were to be seen: The like to this is mentioned in the *Arausican* Council. There were certain Women that imagined they rode upon Beasts in the Night, and that they had *Diana* and *Herodius* in company with them, besides a Troop of other Persons; the Council giveth this Sentence on it; *Satanas qui se transfigurat in Angelum Lucis, transformat se in diversarum personarum species, &*

mentem quam captivam tenet, in somnis deludit. Satan transforms himself into the likeness of divers Persons, and deludes the Souls that are his Captives with Dreams and Fancies; see Dr. *Willet* on *1 Sam. 28. p. 165.* What Credit can be given to those that say they can turn Men into Horses? If so, they can as well turn Horses into Men; but all the Witches on Earth in Conjunction with all the Devils in Hell, can never make or unmake a rational Soul, and then they cannot transform a Bruit into a Man, nor a Man into a Bruit; so that this Transmutation is fantastical. The Devil may and often does impose on the Imaginations of his Witches and Vassals, that they believe themselves to be Converted into Beasts, and reverted into Men again; as *Nebuchadnezzar* whilst under the Power of a Dæmon really imagined himself to be an Ox, and would lye out of Doors and eat Grass: The Devil has inflicted on many a Man the Disease called *Lycanthropia*, from whence they have made lamentable Complaints of their being Wolves: In a word, there is no more Reality in what many Witches confess of strange things seen or done by them, whilst Satan had them in his full Power, than there is in *Lucian's* ridiculous Fable of his being Bewitched into an *Asse*, and what strange Feats he then played; so that what such persons relate concerning Persons and Things at Witch-meetings, ought not to be received with too much Credulity.

I could mention dismal Instances of Innocent Blood which has been shed by means of the Lies of some Confessing Witches; there is a very sad Story mentioned in the Preface to the Relation of the Witchcrafts in *Sweedland*, how that in the Year 1676, at *Stockholm*, a young Woman accused her own Mother (who had indeed been a very bad Woman, but not guilty of Witchcraft,) and Swore that she had carried her to the Nocturnal Meetings of Witches, upon which the Mother was burnt to Death. Soon after the Daughter came crying and howling before the Judges in open Court, declaring, that to be revenged on her Mother for an Offence received, she had falsely accused her with a Crime which she was not guilty of; for which she also was justly Executed. A most wicked Man in *France* freely confessed himself to be a Magician, and accused many others, whose Lives were thereupon taken from them; and a whole Province had like to have been ruined thereby, but the Impostor was discovered: The Confessing pretended Wizzard was burnt at *Paris* in the year 1668. I shall only take notice further of an awful Example mentioned by A. B. *Spotswood* in his History of *Scotland*, p. 449. His words are these, 'This Summer (*viz.* Anno 1597.) there was a great business for the Tryal of Witches, amongst others, one *Margaret Atkin* being apprehended on suspicion, and threatned with Torture, did confess herself Guilty; being examined touching her Associates in that Trade, she named a few, and perceiving her Delations find Credit, made offer to detect all of that sort, and to purge the Country of them; so she might have her Life granted: For the reason of her Knowledge, she said, *That they had a secret mark all of that sort in their Eyes, whereby she could surely tell, how soon she looked upon any, whether they were Witches or not*; and in this she was so readily believed, that for the space of 3 or 4 Months she was carried from Town to Town to make Discoveries in that kind; many were brought in question by her Delations, especially at *Glasgow*, where *diverse Innocent Women, through the Credulity of the Minister Mr.* John Cowper, *were condemned and put to Death*; in the end she was found to be a meer deceiver, and sent back to *Fife*, where she was first apprehended: At her Tryal she affirmed all to be false that she had confessed of herself or others, and persisted in this to her Death, which made many fore-think their too great forwardness that way, and moved the King to recall his Commission given out against such Persons, discharging all Proceedings against them, except in case of a voluntary Confession, till a solid Order should be taken by the

Estates touching the form that should be kept in their Tryal.' Thus that famous Historian.

2. *If two credible Persons shall affirm upon Oath that they have seen the party accused speaking such words, or doing things which none but such as have Familiarity with the Devil ever did or can do, that's a sufficient Ground for Conviction.*

Some are ready to say, that Wizzards are not so unwise as to do such things in the sight or hearing of others, but it is certain that they have very often been known to do so: How often have they been seen by others using Inchantments? Conjuring to raise Storms? And have been heard calling upon their Familiar Spirits? And have been known to use Spells and Charms? And to shew in a Glass or in a Shew-stone persons absent? And to reveal Secrets which could not be discovered but by the Devil? And have not men been seen to do things which are above humane Strength, that no man living could do without Diabolical Assistances? *Claudia* was seen by Witnesses enough, to draw a Ship which no humane Strength could move. *Tuccia* a Vestal Virgin was seen to carry Water in a Sieve: The Devil never assists men to do supernatural things undesired. When therefore such like things shall be testified against the accused Party not by *Spectres* which are Devils in the Shape of Persons either living or dead, but by real men or women who may be credited; it is proof enough that such an one has that Conversation and Correspondence with the Devil, as that he or she, whoever they be, ought to be exterminated from amongst men. This notwithstanding I will add; It were better that ten suspected Witches should escape, than that one innocent Person should be Condemned; that is an old saying, and true, *Prestat reum nocentem absolvi, quam ex prohibitis Indiciis & illegitima probatione condemnari*. It is better that a Guilty Person should be Absolved, than that he should without sufficient ground of Conviction be condemned. I had rather judge a Witch to be an honest woman, than judge an honest woman as a Witch. The Word of God directs men not to proceed to the execution of the most capital offenders, until such time as upon searching diligently, the matter is *found to be a Truth, and the thing certain, Deut. 13.14, 15.*

An Acquaintance of mine at *London,* in his description of *New-England* declares, that as to their Religion, the people there are like Mr. *Perkins*; it is no dishonour to us, if that be found true: I am sorry that any amongst us begin to slight so great a Man, whom the most Learned in Foreign Lands, speak of with Admiration, on the account of his polite and acute Judgment: It is a grave and good Advice which he giveth in his Discourse of Witchcrafts (Chap. 7. Sect. 2.) wherewith I conclude; 'I would therefore wish and advise all Jurors who give the Verdict upon Life and Death in the Court of Assizes, to take good heed, that as they be diligent in zeal of God's glory, and the good of his Church, in detecting of Witches, by all sufficient and lawful means, so likewise they would be careful what they do, and not to condemn any party suspected upon bare Presumptions, without sound and sufficient Proofs that they be not guilty through their own Rashness of shedding Innocent Blood.'

Boston, New-England, Octob. 3. 1692.

POSTSCRIPT.

The Design of the preceding *Dissertation*, is not to plead for Witchcrafts, or to appear as an Advocate for Witches: I have therefore written another Discourse, proving that there are such horrid Creatures as Witches in the World; and that they are to be extirpated and cut off from amongst the People of God, which I have Thoughts and Inclinations in due time to publish; and I am abundantly satisfied that there have been, and are still most cursed Witches in the Land. More than one or two of those now in Prison, have freely and credibly acknowledged their Communion and Familiarity with the Spirits of Darkness; and have also declared unto me the Time and Occasion, with the particular Circumstances of their Hellish Obligations and Abominations.

Nor is there designed any Reflection on those worthy Persons who have been concerned in the late Proceedings at *Salem*: They are wise and good Men, and have acted with all Fidelity according to their Light, and have out of tenderness declined the doing of some things, which in our own Judgments they were satisfied about: Having therefore so arduous a Case before them, Pitty and Prayers rather than Censures are their due; on which account I am glad that there is published to the World (by my Son) a *Breviate of the Tryals* of some who were lately executed, whereby I hope the thinking part of Mankind will be satisfied, that there was more than that which is called *Spectre Evidence* for the Conviction of the Persons condemned. I was not myself present at any of the Tryals, excepting one, *viz.* that of *George Burroughs*; had I been one of his Judges, I could not have acquitted him: For several Persons did upon Oath testifie, that they saw him do such things as no Man that has not a Devil to be his Familiar could perform: And the Judges affirm, that they have not convicted any one meerly on the account of what *Spectres* have said, or of what has been represented to the Eyes or Imaginations of the sick bewitched Persons. If what is here exposed to publick view, may be a means to prevent it for the future, I shall not repent of my Labour in this Undertaking. I have been prevailed with so far as I am able to discern the Truth in these dark Cases, to declare my Sentiments, with the Arguments which are of weight with me, hoping that what is written may be of some use to discover the *Depths of Satan*; and to prevent innocent ones having their Lives endangered, or their Reputations ruined, by being through the Subtility and Power of the Devils, in consideration with the Ignorance and Weakness of Men, involved amongst the Guilty. It becomes those of my Profession to be very tender in Cases of Blood, and to imitate our Lord and Master, *Who came not to destroy the Lives of Men, but to save them.*

I likewise design in what I have written, to give my testimony against these unjustifiable ways of discovering Witchcrafts, which some among us have practised. I hear that of late there was a *Witch-cake* made with the Urine of bewitched Creatures, as one Ingredient by several Persons in a place, which has suffered much by the Attack of Hell upon it: This I take to be not only wicked Superstition, but great Folly: For tho' the Devil does sometimes operate with the *Experiments*, yet not always, especially if a *Magical Faith* be wanting. I shall here take occasion to recite some Passages in a Letter, which I received from that Eminent pious and learned Man, Mr. *Samuel Cradock*; during my abode in *London*; the Letter bears date *Febr. 26. 1690*. Then take it in his own Words, which are these; 'We have at this present one in our next Town, who has a Son who has strange Fits, and such as they impute to Witchcraft: He come to consult with me about it, but before he came, he had used a means which I should never had directed him unto, *viz*. He took the Nails of his Son's Hands and Feet, and some of his Hair, and mixed them in Rye-Paste with his Water, and so set it all by the Fire till it was consumed, and his Son (as he says) was well after, and free from his Fits for a whole Month, but then they came again, and *He tried that means a second time, and then it would not do*; He removed his Son into *Cambridgeshire* the next County, and then he was well, but as soon as he brought him home he was afflicted as before. The Boy says, He saw a thing like a Mole following of him, which once spoke to him, and told him he came to do the Office he was to do: I advised his Father to make use of the Medicine prescribed by our Saviour, *viz*. Fasting and Prayer. Here have been others in this Town, that though they were under *Ill-handling* as they call it: One Family had their Milk so affected, that they could not possibly make any Cheese, but it hov'd and swelled, and was good for nothing: They are now rid of that trouble, but how they got rid of it I do not know': Thus my Letter. By which it is evident that Towns in *England* as well as *New-England* are molested with *Dæmons*, only I wish that the Superstitions practiced in other places to get rid of such troublesome Guests had never been known, much less used amongst us or them.

Some I hear have taken up a Notion, that the Book newly published by my Son, is contradictory to this of mine: 'Tis strange that such Imaginations should enter into the Minds of Men: I perused and approved of that Book before it was printed; and nothing but my Relation to him hindred me from recommending it to the World: But my self and Son agreed unto the humble Advice which twelve Ministers concurringly presented before his Excellency and Council, respecting the present Difficulties, which let the World judge, whether there be anything in it dissentany from what is attested by either of us.

It was in the Words following:—

The Return of several Ministers consulted by his Excellency, and the Honourable Council, upon the present Witchcrafts in *Salem* Village.

Boston, *June 15, 1692.*

I. The *afflicted State of our poor Neighbours, that are now suffering by Molestations from the Invisible World, we apprehend so deplorable, that we think their Condition calls for the utmost help of all Persons in their several Capacities.* II. *We cannot but with all Thankfulness acknowledge, the Success which the merciful God has given unto the sedulous and assiduous Endeavors of our honourable Rulers, to detect the abominable Witchcrafts which have been committed in the Country; humbly praying that the discovery of these mysterious and mischievous Wickednesses, may be perfected.* III. *We judge that in the prosecution of these, and all such Witchcrafts, there is need of a very critical and exquisite Caution, lest by too much Credulity for things received only upon the Devil's Authority, there be a Door opened for a long Train of miserable Consequences, and Satan get an advantage over us, for we should not be ignorant of his Devices.* IV. *As in Complaints upon Witchcrafts, there may be Matters of Enquiry, which do not amount unto Matters of Presumption, and there may be Matters of Presumption which yet may not be reckoned Matters of* Conviction; *so 'tis necessary that all Proceedings thereabout be managed with an exceeding tenderness towards those that may be complained of; especially if they have been Persons formerly of an unblemished Reputation.* V. *When the first Enquiry is made into the Circumstances of such as may lie under any just Suspicion of Witchcrafts, we could wish that there may be admitted as little as is possible, of such Noise, Company, and Openness, as may too hastily expose them that are examined: and that there may nothing be used as a Test, for the Trial of the suspected, the Lawfulness whereof may be doubted among the People of God; but that the Directions given by such judicious Writers as* Perkins *and* Bernard, *be consulted in such a Case.* VI. *Presumptions whereupon Persons may be committed, and much more Convictions, whereupon Persons may be condemned as guilty of Witchcrafts, ought certainly to be more considerable, than barely the accused Person being represented by a Spectre unto the Afflicted; inasmuch as 'tis an undoubted and a notorious thing, that a Dæmon may, by God's Permission, appear even to ill purposes, in the Shape of an innocent, yea, and a vertuous Man: Nor can we esteem Alterations made in the Sufferers, by a Look or Touch of the Accused to be an infallible Evidence of Guilt; but frequently liable to be abused by the Devil's Legerdemains.* VII. *We know not, whether some remarkable Affronts given to the Devils, by our disbelieving of those Testimonies, whose whole force and strength is from them alone, may not put a Period, unto the Progress of the dreadful Calamity begun upon us, in the Accusation of so many Persons, whereof we hope, some are yet clear from the great Transgression laid unto their Charge.* VIII. *Nevertheless, We cannot but humbly recommend unto the Government, the speedy and vigorous Prosecution of such as have rendered themselves obnoxious, according to the Direction given in the Laws of God, and the wholesome Statutes of the* English *Nation, for the Detection of Witchcrafts.*

CPSIA information can be obtained
at www.ICGtesting.com
Printed in the USA
LVHW082136151022
730803LV00011B/384